Communicating
ADVICE

This book is part of the Peter Lang Media and Communication list.
Every volume is peer reviewed and meets
the highest quality standards for content and production.

PETER LANG
New York • Bern • Frankfurt • Berlin
Brussels • Vienna • Oxford • Warsaw

Communicating

ADVICE

Peer Tutoring and Communication Practice

Wendy Atkins-Sayre and Eunkyong L. Yook, Editors

PETER LANG
New York • Bern • Frankfurt • Berlin
Brussels • Vienna • Oxford • Warsaw

Library of Congress Cataloging-in-Publication Data

Communicating advice: peer tutoring and communication practice /
edited by Wendy Atkins-Sayre, Eunkyong L. Yook.
pages cm
Includes bibliographical references and index.
1. Peer teaching. 2. Tutors and tutoring.
3. Communication and education. 4. Communication—Study and teaching.
I. Atkins-Sayre, Wendy. II. Yook, Eunkyong Lee.
LB1031.5.C66   371.39'4—dc23   2015016343
ISBN 978-1-4331-2854-7 (hardcover)
ISBN 978-1-4331-2853-0 (paperback)
ISBN 978-1-4539-1617-9 (e-book)

Bibliographic information published by **Die Deutsche Nationalbibliothek**.
Die Deutsche Nationalbibliothek lists this publication in the "Deutsche
Nationalbibliografie"; detailed bibliographic data are available
on the Internet at http://dnb.d-nb.de/.

To our families

To Ward, Gillian, and Owen for showing me how family support can provide the perfect model for so many other relationships. Thanks for encouraging me, even through long hours, distracted evenings, and an endless workload.
    —Wendy

To my family: Ken, Chris, Kari for the consistent support, encouragement, and solace provided over the years as we forged our group identity as a family of first generation Korean Americans. You have made everything possible.
    —Eunkyong

CONTENTS

FOREWORD

Communication and Peer Tutoring

Christopher Bell and Sherwyn Morreale

At the collegiate level, the value of peer tutoring, both for the tutor and the tutee, cannot be overstated. Colvin (2007) broadly states that "peers are often considered the most powerful influence in undergraduate education, even more so than advisors and instructors" (p. 166). It takes time to enact real learning; critical foundational matter must be understood in order to build more advanced concepts. Tutoring, particularly peer tutoring, can supplement an instructor's capacity to assist student learning at various stages along the way. Peer tutoring provides an opportunity for students of different skill levels to come together to learn course material—a valuable enterprise for both sides of the tutoring equation. The student being tutored is given a chance to learn from someone who may use different language, examples, or instructional methods than the professor. As a result, the material may "click" for the tutee in a new way. The student doing the tutoring strengthens his/her own grasp of the concepts and reinforces her/his knowledge of key principles by explaining them to someone else. Far beyond the amorphous "learning leadership skills," this exchange may not only help the tutor retain important information, it also can reveal gaps in the tutor's knowledge that need to be shored up. Topping (1996) reminds us that "Just preparing to be a peer tutor has been proposed to enhance cognitive processing in the tutor—by increasing attention to and motivation for the task, and necessitating review of existing knowledge and skills" (p. 324). This benefit is echoed by Roscoe & Chi (2007), who state that tutors, "*metacognitively reflect* upon their own expertise and comprehension, and *constructively build* upon their prior knowledge by generating inferences, integrating ideas across topics and domains, and repairing errors" (p. 541, emphasis original).

Hall & Stegila (2003) further explain that "to be most effective, students must be taught roles in the instructional episode; to be systematic, elicit responses, and provide feedback" (p. 1). A peer tutor who can elicit responses and provide feedback will foster a more conducive learning environment for peers, and that leads to more positive learning outcomes. While new or poorly-trained tutors might "give shorter answers, and tend to concentrate on the 'concrete,' rather than explaining, or elaborating on conceptual connections ... a well-coached tutor tends to give more 'explanatory' responses in the same way that a 'good' teacher can direct thought processes through the use of questioning and/or conversation" (Galbraith & Winterbottom, 2011, p. 323).

Undoubtedly, the more effectively peer tutors communicate, the more each student (both tutor and tutee) will benefit from the tutoring process. To elaborate, "establishing a good rapport between students and tutors is the most important factor in the success of tutoring ... interpersonal skill is especially important in tutoring actions" (Morillas & Garrido, 2014, p. 95). In this context, interpersonal skill is defined as "promoting critical spirit, motivation and confidence, recognizing cultural diversity and individual needs, and creating a climate of empathy and ethical commitment" (Torra et al., as cited in Morillas & Garrido, 2014, p. 95). Indeed, the ability to use communication to establish rapport is essential. Hawkins (1982, as cited cited in "Falchikov & Blythman, 2001) posits that learning, in the peer tutoring context, stems from its social nature; it is the "sharing in the work of the system between two friends who trust each other" (Hawkins, 1982, p. 29, as cited in Falchikov & Blythman, 2001, p. 4) that allows for tutoring to be effective. A peer tutor then is a trusted friend with effective communication skills, who is not simply clarifying or supplementing course material, but also is providing encouragement, emotional reassurance, inspiration, and a safe environment in which to ask questions. These more positive student-to-student communication interactions tend to correlate with more positive classroom climates and more in-class participation (Frisby & Martin, 2010), both necessary components of effective teaching and learning in higher education.

Clearly, peer tutoring is of much value to the educational enterprise, and communication is vital to the administration of tutoring duties and to the effectiveness of the entire tutoring process. The tutor-tutee interaction *is* a communication interaction, and effective interpersonal communication skills are not just necessary, they are essential. Given this reality, the volume you hold in your hands is a central repository of theory and practice in higher education tutoring. It is divided into three sections, with practical exercises, training strategies, and advice interspersed among the sections. The result is a practical and useful guide to building a successful tutoring program, from staffing to training to implementation.

The first section focuses on the selection and training of tutors. First, in Chapter 1 ("Training the Trainers: Improving Peer Tutoring through Communication Education"), Atkins-Sayre and Yook provide a compelling argument for the inclusion of communication education in peer tutor training, regardless of discipline. Given the importance of establishing rapport to the learning objectives of a peer tutoring relationship, this communication training is paramount to success. Turner and Sheckels, in Chapter 2 ("Tutors, Directors, and Research: Proactively Building Professional Foundations"), then detail three areas about which tutoring programs should be concerned for maximum effectiveness: the quality of tutoring provided, appropriate evaluation of tutoring center directors, and research into peer tutoring processes. In Chapter 3 ("Building an Effective and Supportive Peer Tutoring Team"), Beebe follows with a reminder that quality teamwork contributes to tutor success, laying out a step-by-step method for developing a well-organized and competent peer tutoring team. Chapter 4 ("Making Sure the Work Is *Good* Work"), by Hess, considers the role ethics plays in the tutoring process, as we seek to produce service-oriented tutors. Finally, Bevan and Waldeck provide useful advice about managing the inevitable conflicts that arise in the peer tutoring relationship, in Chapter 5 ("Managing Conflict in the Peer Tutoring Context").

The second section turns to the other half of the tutoring equation, the tutee. Palmerton opens the discussion, in Chapter 6 ("Working with Diverse Clientele"), with a frank look at diversity as it relates to tutoring, including a valuable set of guidelines to share with tutors regarding engagement with culturally diverse students. Brown, King, and Venette continue this line of thought in Chapter 7 ("Learning Styles: Rounding the Cycle of Learning in the Context of Peer Tutoring"), moving the discussion from cultural diversity into multimodal diversity of learning styles—another area about which peer tutors must be aware. As tutoring centers are charged with the task of aiding student retention, building connections with first-year students is vital, and Seiler provides useful tools in Chapter 8 ("Connecting with the First Year

Student") for connecting with that population. As anyone who has worked with peer tutors can attest, dealing with student communication apprehension and communication anxiety can be a difficult challenge; Dwyer's suggestions in Chapter 9 ("Helping Students Conquer Anxiety in the Session"), for alleviating this stress, will be pertinent for peer tutors and for their training. Wright finishes up this section, in Chapter 10 ("Online Communication for the Savvy Tutor"), with training tools for preparing peer tutors to enter the ever-expanding world of online tutoring.

The last section deals with the tutoring space itself, the environment, both physically and philosophically. Omdahl returns to interpersonal communication, in Chapter 11 ("Building Trust in Tutoring through Effective Interpersonal Communication"), as a method for building trust as a tutor, regarding both confidentiality and the minimization of the stigma colloquially associated with receiving tutoring. *Ethos*, that most ephemeral of Aristotle's basic rhetorical canons, is considered by Hoerl, Kolb, Gregerson, and Butler in Chapter 12 ("Communicating Ethos at the Center"), giving practical advice for constructing credibility step-by-step before, during, and after a tutoring session. The rhetorical aspects of tutoring philosophy are detailed in Chapter 13 ("Engaging in Effective Instructional Communication Behaviors in the Tutoring Relationship") by Myers, Atkinson, Ball, Goldman, Tindage, and Carton, with examples of how to put rhetorical principles into practice during tutoring sessions. Timmerman's examination of customer service in Chapter 14 ("Peer Tutoring and Customer Service: Students as 'Partial Employees'") is destined to become standard reading for the training of future tutors, as he gives insightful tips about developing tutors as employees. This last section concludes with Ellis and Grimaldi directly reflecting upon feedback, its construction and its uses, in Chapter 15 ("Designing and Delivering Effective Feedback: Making the Most of Your Consultation Time").

Between each section, the editors have included sample cases of various peer tutoring center practices. These brief cases explore everything from staff training, developing team relationships, and creating a staff code of ethics to reflecting on feedback styles and online tutoring needs. The pieces, contributed by peer tutoring center directors, provide specific advice and examples and will be a welcome tool to many center directors.

In all, the practicality and applicability of the information contained in this volume will prove worthwhile and highly useful to anyone who runs a tutoring program or tutoring center, whether it's the first day on the job or the tenth year in the business. Even a casual perusal of the auspicious list of contributing authors suggests this set of essays will become the "go-to" book for anyone with an interest in the opportunities and challenges inherent in peer tutoring. As former directors of tutoring centers and communication centers ourselves, we assuredly attest to the depth and quality of this collection. We say with confidence that it will serve future tutoring professionals in the care and guidance of peer tutors for years to come.

References

Colvin, J. W. (2007). Peer tutoring and social dynamics in higher education. *Mentoring & Tutoring, 15*(2), 165–181.

Falchikov, N., & Blythman, M. (2001). *Learning together peer tutoring in higher education*. London: Routledge/Falmer.

Frisby, B. N., & Martin, M. M. (2010). Instructor-student and student-student rapport in the classroom. *Communication Education, 59*, 146–164.

Galbraith, J., & Winterbottom, M. (2011). Peer tutoring: What's in it for the tutor? *Educational Studies, 37*(3), 321–332.

Hall, T., & Stegila, A. (2003). *Peer mediated instruction and intervention*. Wakefield, MA: National Center on Accessing the General Curriculum. Retrieved from http://aim.cast .org/learn/historyarchive/backgroundpapers/peer-mediated_instruction

Morillas, N. R., & Garrrido, M. F. (2014). The role of tutoring in higher education: Improving the student's academic success and professional goals. *Revista Internacional de Organizaciones, 12*, 89–100.

Roscoe, R. D., & Chi, M. T. H. (2007). Understanding tutor learning: Knowledge-building and knowledge-telling in peer tutors' explanations and questions. *Review of Educational Research, 77*(4), 534–574.

Topping, K. J. (1996). The effectiveness of peer tutoring in further and higher education: A typology and review of the literature. *Higher Education, 32*, 321–345.

ACKNOWLEDGMENTS

An edited volume is, by definition, a product of teamwork. To all of the contributors and supporters of this project, we offer big thanks. Your experience and expertise has made this a valuable collection of essays. Thanks also go to the Department of Communication Studies and the College of Arts and Letters at the University of Southern Mississippi for their generous support of the project through time and money. The Speaking Center at the University of Southern Mississippi has provided continual support and a testing ground for peer tutoring ideas. The Communication Department at George Mason University also supported the project monetarily and, for that, we are very thankful. Carl Brown and Victoria Brown provided invaluable copy editing and indexing assistance. Finally, thanks also go to Meg Turner for her expert assistance in providing her indexing skills in a timely manner.

PART 1
BUILDING A STRONG STAFF

· 1 ·

TRAINING THE TRAINERS

Improving Peer Tutoring through Communication Education

Wendy Atkins-Sayre and Eunkyong Lee Yook

Peer tutoring has increased dramatically on college campuses in recent years, as more colleges and universities see the need to increase services targeted at retaining students and helping students to graduate. Although these centers can be a significant investment for universities, the benefits in terms of student success are noteworthy. Munley, Garvey, and McConnell (2010), for example, found evidence of the positive effect of peer tutoring on grade point average. Yook (2012) also found preliminary evidence of campuses with peer tutoring centers (in this case, communication centers) having higher retention rates. Because of a belief in the positive impact that peer tutoring centers have on college campuses, research has emerged focusing on best practices for running these centers. Resources in specific disciplines give advice for explaining particular material such as mathematics (Hodges & Brill, 2007; Topping, Miller, Murray, & Conlin, 2011) and writing (Murphy & Sherwood, 2008; Ryan & Zimmerelli, 2006). Other peer tutoring resources focus not only on the content of the consulting session in terms of discipline-specific information, but also on the best pedagogical approaches for teaching students (Tindall & Black, 2011). Scholars have even studied the best use of space for creating the right learning environment in peer tutoring settings (Carpenter, 2012).

Most have, however, overlooked one of the main components of the peer tutoring context: communication. This oversight is counter-intuitive and even surprising, as communication training is critical to teacher education. Effective communication is essential to the instructional process because many of the skills required of teachers depend on the ability to communicate effectively, such as communicating interpersonally with students or presenting information in class in a way that students understand (Hunt, Simonds, & Cooper, 2002). Although there are differences, tutoring is a type of instruction and should be studied and explained in terms of instructional communication.

Just as various departments across the disciplines, including the sciences and mathematics, are now acknowledging the importance of communication to their fields (Darling & Dannels, 2003), scholars of peer tutoring must also emphasize the centrality of communication to the peer tutoring process. Because communication is a transactional process whereby meanings are negotiated, it forms the backbone of the successful tutoring process where interaction is key. Especially within the tutoring context, negotiating meaning among interactants in a two-way process is essential to avoid one-way, ineffectual communication (Roscoe & Chi, 2007). Without effective communication, a tutoring session can turn out to be a monologue of content knowledge, as opposed to an engaged dialogue with the goal of learning. If tutoring is conducted ineffectively, students may very well be turned off by the tutor's lack of communication skills and even resist returning for more assistance when needed. Additionally, beyond the classroom, students will be less likely to be engaged learners, seeking to expand learning as they should to fully benefit from their academic experience. To engage students, effective communication in the tutoring process is essential. Whether it is establishing rapport for open communication, connecting with the client, or keeping the communication positive and constructive, peer tutors need advice for creating the best communication climate.

Therefore, this chapter calls for increased attention to communication education about peer tutoring centers on campus, and makes suggestions about how this training can occur. We explore the areas of communication that should be discussed in university-wide tutor training and options for providing training services for other centers. In doing so, we hope to emphasize the centrality of communication to any peer tutoring situation and to bring the contributions of communication education to other disciplines.

The Role of Communication Education in Peer Tutor Training

Part of the motivation for this chapter is that so many peer tutoring resources give advice on communication issues. And yet, research emerging from communication studies is rarely incorporated to develop the practices suggested. A sampling of peer tutoring books, for example, shows discussions about a variety of communication topics, as suggested by those outside of the field of communication. *The St. Martin's Sourcebook for Writing Tutors* (Murphy & Sherwood, 2008) covers topics such as the importance of the interpersonal relationship that develops within the first few minutes of the appointment, getting quiet students to speak up in sessions, and setting the right climate for online tutoring. *The Bedford Guide for Writing Tutors* (Ryan & Zimmerelli, 2006) explores the different communicative roles of the tutor and communicating in difficult situations. *A Tutor's Guide: Helping Writers One to One* (Rafoth, 2005) provides advice for working with non-native speakers and for avoiding dominating the conversation. Gillespie and Learner's (2008) *The Longman Guide to Peer Tutoring* discusses the importance of peer tutoring not only for clear communication with students, but also for the institution's goal. Tindall and Black's (2011) book on peer tutoring, *An Indepth Look at Peer Programs*, emphasizes the central role of communication skills in peer tutoring, which develop into important life skills for the tutor. While it is important that guidebooks such as these discuss communication-related topics, the obvious centrality of communication to the tutoring process should also provide a compelling reason to draw from the research and advice that comes from communication studies. Those who direct peer tutoring centers should also consider partnering with communication educators and researchers in order to develop communication-focused training modules that can provide knowledge and insight from those specifically trained in relevant theory-based communication practices.

There are a number of areas in communication education that provide guidance in training tutoring staffs of other academic centers. For example, communicating effectively with students during a consulting session often presents tutors with challenging situations. Listening is an important communication skill that tends to be eclipsed in training sessions. Effective listening, understanding diverse backgrounds, and dealing with different types of anxieties and learning styles will lead to better decisions when communicating advice to clients (Cuny, Wilde, & Stephenson, 2012). In tutoring contexts, listening is an important skill for the tutor in order to be able to accurately understand the issues the student is facing, as well as decode the accompanying emotional responses, such as fear, anxiety, and disappointment. Accurate detection and understanding allows the tutor to correctly diagnose the overall situation facing the student, so that helpful assistance can be targeted. The scenarios provided in the following paragraphs illuminate the importance of listening, a core communication skill.

For example, a student may come into the campus writing center looking for advice on developing the argument in her paper. After discussing her goals for the session with the tutor, the tutor begins to review the paper with the student. Despite the stated goals of the session, though, the tutor quickly realizes that the paper might not be organized in the most effective way. Shortly thereafter, the tutor attempts to direct the focus of the conversation toward organization. Despite the good intentions of the tutor, the student leaves the appointment frustrated because she feels that the tutor neither listened to her, nor provided the guidance that she was seeking.

In a similar scenario, a communication center tutor meets with a freshman public speaking student. The student comes into the center with a speech topic and some general idea about what she wants to discuss in the speech. The tutor, getting excited about the possibilities for the speech, quickly takes over the draft and begins to explain some of the ways that the student might develop the speech. At the end of the session, as the student walks out of the center, she realizes that the speech is no longer her own; instead, the tutor has drafted a speech that looks nothing like what the student originally planned. In both scenarios, attention to communication strategies for listening, building trust, and getting the student to actively participate in the discussion would have benefitted both the tutor and the student.

This breakdown in communication might be attributed to a lack of effective listening on the part of the tutor and/or a lack of clear communication about the reason for the new focus, despite the good intentions of the tutor. In this case, training the tutor to effectively listen for what guidance the student seeks, skillfully guiding the direction of the appointment when needed, and communicate goals and rationales clearly, could preempt frustrating situations such as those described above.

It is also important to think about the best ways to create a supportive environment through communication during the tutoring session. In order to effectively tutor a client, it is necessary to build credibility and trust between the tutor and the client (Ward & Schwartzman, 2009). Tutors also need to be able to communicate their advice in a way that enhances the learning environment, creating a relationship that leads to collaboration rather than unilateral direction. While the content knowledge of the tutor is important, the ways that tutors give feedback are just as, or arguably even more, important to the success of the tutoring process.

For example, a student comes into the media center seeking advice on his e-portfolio. The tutor launches directly into the appointment, opening the web site and proceeding to comment on the weaknesses of the content, organization, and design. Although the tutor has good feedback, the student leaves the center unmotivated to take that advice because he feels overwhelmed and insulted. The tutor had good intentions and knowledgeable advice, but the way she communicated her message and her inattention to building an environment based on collaboration led to an unsuccessful session.

Finally, another area of communication that is of particular interest to peer tutoring centers is the relationships among the tutoring staff, which are important for establishing a positive overall climate for the tutoring center. If the staff members do not get along, then the center will struggle to create a positive and supportive environment, and ultimately the tutoring quality may suffer. Consequently, creating effective work teams and giving tutors the right tools for managing conflict will be particularly critical. Regardless of how knowledgeable individual tutors are, if they do not work well together, it will not allow for a positive climate among tutors, resulting in frustration and loss of focus and productivity as a group. The effects of this discord could also spill over to the tutoring session.

To illustrate the point, consider another scenario: As a student walks in for his appointment, he can see that some of the tutors at the math center are noticeably upset. Two tutors who consistently show up late for their work hours are late for appointments again. The other staff members, who go to great lengths to be at work on time, are upset at both of the tardy tutors, as well as the math center director who has not taken any action to address the problem. As one of the frustrated tutors begins the appointment with the student, she makes a negative comment about her co-worker. The student finds it hard to concentrate on the math work, distracted by the tension in the air. Had the math lab tutors been trained in the areas of conflict management and the importance of communicating ethically and professionally at all times, this uncomfortable situation may have been avoided.

From start to finish, the peer tutoring session is driven by communication practices. From the time the student walks through the door, then sits down with the tutor and begins working on the project, until the student leaves the center, communication determines the effectiveness of the session. Making sure that peer tutors have thought through and planned for multitudes of possible communication scenarios would benefit any peer tutoring center. Moreover, understanding the theoretical bases for such guidance from communication research will provide depth to their understanding of the context and will further enhance their tutoring skills. Consequently, peer tutoring centers should provide training for strengthening communication skills while tutoring.

Developing a Training Plan

With the first goal of improving communication skills at all peer tutoring centers established, the next step is to determine the best plan. This takes three separate efforts: finding resources for communication education on campus, developing partnerships across campus, and planning training sessions.

There are three possible options for locating training resources. First, peer tutoring centers might choose to work with communication studies faculty on campus in order to train their staff members. Given that many colleges and universities now have some version of communication across the curriculum programs, there should be interest in developing those relationships. Second, in the absence of a communication studies department, peer tutoring centers might consider bringing in a consultant—perhaps a communication studies researcher or even a communication center director—to help them train staff members and develop training materials.

The most desirable option for partnering, however, is working directly with a communication center, assuming it is available on campus. Communication centers are primarily known for their work with students on oral communication assignments. However, as the site of expertise on campus for a broad range of communication skills, these centers can also be a valuable resource in helping to train peer tutors at other centers. By focusing on communication skills such as strengthening interpersonal communication, offering advice to students in the most effective way, communicating competently within a group, using persuasive skills to overcome a negative speaking experience, and empowering students, communication education should become a central concern for strengthening tutoring across the university.

Given this last partnership option, the first discussion that some campuses will need to have is one that focuses on the current and possibly expanded role of their communication center. The task of redefining the role of the communication center for tutoring centers will require introspection and honest discussions about a given communication center's identity. While some communication centers give advice in the various areas of communication studies (interpersonal, small group, public speaking, conflict, etc.), others primarily tutor public speaking. Although those centers might not currently offer tutoring in all of these areas, they might choose to work with other peer tutoring centers on campus to provide communication training for other staffs.

In order to do this work, however, communication center staffs would need to conduct additional staff training and development on the communication aspects of tutoring. Most communication centers provide campus workshops on communication topics, providing relevant experience for this type of peer tutor training. After learning about the particulars of the discipline/tutoring centers with which they are working through meetings with various academic center directors, communication center directors and staff members would need to identify relevant communication research that matches the training needs of the tutoring centers. They would then need to create workshops and materials for the workshops with that particular audience in mind.

Once the overall decision about the revised role is reached through a reflection of the identity and the mission of the communication center vis-à-vis the campus overall mission, the rationale for the changed role would be suggested to administration for their support, using arguments such as those included earlier in this chapter. The nature of the changed role would be described during this process.

The second challenge to this issue is developing partnerships across campus. Faculty and other peer tutoring centers are important stakeholders in this newly conceptualized role of communication centers, so communication centers would also need to first do some outreach to faculty in other departments on campus. Partnering with those knowledgeable in the content areas for tutoring might afford an opportunity for a deeper understanding of the needs of the various tutoring centers as well as more sustained and effective outreach and relationships with other departments and tutoring centers. Partnering would not only open channels of understanding with faculty members, but also facilitate faculty buy-in and support for the new suggested role of the communication center on their campus.

Partnering with other peer tutoring centers, in addition to the administration and faculty as mentioned above, is of utmost importance. Communication centers are often misunderstood to be focused only on improving public speaking skills, and even more specifically, to be focused solely on delivery improvement. Consequently, it might be necessary to clarify what the center can offer in terms of wider communication training on topics such as conflict management, communication climate, leadership, and listening. This is, of course, a good opportunity for communication centers to increase campus awareness about their services, but also to bring attention to the kinds of communication skills that are important to effective communication. Despite the wider offerings of the center, if the training with other centers is to happen, it will mean that communication centers need to reach out to other peer tutoring centers and explain what this training might entail. Other types of centers might also request this service of communication centers. Campus centers for teaching and learning and student success centers might also provide a good starting point for developing these partnerships.

Finally, the training module itself would need to be developed. There are several options for providing services to other centers. While different in format, in terms of content all of these options would be communication-based, providing theoretical support for best practices for tutoring, and based on relevant communication theories. First, a communication center might provide workshops, not unlike those offered to the general student body, that would target peer tutors in various academic centers on campus. Those workshops could either be formulated for particular centers, or be general enough such that peer tutors from any center could benefit from them. The workshops should cover topics needed for successful tutoring such as building trust between client and tutor, communicating effective and supportive feedback, speaking to students with diverse needs, or getting students engaged in a tutoring session (many of the topics covered in subsequent chapters in this volume). While these topics are primarily about communication with the client, workshops might also focus on communication within the center covering topics such as managing conflict in the center, building an effective staff team, and communicating ethically.

Second, communication centers might provide active learning activities in which tutors would participate in role-playing, and other experiential learning such as skits and simulations. Kolb's (1984) experiential learning theory, which includes the cycle of concrete experience, active experimentation, reflective observation, and abstract conceptualization, serves as the basis for experiential training. For example, carefully created scenarios for role-playing and subsequent analysis and discussion can guide tutors in understanding the difference between tutoring behaviors conducive to successful learning and poor tutoring behaviors that could leave the student feeling frustrated and disempowered. This understanding would allow the math or writing tutor, who is gifted in mathematical or writing ability but perhaps lacking competence in communication, to gain the communication knowledge and skills to combine both content knowledge and communication competence for successful tutoring.

Third, communication centers might assist in the development of peer tutoring communication rubrics to be used by an academic center's own tutors to assess the communicative skills of the staff. Continuous assessments and efforts to improve are needed to enhance communication skills, so building a rubric that is custom-tailored to the needs of the center and the content area for assessment is important. The rubric-building exercise might be completed together with the center's tutors, following a workshop for that center. Involving the center's tutors will clarify understanding of the assessed skills, and also increase commitment to use the rubric to ultimately help the students improve. As a starting point, we have included a generic rubric in Case 8.

Fourth, using the created rubric, communication center tutors might be paired up with other peer tutors to observe and provide feedback on communicative skills. This could happen within a two to three week period after an initial workshop, and would only require that tutors from the two centers be matched up during appointments. Allowing a time immediately following the observation to have the tutors discuss the session ensures that it becomes a collaborative, self-reflective exercise, rather than simply an observation by an outsider. Tutors can sometimes learn just as much, or even more, when they give feedback about observations, compared to when they are the recipients of feedback. Meta-communication about observed communication, accompanied by discussions to clarify communication concepts and guide competent communication, will lead to a thoughtful and deliberate communication approach over time. An additional benefit of this exercise is that tutors can practice giving each other feedback in a positive tone which, when translated to the tutoring context, will be much more conducive to student compliance and ultimate improved learning, as opposed to feedback that may be content-rich but delivered with less-than-competent communication skills.

Although it is preferable for communication center staffs to be directly involved in this training, it may be the case that some peer tutoring centers would be more comfortable training their own staff members to observe and give feedback on tutoring sessions. Ultimately, this would be the goal of the training—to give the staff enough information to be able to recognize communication strengths and weaknesses, so as to enable metacognition and meta-communication about their tutoring skills. Additionally, as mentioned earlier in this section, it would be possible to do all of this work with a communication studies consultant or department, in the absence of a communication center.

Other than the above-mentioned models, alternative training models may emerge that are particularly well suited to individual institutions. It may be useful, for example, to have the staffs of each of the centers discuss the training options that would be most helpful to them together with their directors, to allow them to select the most fitting for their specific circumstances. As a starting point, however, it would be useful to have particular training models in mind when first developing communication training for peer tutoring centers.

Conclusion

Training peer tutors to be effective communicators has its advantages. However, as with any new endeavor, there may be some initial stumbling blocks. Peer tutoring centers with established training models, for example, may initially be resistant. These centers may feel comfortable with the status quo and not willing to make any changes to their current tutor training. It is also possible that they feel threatened by the new centrality of communication in peer tutor training. Consequently, focusing on the advantages to training in communication is important.

For example, this education can be extremely useful for other tutoring centers, as successful communication of ideas is just as important as the content of tutoring. Communication has its own theories and content areas, but it also has a uniquely transferable aspect. It can provide insight into effective means to relay that content, so it is a field that can be particularly amenable and useful to all fields of study. Communication theories, especially from instructional communication and communication education, would benefit other tutoring centers, and these theories should guide tutoring pedagogy.

Second, in tough budgetary times, there are advantages to increasing coordination and cooperation among various campus services and highlighting the numerous ways that the services benefit the wider campus through the synergy created. Enhanced coordination and effective utilization of resources will improve the overall institutional effectiveness. By offering training services to other peer tutoring centers on campus, communication centers (or, in some cases, departments) would find another way to practice their area of expertise, making themselves even more instrumental to the overall academic success of students and the entire campus. More students can benefit from effective tutoring, resulting in increased traffic to various tutoring centers, increasing the likelihood that students will succeed academically.

A somewhat smaller added potential benefit is that with more frequent interaction between tutoring centers, understanding about the importance of communication among the tutors of those tutoring centers will be enhanced, possibly increasing traffic to communication centers by the peer tutors themselves. In the same light, communication center tutors might also be more likely to use other centers themselves as they build partnerships with other tutors across campus.

Third, and of course most importantly, this would be a way to ensure that peer tutoring centers are communicating in the most effective way with students, therefore aiding student retention. More effective tutoring centers, in which tutors communicate successfully with tutees and with each other, will create a climate that will induce students to seek help without hesitation, which is the first (and arguably the most important) step in promoting student success and retention. Although it will likely take substantial efforts to reconceptualize the role of communication education on campus and to implement such coordinated training, the results will be well worth the effort. Institutions of higher education and their students will ultimately reap the benefits of effective and coordinated student academic support for student success.

References

Carpenter, R. (Ed.). (2012). *Cases on higher education spaces: Innovation, collaboration, and technology.* Hershey, PA: Information Science Reference.

Cuny, K. M., Wilde, S. M., & Stephenson, A. V. (2012). Using empathetic listening to build relationships at the center. In E. Yook & W. Atkins-Sayre (Eds.), *Communication centers and oral communication programs in higher education: Advantages, challenges, and new directions* (pp. 249–256). Lanham, MD: Lexington Books.

Darling, A. L., & Dannels, D. P. (2003). Practicing engineers talk about the importance of talk: A report on the role of oral communication in the workplace. *Communication Education, 52,* 1–16.

Gillespie, P., & Learner, N. (2008). *The Longman guide to peer tutoring.* New York, NY: Longman.

Hodges, C. B., & Brill, J. M. (2007). Developing a training program for instructional assistants within a large-scale emporium-based environment: A nine-year evolution towards systemic change. *International Journal of Teaching & Learning in Higher Education, 19*(1), 93–104.

Hunt, S. K., Simonds, C. J., & Cooper, P. J. (2002). Communication and teacher education: Exploring a communication course for all teachers. *Communication Education, 51,* 81–94.

Kolb, D. A. (1984). *Experiential learning: Experience as the source of learning and development.* Englewood Cliffs, NJ: Prentice-Hall.

Munley, V. G., Garvey, E., & McConnell, M. J. (2010). The effectiveness of peer tutoring on student achievement at the university level. *American Economic Review, 100,* 277–282.

Murphy, C., & Sherwood, S. (Eds.). (2008). *The St. Martin's sourcebook for writing tutors.* Boston, MA: Bedford/St. Martin's.

Rafoth, B. (Ed.). (2005). *A tutor's guide: Helping writers one to one.* Portsmouth, NH: Boynton/Cook.

Roscoe, R., & Chi, M. (2007). Understanding tutor learning: Knowledge-building and knowledge telling in peer tutors' explanations and questions. *Review of Educational Research, 77,* 534–574.

Ryan, L., & Zimmerelli, L. (2006). *The Bedford guide for writing tutors.* Boston, MA: Bedford/St. Martin's.

Tindall, J. A., & Black, D. R. (2011). *An indepth look at peer programs.* New York, NY: Routledge.

Topping, K., Miller, D., Murray, P., & Conlin, N. (2011). Implementation integrity in peer tutoring of mathematics. *Educational Psychology, 31*(5), 575–593.

Ward, K., & Schwartzman, R. (2009). Building interpersonal relationships as a key to effective speaking center success. *Journal of Instructional Psychology, 36,* 363–372.

Yook, E. L. (2012). Communication centers and retention in higher education: Is there a link? In E. Yook & W. Atkins-Sayre (Eds.), *Communication centers and oral communication programs in higher education: Advantages, challenges, and new directions* (pp. 3–12). Lanham, MD: Lexington Books.

· 2 ·

TUTORS, DIRECTORS, AND RESEARCH

Proactively Building Professional Foundations

Kathleen J. Turner and Theodore F. Sheckels

Peer tutoring is increasingly conducted on college or university campuses in centers of one sort or another (see, for example, Dvorak, 2001). That institutional positioning helps boost the political significance of peer tutoring. However, although such centers are now in vogue, they may not be in the near future. Reasons for the tenuous nature of such peer tutoring centers are varied, including changes in academic leaders and their philosophies or in academic trends. Additionally, consider the political situation of peer tutoring in the context of academic institutions that value either first teaching and then research or first research and then teaching. Peers are, of course, not professors, not even instructors. Tutoring is not teaching; it is usually provided by students (undergraduates or graduates) rather than faculty, and it is often perceived as needed only by those who are struggling to learn, not by the students to whom teachers point with pride. In a teaching-focused environment, peer tutoring may be marginal. Peer tutoring, furthermore, does not seem to be an arena where research might be either conducted or focused. In a research-focused environment, peer tutoring may seem irrelevant. An added challenge is that these centers are frequently directed by professionals who lack tenure-track status. Indeed, often, they may even lack a terminal research-oriented degree. Their status may be tenuous, and so may the status of the centers.[1]

Those involved in improving the pedagogy of peer tutoring can bemoan its weak political situation, even crusade against it. Why should peer tutoring be positioned so weakly? After all, it may positively affect the careers of many students, ranging from those who are excelling to those who are indeed struggling. Insofar as it helps the latter group, it may improve the retention numbers that are important to an institution's image as well as its *U.S. News & World Report* rating. But, short of a crusade, what can be done?

There are indeed ways that those who are professionally responsible for peer tutoring can take the initiative to improve this political situation. Despite the political quagmires facing peer tutoring centers and their directors, one particular type of peer tutoring center, the communication center, has been proactive in analyzing and creating ways for these centers to increase their academic ethos. This chapter reports on the efforts that the National Association of Communication Centers (NACC) has made to strengthen the enterprise at three points where it might be considered vulnerable: the quality of the tutoring the peers provide, the job security of those who direct centers, and the need for peer tutoring processes to be the focus of research. Over the past several years, NACC has been proactive on these fronts, and its initiatives provide guidance for other types of centers.

The precise action NACC took is less important than first, the process it followed, and second, some general characteristics of the efforts. In other words, what NACC did reflects the situation of communication or speaking centers, which is somewhat similar to that of writing centers but rather different from that of subject tutoring centers. Both the process and the products, however, can provide insights that are useful for all peer tutoring enterprises. This chapter contains a discussion of the process first, then of the problems and key characteristics of the solutions involved in each effort.

Process

Communication centers, or speaking centers as they are alternatively called, are well served by two national organizations. The National Communication Association (NCA) is the professional organization of the communication discipline in the United States, with almost 8,000 members. It has met annually since 1914, and its meetings bring together the many facets of the discipline. Therefore it offers important, albeit limited, opportunities for communication center directors to meet, share ideas, and present research.

In 2001, NCA sponsored a summer conference focused on several new directions in pedagogy, peer tutoring in communication centers among them. Those involved in that strand decided to meet again and, thus, NACC was formed. Annually, NACC offers two days of sessions focused on communication centers, and it also provides many opportunities for the peer tutors themselves to share their ideas.

The scheduling of NCA conventions in the fall and NACC conferences in the spring facilitated a collegial process that developed the three efforts outlined below. Those meeting at NCA identified a problem; those charged with developing a response conducted discussions at the next NACC; they presented a draft solution and a revised draft solution at the next NCA for the endorsement of the NCA communication centers unit; and they presented this endorsed solution at the following NACC for that group's adoption. The precise pattern is less important than the fact that it involved considerable input from directors gathered at these two national meetings. The fact that there are two annual meetings sped the process along, as did the authors' willingness to revise "on the fly" between an early convention session and a later one. The process moved along with alacrity, in part by reducing the tendency characteristic of more drawn-out processes: frequently revisiting matters already discussed and determined by the group.

Of course, not all peer tutoring efforts have the luxury of holding two professional gatherings per year, but a myriad of electronic means can stimulate and simulate the steady dialogue that occurs in face-to-face meetings. Regardless of how the dialogue is created and sustained, the key is to have open discussion, for the crafted solution needs to respond to multiple situations and must be owned by the peer tutoring directors at large. It will likely fail if it is perceived as either specific to only certain kinds of institutions, or reflective only of the needs and concerns of a subgroup.

The process described here resulted in widespread support for documents concerning peer tutor certification and the evaluation of center directors, as well as a journal featuring research on peer tutoring practices. The problems and solutions for each of these aspects of the centers' enterprise are outlined below.

Peer Tutor Certification

The Problem

As peer tutoring grows, public suspicion may diminish, but it still lurks. Students wonder if their peers can really help them; parents wonder, too. Faculties often are suspicious. Some English Department faculty, for example, make disparaging comments about writing centers because peers cannot possibly offer feedback that is of the same quality as first-year composition instructors. In this still skeptical context, it is important to be able to argue that the peer tutors are trained to be highly capable at their job. The tutor certification procedure we developed helps directors make this very argument.

Tutors—e.g., those a parent might hire privately to help a struggling student with calculus—can be certified through a national organization, but those are typically not peer tutors—i.e., fellow students. Peer tutors do, of course, exist for subject areas, and subject area peer tutors can also be certified, primarily through the College Reading and Learning Association (CRLA). However, the authors believe that CRLA certification, on which many writing centers rely because there is no alternative, does not offer the best model for communication centers (nor, perhaps, subject-area tutoring) for two related reasons.

First, the CRLA procedures focus exclusively on tutoring for students who are struggling, thus emphasizing remedial assistance. Yet like many peer tutoring centers, communication center tutoring is not remedial. Their assumption is that anyone who wants to improve their communication can use the peer tutor's services. The peer communication tutor, then, functions analogously to the faculty peer who looks at a manuscript or presentation another faculty member is developing. As in the case of the scholarly peer review process, the authoring faculty member is not seeking remediation; rather, she/he is seeking the advice of a peer who is a bit savvier. The assumption is that the sheer act of reviewing by a different set of ears or eyes, trained by experience in academe and the discipline, helps to improve the scholarly work. Peer tutoring, then, is termed such not just because the people involved are peers but also to suggest that it mirrors what routinely occurs in academe among faculty colleagues when experienced faculty assist their colleagues through peer review. To fill the need for tutoring based on an assumption and approach that was different from that of the CRLA, the NACC-adopted certification procedure was developed, first and foremost, for genuine, non-remedial peer tutoring.

The second reason CRLA certification guidelines did not work well for communication centers was that although useful, they were applicable to tutoring in general, not tutoring in communication. In contrast, the document the authors developed, with considerable input from our peers, insists that certified programs feature training that covers not only general principles (e.g., how to begin a session) but also communication-specific principles. In other words, those centers that wish to be certified need to train not just peer tutors, but peer tutors in communication.

The discipline of rhetoric highlights the theoretical work of many post-1900 thinkers, some of whom, such as Foucault, Bakhtin, and Derrida, academe might even not label rhetoricians. Nonetheless, Aristotle's influence continues: the frameworks he established are still used, extended over the years by ideas derived from others. So, in recognition of the continuing validity of Aristotelian principles, the certification procedure insists that tutors receive communication-specific training in the areas of invention (*inventio*), disposition (*dispositio*), style (*elocutio*), memory (*memoria*) and delivery (*pronunciatio*). But in doing so, the certification document does not prescribe a particular mode of training: training could be in a class, for example, or it could be heavily on-line. This new certification document also contains some common sense basic guidelines—e.g., peer tutors need to be eased into the endeavor, often by shadowing experienced ones, and peer tutors need to be systematically assessed.

Key Characteristics of the Solution

As discussed earlier, our development of the certification procedure relied on two key principles: first, certification should be of genuine peer tutors, not of tutors who work mainly with struggling students; second, certification should be discipline-specific. General tutoring principles exist, but tutors who know how to manage a session provide little support if they do not know the specific aspects of the content area in which assistance is sought as well as the choices they have in approaching those aspects in a given peer tutoring session.

We designed a procedure by which tutor training programs at communication centers can earn certification. After proceeding through such programs, individual tutors can then receive certificates proclaiming that they have successfully completed a communication tutor training program certified by the NACC. To earn this certification, directors submit materials indicating first, how they select their tutors; second, how they train their tutors; and third, how they continually evaluate their tutors. The second area (arguably the core) requires documentation of the amount of time in training, the modes of training, and the topics covered by training.

Although specific training topics will obviously vary from a communication center to another kind of peer tutoring center, the authors believe that four fundamental matters should be discussed in peer tutor training, regardless of the type of center. First, how does the center see itself? Tutors need to understand a center's particular mission, which might vary from helping students enrolled in a basic course to assisting students across the curriculum, including those presenting research in capstone courses. Second, how do tutors conduct an effective tutoring session? Tutors need to understand how to begin and end a session and how to deal with a range of clients, including those who are highly anxious, those who are resistant to suggestions, and those who expect the tutors to do all the work. Third, how should tutors address the issues common in the particular academic field? Tutors need to understand the fundamentals of the area as well as the alternatives available to address them. Fourth, how do tutors undertake the administrative work necessary to keep a center running smoothly? Tutors need to understand how to get on the payroll, how to create and file reports on sessions, and how to operate whatever technology the center may have.

As this summary suggests, the certification procedure must require rigor. Peers, parents, and faculty who are suspicious must be assured that training is comprehensive and substantial. While most may never be privy to the particulars, they will appreciate the "certified by" message. That message, by itself, implies quality, much as "The Good Housekeeping Seal of Approval" did decades ago. The procedure NACC approved was designed to ensure that "certified by" meant rigor, and therefore quality.

Evaluation of the Peer Tutoring Director

The Problem

Peer tutoring centers have directors with diverse roles and status within an institution. At a few institutions, the director is a tenured member of the faculty with the rights, privileges, and respect that accompany that status. However, at far more numerous institutions, the director is in a faculty or administrative position that is not tenured. In some cases, although well-qualified to direct a peer tutoring effort, the director may not have a doctorate, and, in still other cases, the director might even be less than full-time. Thus, many directors find themselves in vulnerable positions.

Given this vulnerability, evaluation is a highly sensitive matter; it can be their friend or foe, depending on how it is conducted. The matter might be left to the discretion of the chairs and/or deans to whom these directors report; however, since those administrators are probably less than sure how to proceed given the multifaceted and unique jobs of center directors, there is an opportunity for national entities, such as NCA and NACC, to be proactive and provide an appropriate evaluation process.

Key Characteristics of the Solution

Any process must be flexible to be appropriate for a wide variety of institutional situations. That flexibility entails recommending far more often than prescribing. For example, we believe that, at least at some points, evaluation by someone external to the institution and very knowledgeable about peer tutoring and peer tutoring centers would be valuable. However, requiring that could quickly result in the entirety of the solution being rejected, if the use of such an external evaluator is either alien to the particular institution's culture or beyond its budget.

Being flexible does not, however, mean being indecisive or inconsistent. Thus, the solution that NCA endorsed and NACC adopted argues that the initial step in sound evaluation should be a mutually agreed-upon job description. The document the authors developed lists the many tasks a director might be expected to undertake. The expectation is that the director and his or her superiors will develop a job description specific to the academic institution. The list in the evaluation document is intended to be heuristic. Aided by the feedback of our colleagues at crucial points, we made every attempt to make the document both inclusive in content and flexible in language.

For example, most job descriptions for directors of peer tutoring centers will be a combination of administrative and teaching responsibilities. The precise mix will vary significantly from institution to institution. The important thing is that whatever the balance is, the evaluation should reflect the mix proportionally. A director who teaches few classes should be evaluated primarily for administrative aspects; conversely, a director who is primarily a classroom teacher should be assessed primarily for pedagogy. Superior abilities are rightly expected across the board, but given the complexities of a directorship few people display excellence in every element of their job. The principle insisted upon here is that a person who is performing excellently in the major portion of the job ought not to suffer an overall mediocre evaluation because there are questions about performance in the minor portion.

Another principle involves how teaching is defined. A director may well have conventional classroom teaching assignments; however, a great deal of instruction typically occurs in the context of the peer tutoring center. Tutors need to be instructed in the content as well as the practice of tutoring—both initially and on an on-going basis. In addition, some directors provide instruction to other faculty as well. They may, for example, offer faculty development workshops at which they teach their peers pedagogically sound approaches to such classroom matters as conducting effective discussions or ways of assessing presentations. Therefore, a director's evaluation as an instructor should include not just classroom teaching but activities both in the center with peer tutors as students and outside the center with fellow faculty as the audience. Should instruction extend to other audiences—e.g., admissions guides, staff members, community groups—this teaching also needs to be incorporated into the director's evaluation. Teaching is teaching, after all: the most traditional form ought not to be the only one privileged over others when a peer tutoring director is often engaged in varied instructional roles with various audiences.

The evaluation procedure created by the authors has two parts: the evaluation of the combined teaching-administration role and the evaluation of "intellectual work." The term was not ours; rather, it's derived from Ernest Boyer's (1990) rethinking of higher education. It has been embraced by the Modern Language Association Committee on Professional Service (1996) and several non-language academic disciplines (e.g., Diamond & Adam, 1995), and it has been used in evaluation procedures drafted by writing center groups (Council of Writing Program Administrators, 1998). Although not the traditional conception of research, the term has currency in academe.

Using the term "intellectual work" is not a way of avoiding rigor or excellence; rather, it is a way to expand the substance on which evaluations are based. The evaluation of research involves peer review; so too should the evaluation of intellectual work. Rather than being conducted through anonymous readers' reports, the evaluation is instead focused on how one's peers assess the materials the director has developed. The effort might be a tutor training manual that one's peers at NACC or a comparable organization find exemplary, or it might be workshop materials that one's institutional peers find valuable in their classrooms. Rubrics for informative speeches across the curriculum would be another example of intellectual work, and they would be judged on whether or not they reflected an understanding both of essential communication principles and of the different disciplines derived from the director's systematic investigation of those disciplines. Internet materials for students to use would also be considered intellectual work, and the number of hits would be one way to demonstrate their utility. Other means might be devised to gather additional means of assessment, including gauging the number of hits from beyond the institution and how often colleagues elsewhere have asked if they can borrow materials or link to particular sites.

The use of the term intellectual work, rather than research, is crucial in assessing the contributions of center directors. Many directors of peer tutoring centers do not have research doctorates: they are not trained to engage in research *per se*. Even those who are thus equipped spend much of their time creating materials that will not find their way into publication, but that nonetheless evidence intellectual rigor. Directors may produce high-quality professional work, work that actually might affect more people than an article in a peer-reviewed journal. An appreciation of intellectual work embraces these valuable contributions to higher education at the particular institution and, often, beyond.

Research

The Problem

Why is there limited research on peer tutoring? There are a number of reasons. First, those who direct peer tutoring are often too busy directing and doing other administrative activities to do research on the subject. Second, those who direct peer tutoring are often not trained to be researchers. When urged to do research, directors often say, "I'd like to, but...." A third problem—one that discourages many from trying—is that there seems to be minimal interest in the subject, with a stream of writing center work inspired by Ken Bruffee's (1972/2006) approach to pedagogy being the noteworthy exception. Although vital to academic survival at many academic institutions, peer tutoring is often not regarded as a sufficiently prestigious subject nor as a sufficiently disciplinary subject: In education, it is a marginal area and in English, it is buried in composition studies and probably lurks behind other topics more related to classes *per se*. In communication, the situation is similar—buried in or lurking behind studies of the basic course.

Being viewed as a marginal subject means that peer tutoring research has a difficult time finding presentation outlets and an even more difficult time finding publication outlets. Our writing center colleagues, who have been offering peer tutoring since the late 1970s, have gradually developed several venues such as *The Writing Center Journal*, *The Writing Lab Newsletter*, and *Praxis*, but they are primarily for writing center research (and have, not coincidentally, created some of the most valuable research currently available). (A full listing of writing-focused journals is available at the Writing Program Administrators' website.) In the case of communication centers, the subject's few slots in the NCA program helped gain visibility; the two-day NACC conference provided even more. But there is a pecking order in academe among conferences, and NACC lacks NCA's prestige as well as that of other communication discipline meetings that have emerged for specific communication areas—e.g., the Rhetoric Society of America (RSA) meeting for rhetorical scholars.

The more crucial problem, however, is rooted in the fact that, regardless of how prestigious the conference, publication trumps presentation. In communication, the publication channels for peer tutoring research have been few. The *Basic Course Yearbook* focuses on material on the basic course; *Communication Education* has largely excluded peer tutoring and communication centers; writing center–oriented journals, not surprisingly, privilege material on writing centers. Notwithstanding its title, the annual Conference on College Composition and Communication as yet focuses primarily on writing, despite occasional efforts to bring communication as the communication discipline defines it into the fourth of the "Four Cs" effort.

So, the problem has been two-fold: first, getting directors—and others—to the professional point at which they could do research; second, finding places beyond the NACC and NCA conferences for good research to be disseminated. Given the academic preparation and the job descriptions of many directors, it may not be an easy task to get directors to the point where they are researchers able to wield whatever research methodology they may choose. These directors nonetheless have a great deal of intellectual work worth sharing, from accounts of what a particular institution does in the face of common challenges, to analyses of practices that are arguably "best," at least for a sizeable number of institutions. So finding a place in print for *praxis* as well as more traditional research presented a third problem.

Key Characteristics of the Solution

The solution was to develop the *Communication Centers Journal*. The idea was born at an NCA meeting, and developed through conversations at both NACC and NCA. At the time of our writing this chapter, the journal now has an initial editor, an initial editorial board, and an initial editorial philosophy. Developing a journal, however, does not necessarily solve the problem, as a journal can quickly develop a reputation as a place that only publishes work that is otherwise unpublishable. The problems facing those who wanted to publish on peer tutoring in communication were largely systemic: rejections were based much more on a piece's not being appropriate for an existing outlet than on a piece's quality. Developing a journal is, then, a necessary initial step in addressing these systemic problems.

Nonetheless, because communication centers are not at the top of the discipline's hierarchy, many might very quickly dismiss the *Communication Centers Journal* without careful attention to the process of its design and development. Care was taken on various levels to preempt these potential perceptions and to clear the groundwork for establishment of a high quality peer-reviewed journal. First, the editorial board features not just peer tutoring or communication centers experts but also well-known people from cognate areas within the extended communication discipline. Scholars known for their work in such areas as interpersonal communication, group communication, and assessment are on the board and are ready to review manuscripts that relate to their fields of expertise. So are basic course leaders, long-serving department chairs, and, more generally, disciplinary leaders, including two past presidents and the current president of NCA. One looking at the board would have a very difficult time characterizing the journal as a place where lesser-known scholars dump lesser-quality work that would likely be rejected elsewhere.

Second, the editorial philosophy stresses rigor. The stated philosophy makes it clear that research reports will have to meet the different but equally rigorous standards applied across the communication discipline for quantitative, qualitative, rhetorical, and critical work, with no cursory literature reviews, no unacceptably small sample sizes or claims of significance without statistical proof, and no application of superficial or outdated theory. Pieces that talk about *best practices* must make the case that whatever is being outlined is not only significant but sufficiently generalizable. Of course, the proof will be in what the journal publishes, but the philosophy strongly suggests that the *Communication Centers Journal* will feature high-quality pieces that were not publishable elsewhere simply because of their focus on peer tutoring processes.

Third, the journal distinguishes between research and *praxis* by offering two distinct sections, one for each category of intellectual work. Doing so achieves two goals: First, it prevents those who would dismiss research articles in the journal because they appeared mixed in with *best practices* pieces from doing so (or, at least, doing so quickly). The journal sends the message that communication centers scholars value both types of intellectual work while recognizing the differences. And the journal's editorial philosophy stresses rigor for both types, while making it clear that the questions one would ask of a research piece should be different from those that one would ask of a *praxis* piece.

Having two parts—in particular, a *praxis* section—provides an outlet for those involved in peer tutoring centers who do not have the background or inclination to engage in traditional research but who nonetheless can share their excellent practical ideas translated into intellectual work. These directors are, at present, doubly disenfranchised—both because they are working on an unpopular topic and because they are sharing pragmatically grounded ideas. Because of the kinds of people in academe who have often been asked or volunteered to direct peer tutoring, these professional colleagues, who are capable of directing peer tutoring practices but not trained as empirical researchers, are numerous. The structure of the *Communication Centers Journal* gives them a voice and allows their important practical ideas to reach the audience that needs to hear them to escape the unfortunate *reinventing the wheel* situation in which peer tutoring centers have often found themselves.

The *Communication Centers Journal* has the obvious potential to extend and strengthen communication center research. In this way it serves the same function as journals specific to writing centers have. As other areas of peer tutoring emerge, they too should follow suit and make sure that there exist appropriate outlets for the research that will strengthen and professionalize their effort.

Conclusion

Being proactive, by definition, means recognizing that there is a problem and acting before there is a crisis. Doing so allows one to maintain a certain level of control over the solution. That control will, of course, facilitate arriving at an ultimate solution that serves the interests of the peer tutoring enterprise. The solution must be perceived by others in academe as rigorous and appropriate, so that it is not framed as overly serving the interest of the centers. In concluding, the authors would like to stress that proactive measures must exhibit professionalism if they are to avoid being suspect and, perhaps, then rejected.

Being proactive will be seen as simply being ahead of others if it is not accompanied by professionalism. The advantage of being ahead of others vanishes very quickly if the professionalism is not there. So, what is professionalism in this case? We would suggest that it has four features. First, whatever is developed in response to whatever problems exist should go through a process that is collegial, and thereby inclusive of as many insights and perspectives as possible. Second, whatever is developed should be branded to the extent possible by the appropriate professional organizations—in communication's case, endorsement by an NCA unit and adoption by NACC. Third, whatever is developed should be thorough and comprehensive. Anyone who is interested in the certification and evaluation procedures (and the journal issues as they emerge) can view them at the NACC website (commcenters.org). We worked to balance conciseness, cohesiveness, and coherence. We did not want it to be easy for anyone who wanted to be critical to say, "What about this?" or "What about that?" Fourth, whatever is developed should be rigorous. Again, we invite those reading this chapter to go to the NACC website. They will find rigor in the language we use to talk about the certification of tutors, the assessment of directors, and the manuscripts we hope to see in the *Communication Centers Journal*. They will also find rigor in the awareness these products evince of the academic support area. The authors did not cite studies for the sake of citing studies or refer to extant procedures for the sake of doing so; rather, we situated what communication centers were doing in significant work that was relevant, whether it supported what we were doing (e.g., Boyer, 1990) or proceeded along a course we wished to avoid (e.g., CRLA's website).

Thus, the title of this chapter includes the word "professional." The word does not mean we necessarily want to transform amateurs into professionals, for one of the highlights of working with peer tutors is the contagious enthusiasm they exhibit and the energy they bring because they are new to an important endeavor. They may be naively unaware of some of the politics entailed in the effort; so be it. But peer tutoring advocates must be aware of the politics. This chapter is driven by such an awareness. One can respond to political realities by lamenting them and, then either wishing them away or defying them. Neither course strikes us as useful. Rather, it is better to recognize them and to be professionally proactive in response. Peer tutoring can then be ahead and stay ahead of others because the groundwork that was created was solid.

References

Boyer, E. L. (1990). *Scholarship reconsidered*. Stanford, CA: Carnegie Foundation for the Advancement of Teaching.

Bruffee, K. (2006). *A short course in writing: Composition, collaborative learning, and constructive reading*. New York, NY: Longman. (Original work published 1972)

Council of Writing Program Administrators (1998). *Evaluating the intellectual work of writing administrators*. Retrieved from http://www.wpacouncil.org/positions/intellectual work. html.

Diamond, R. M., & Adam, B. E. (1995). *The disciplines speak*. Sterling, VA: Stylus Publishing.

Dvorak, J. (2001). The college tutoring experience. *The Learning Assistance Review*, 6, 33–46.

Modern Language Association Commission on Professional Service. (1996). *Making faculty work load visible: Reinterpreting professional service, teaching, and research in the fields of language and literature*. New York, NY: Modern Language Association.

Note

1. We base this observation on the statuses of our colleagues in both speaking and writing centers as well as those in related tutoring centers. To our knowledge, there is no systematic survey of tutoring directors to provide hard data.

· 3 ·

BUILDING AN EFFECTIVE AND SUPPORTIVE PEER TUTORING TEAM

Steven A. Beebe

Peer tutoring centers function best when staff members work collaboratively as an effective and supportive team. Although tutoring others is often a one-on-one instructional activity, there are benefits to working as a team to achieve the goals of a peer tutoring center. Yet teamwork typically doesn't just happen without careful coordination and planning. This chapter presents practical strategies to develop a well-functioning peer tutoring team. After identifying why working together as a team is important, teamwork is defined and the characteristics of effective teamwork are delineated. The chapter then presents the skills, techniques, and strategies for developing an effective peer tutoring team. Since peer tutors often collaborate during meetings, how to organize, lead, and participate in meetings is presented. Finally, how to avoid groupthink in teams and achieve team consensus when there are differences of opinion is presented. The overall goal of this chapter is to identify the key skills and principles to ensure that peer tutoring centers operate as a collaborative community.[1]

The Importance of Teamwork in an Effective Peer Tutoring Program

It is not just peer tutoring centers that benefit from teamwork; most work that is accomplished can be enhanced when there is collaboration and carefully crafted teamwork. Why do we spend so much of our workday collaborating with others? And why is it important to develop team skills? The simple fact is two heads are indeed better than one (most of the time). An effective peer tutoring team can capitalize on the energy of others (which is often called synergy) and this energy can enhance the overall effectiveness of the team. It is important to develop teamwork skills because research suggests that when we collaborate we usually (but admittedly not always) end up with a better outcome (Rico, Sanchez-Manzanares, Gil, & Gibson, 2008). The reason that teams can be so successful is because they usually have more information; stimulate creativity; enhance recall of information because participants are actively involved in the process; are more satisfied with the outcome (Strubler & York, 2007); and learn about themselves through feedback from others (Argyle, 1991; Maier, 1967; Wilke & Meertens, 1994).

Peer tutoring centers can thus be enhanced if peer tutors are trained to work together rather than seeing their work as isolated from the overall goals of the center. But if all of these advantages occur when we collaborate, why do we sometimes become frustrated when working in teams? The answer: because there are also disadvantages when we collaborate with others. One person may dominate; there may be pressure to conform; too few people may actually do the work (Stark, Shaw, & Duffy, 2007); and it takes more time to work collaboratively than it does collectively (Beebe & Masterson, 2015).

Although peer tutoring is primarily a dyadic activity with a peer tutor working with a learner, it is important for peer tutors to view their work as a collaborative process. Members of a peer tutoring team work with others to achieve the overall goals of the peer tutoring center. Understanding how individual tutorial roles link with the larger goal of a peer tutoring program can enhance both the individual tutor-learner relationship, as well as help the entire peer tutoring program to operate more efficiently and effectively and achieve the goals of the center. From time to time there are disagreements and conflicts that occur within a peer tutoring team. Understanding and applying teamwork skills and principles can help manage differences when they arise as well as address issues before they erupt into more destructive communication challenges.

Definition of Teamwork

A team is a coordinated group of individuals organized to work together to achieve a specific, common goal (Beebe & Masterson, 2015). A peer tutoring team includes all of the individuals involved in achieving the goal of enhancing learning between tutor and learner. Investing the time in understanding and applying principles of teamwork can not only be beneficial to those who administer a peer tutoring center, but also pays dividends for the student learners as well. Precisely what do effective peer tutoring teams do? Stated succinctly, they have clearly defined responsibilities, explicit rules for operation, well-defined goals, and clear methods of coordinating their work.

Teams develop clearly defined responsibilities for team members

Each member of the peer tutoring team needs to know both what their individual responsibilities are as well as the responsibilities of other team members. On a sports team, for example, most team members have specifically assigned duties such as shortstop, pitcher, quarterback, or fullback. A peer-tutoring team member's duties and roles should be explicitly spelled out. Team members may perform more than one function or role, but they nonetheless have well-defined duties (Brodbeck & Greitemeyer, 2002).

Teams have clearly defined rules for team operation

In a well-functioning team, team members develop explicit rules for how the work should be done (Shimanoff, 1980). A rule is an explicit procedure and prescribed behavior that helps the team achieve its goals. For example, a peer tutoring team may establish a rule that if someone is going to be absent he or she should tell another team member. Team members should know what the rules are and be aware of how those rules affect the team.

Teams develop clear goals

One of the hallmarks of any team is having a clear goal. Peer tutors should know not only what their individual goal is, but also what the overall goal of the peer tutoring team is (Hoegl, 2003). The clearest team goals are stated in ways that the goal can be measured, such as to increase learner satisfaction with tutoring sessions, or to see more repeat appointments. Having a peer tutor view him or herself as contributing to a larger goal will help foster teamwork.

Teams develop a way of coordinating their efforts

Effective teams spend time discussing how to accomplish the goals of the team. They work together. Their work is coordinated to avoid duplication of effort. Peer tutor members should periodically come together to talk about common problems and also provide development opportunities (Mierlo, Rutte, Kompier,

& Kompier, 2005). Are there common strategies for leading a peer tutoring session? Are there ways of assessing learning that all team members should follow? Team training should focus on how team members work both individually but also collectively in achieving the clear goals that are developed.

Developing an Effective Peer Tutoring Team

There is a difference between simply knowing what an effective team does and coaching a team to be effective. This section describes how peer tutoring teams can develop the characteristics of effective teamwork. This information can be useful when developing peer tutoring training programs. Precisely what does an effective peer tutoring team do when applying principles and practices of effective teamwork? Peer tutoring teams should be able to develop a clear mission statement, clarify who does what by explicitly discussing team member roles, identify and clarify team norms, and participate in the development of team ground rules.

Developing a Team Mission Statement

A team mission statement is a concise description of the overarching goals or desired outcomes of the team. A clearly-worded mission statement not only helps a team achieve the task by knowing whether it is on task or off task, but also lets the team know when it has completed the task. It is best for tutoring teams to participate in the development of a mission statement rather than having one thrust upon them (Beebe & Masterson, 2015). Because there are likely to be team members who leave and others who join the team, it is useful for a peer tutoring team leader to periodically revisit the team mission statement. Whereas the goals of the team and specific learning objectives are typically more specific than a mission statement, the overall mission statement provides a "north star" to guide the peer tutoring team.

A well-worded team mission statement includes six elements. First, it should be specific—it should clearly describe what the team should accomplish. Although team goals and objectives are even more specific, a mission statement should clearly describe what the team does. Second, it should be measurable. The team must be able to assess whether the mission was achieved. Third, it should be attainable—the mission statement should be realistic. Fourth, it should be relevant—the mission should be appropriate to what the team has been assigned to do. Fifth, it should be time bound—teams should set a deadline or time frame for achieving the mission. Finally, it should be a bit of a challenge, so as to stretch the team. If the mission is too simple, it won't inspire the team to do its best work. In summary, a good team mission statement should pass the SMARTS test—it should be Specific, Measurable, Attainable, Relevant, Time bound, and should Stretch the team (Katzenbach & Smith, 1993; Scholtes, Joiner, & Streibel, 1996). Here are examples of SMART team mission statements:

- Our team will increase reading comprehension for students at our school by 10 percent within six months.
- Our team will enhance student performance on math exams within four months.
- Our team will assist in increasing the passing rate on standardized test scores by 10 percent by the end of the academic year.

Because the team mission statement guides the team in all they do, it is best if teams develop their mission statements early in their history rather than later.

Developing Clear Peer Tutoring Team Roles

How to communicate with others in a team is a function of the team member's role. A role is the consistent way a person communicates with others in a team based on expectations people have for themselves and others (Beebe & Masterson, 2015). It is impossible not to have a role; but the role may be unclear, changing, or unproductive in helping the team achieve its mission. It is important to have explicit conversations about who does what and when they should perform specific tasks. A team member's role is based upon their expectations of themselves and the expectations others have for them. There is also evidence that a team member's personality and the personality characteristics of other team members has a major influence on team role development (Halfhill, Sundstrom, Lahner, Calderone, & Nielsen, 2005).

A team role is worked out jointly between a team member's own expectations about him or herself and the expectations of others. So one of the ways to develop team roles is to have a team conversation about role expectations, duties, and how the individual team-member responsibilities are linked to the overall goal of the team. A team member's role can be classified into three broad categories: task roles, social roles, and individual roles.

Task roles

Task roles are those behaviors that help the team achieve its goal and accomplish its work; training team members to perform their specific tutorial functions, reading to learners, fulfilling administrative duties, writing reports, and working one-on-one with students are examples of task roles. Each of these behaviors help the team accomplish its mission by performing specific tasks that are assigned or emerge from the work that needs to be done. Training sessions or instructional materials that teach peer tutors how to perform their task roles is vital to a peer tutoring center achieving its overall mission. It is important for peer tutors to know not only their own role but also the roles of other team members, especially if team members have differing assignments among them.

Social roles

Social roles focus on behaviors that manage relationships and affect the team's climate. These roles help manage interpersonal relationships, resolve conflict, and enhance the flow of communication. Soothing hurt feelings and helping the team celebrate its accomplishments are examples of social role behavior. Training sessions that focus on such skills as listening, conflict management, and developing a supportive team climate will help develop positive social roles within the team. Although social roles typically develop naturally based on the talents, skills, and personalities of individual team members, team training sessions that discuss the importance of social roles can ensure that these important team roles are met.

Individual roles

Individual roles are those that focus attention on the individual, rather than the team (Beebe & Masterson, 2015). These are roles that do *not* help the team; instead, they emphasize individual accomplishments and issues rather than those of the entire group. It is useful for team members to not only know what roles to perform (task and social roles) but also what team roles are counterproductive to the team. Dominating team discussions to talk about personal issues or concerns, always telling jokes that routinely get the team off track, and constantly complaining or whining about how their individual needs aren't being met are examples of individual roles. Individual roles are to be avoided.

When training peer tutoring teams it is useful to include information about team roles. Reviewing specific, individual responsibilities and expectations with each team member and showing how the individual actions contribute to achieving the overall mission of the team should be a key element in peer tutoring training.

How to Identify and Understand Team Norms

Team norms are standards that determine what constitutes appropriate and inappropriate behavior in a group (Beebe & Masterson, 2015). Common team norms help develop team coordination and cooperation. Norms reflect normal behavior in the group. They influence how group members are supposed to behave—everything from the type of language that is acceptable to the casualness of the clothes that team members wear. Norms can evolve into more formal rules, which are more explicit prescriptions that spell out how group members should interact.

Norms can be identified by observing the group. Listen and observe any repeated verbal or nonverbal behavior patterns. Note, for example, consistencies in the way people talk or dress. To help you spot norms in your groups, consider the following questions:

- What are group members' attitudes toward time (do meetings and tutoring sessions start and stop on time)?
- How do team members dress for tutoring sessions?
- Is it acceptable to use informal language, slang terms, or colloquialisms?
- What kind of humor is acceptable?
- How do team members treat the leader or supervisor?

Noting when someone breaks a norm can also help you spot a norm. If a peer tutor waltzes into a training session 20 minutes late and a colleague frowns or looks at his or her watch, that is a sure sign that a norm has been violated. The severity of the punishment corresponds to the significance of the norm (Shaw, 1981). Mild punishment is usually unspoken, such as nonverbal glances or a frowning stare. More serious punishment can be a negative comment about the behavior in front of other team members. You do not have to worry about whether teams will have norms or not; norms emerge naturally. You should, however, monitor the team norms to ensure that individual behavior of team members does not distract from the work of the team, or to note whether an unproductive team norm has developed (such as it is normal for peer tutors to be late for tutoring sessions) that the group should discuss.

When providing training about team norms it is useful to make sure team members are aware of how the existing norms affect individual team members, as well as how norms have an effect on the entire team. Spending time identifying and clarifying norms will help team members be more comfortable when communicating with each other. Being aware of team norms helps team members feel more confident and comfortable when interacting with each other.

Developing Team Ground Rules

Team ground rules are explicit, agreed on prescriptions for acceptable and appropriate behavior. Whereas norms develop organically without explicit discussion, ground rules are discussed and may be written down to ensure that they are clear and that team members are in compliance with them. Just as there are rules that sports teams follow to score points, an effective peer tutoring team takes the time to develop clear rules to organize routine tasks and procedures. Rules help keep order so that meaningful work can be accomplished. Rules also state what the team or organization values. Honesty, fairness, starting and stopping meetings on time, and personal safety are typical values embedded in team ground rules.

To develop ground rules, the team leader should facilitate a discussion to establish the ground rules early in the formation of a peer tutoring team. Teams clearly operate better if team members develop their own ground rules rather than having them imposed from "on high." Some questions that can help a group develop clear and appropriate ground rules are:

- How should we record the successes of our accomplishments?
- When we meet together, who should set the meeting agenda?
- How long should our meetings last?
- Should we have a regular meeting time and place?
- What should a member do if he or she can't attend a meeting?
- When we disagree, how should we make our decisions—by majority vote or consensus?
- What kind of climate do we want in our meetings?
- What other kinds of rules or guidelines do we need to develop?

These questions may result in the following typical team ground rules:

- Each of our peer tutoring sessions will begin on time.
- Each team member is expected to attend each staff meeting.
- Each team member will be prepared for every meeting.
- During meetings, only one person will speak at a time.
- We will work together to manage conflict when it arises.
- If we get off the agenda during a peer tutoring meeting, and someone notices that we are off the agenda, we will return to the agenda.
- We will agree to make a written note of issues or topics that we discuss that are not on the agenda and will return to the topic at a later time.

- We will make decisions by consensus rather than a simple majority vote.
- Each team member will follow through on individual assignments.

Teaching team members how to establish their missions, roles, norms, and ground rules will help manage team uncertainty about what team members should do and how they should behave. Besides prescribing specific behaviors, teamwork can be enhanced if team members are able to accurately describe and predict how teams usually discuss issues and topics.

Understanding Team Phases: How Teams Develop Over Time

Some researchers have found that teams go through certain phases or sequences of talk when they meet to solve a problem or discuss an issue (Furst, Reeves, Rosen, & Blackburn, 2004; Wheelan, Davidson, & Tilin 2003). Researchers do not agree on the exact nature of these phases, or even the number of phases. Some researchers have found three phases, while most have found four. One of the most descriptive four-phase models was developed by group communication researcher Aubrey Fisher (1970). His four phases of group talk are: (1) orientation, (2) conflict, (3) emergence, and (4) reinforcement.

Orientation

As you might suspect when people first get together in a team, they become oriented to what they are doing. During the orientation phase, team members become oriented to at least two things: who is on the team and what they will be doing. When a team is first started, there is usually high uncertainty about how the team will be organized, who is in charge, and exactly how things will work. Research on the orientation phase suggests that your communication is directed at orienting yourself toward others as well as to the team's task. Another name for this first phase is primary tension. This is the tension that results from the uncertainty and discomfort people experience when they meet for the first time (Chang, Bordia, & Duck, 2003; Gersick, 1989; Gersick & Hackman, 1990; Poole, 1983; Scheidel & Crowell, 1994). Some team members who do not like uncertainty at all and are eager to start sorting things out will suggest an agenda: "Hello, my name is Steve. Let's start by introducing ourselves." Other group members are quite content to simply sit quietly in the background and let others take the lead. As people begin to become acquainted and group members start talking about the purpose of the meeting, typical groups experience the second phase—conflict.

Conflict

People are different. That unprofound observation has profound implications for human communication, and nowhere is it more evident than in a group discussion after the group gets down to business. The conflict phase typically, but not always, follows the orientation phase. During the orientation phase, group members form opinions about what the group should be doing and who should be doing it. As the group becomes more comfortable and oriented, they start asserting these opinions. They have tested the water in the first phase and are now ready to jump in.

The conflict phase is necessary for both the purpose of solving problems and maintaining group relationships. If there is no conflict it usually means people are not being honest about how they really feel. Lack of conflict and a climate where team members seem to agree about most things without challenging ideas is called groupthink. We will discuss how to avoid groupthink later in the chapter. When ideas are not challenged and tested, the group usually makes flawed decisions. Also, honest yet tactful expression of personal disagreement is more likely to foster genuine rather than phony relationships. You can take some comfort in knowing that conflict is an expected part of group deliberations.

Emergence

You know you are in the emergence phase when decisions begin to be made and the group begins to solidify a common point of view. Though conflict is still a part of the third phase, what sets the emergence phase apart from the conflict phase is the way in which group members manage the conflict. Norms, roles, ground rules, and leadership patterns that have been established in the team help the group get work accomplished. In the emergence phase, a team settles on norms and moves toward consensus or agreement.

Reinforcement

Team members become more unified in the fourth phase, the reinforcement phase. During the orientation, conflict, and emergence phases team members struggle through getting acquainted, developing cohesiveness, competing for status and prominence, and puzzling over issues and actions the team could take. The team eventually emerges from those struggles (phase three) and develops a new sense of direction. This accomplishment results in a more positive feeling about the group. The team more clearly develops a sense of "we." In fact, one of the ways to identify the reinforcement phase is when team members use more collective pronouns to talk about the group (we, us, our) than personal pronouns (I, me, my).

Although there are four distinct phases that groups can experience, all teams do not neatly process through these phases in exactly the same way. The descriptive approach to group problem solving has identified these phases and can help provide a general overview of how many groups operate, but more recent research suggests some groups do not go through these phases at all (Chang, Bordia, & Duck 2003; Gersick, 1989; Gersick, & Hackman 1990; Poole, 1983; Scheidel & Crowell, 1994).

Some teams may simply get stuck in orientation. Conversely, some teams seem to spend more time in the conflict phase, perhaps bouncing between orientation and conflict. Eventually something will emerge (phase three) from the team even if it is not a wise decision or quality solution. The team may decide, for example, to disband and never meet again because the members are so dysfunctional. Something emerged—the group members quit—but that is not the reason the group was formed. Reinforcement is likely to occur because we like to make sense out of what happens to us. Even if the group disbands, we are likely to celebrate its demise or reinforce the decision to disband. Many groups, especially those that emphasize efficiency and productivity, may very quickly gloss over the reinforcement aspects of group celebration. Wise team leaders and participants make sure that victories are celebrated and both team and individual efforts are recognized. The resulting cohesiveness and positive feelings from such celebrations will be helpful as the group prepares for its next task. It becomes oriented all over again, experiences conflict, has something emerge as a course of action, and reinforces the action. Again, these phases may not occur in as orderly or predictable a manner as it appears, but most groups do experience some elements of these phases.

How to Lead Peer Tutoring Meetings

Peer tutoring staffs generally have regular meetings for training and decision-making. Meetings are the ever-present format for collaborating in most contemporary organizations (Johnson, Bettenhausen & Gibbons, 2009). For a meeting to be productive, the group or team should be small enough so that each participant can contribute to the conversation (Bonito, 2006; Hopthrow & Hulbert, 2005). Meetings should have a specific goal—an agenda that identifies what will be discussed, as well as interactive conversation that is focused on achieving the meeting goal.

Meetings are more productive if participants are aware of their own behaviors (Beebe & Masterson, 2015). Using and interpreting verbal and nonverbal symbols is also vital for meeting effectiveness as well as listening and responding to those messages with sensitivity. Because of the complexity and uncertainty of several people collaborating, being able to adapt message content and message structure is essential.

The following is a list of the top ten meeting problems participants often complain about (Mosvick & Nelson, 1987).

1. Getting off the subject
2. No goals or agenda
3. Too lengthy
4. Poor or inadequate preparation
5. Inconclusive
6. Disorganized
7. Ineffective leadership
8. Irrelevant information discussed
9. Time wasted during meetings
10. Starting late

Each of these meeting problems boils down to the two essential things meetings need in order to be effective: structure and interaction (Beebe & Masterson, 2015). Group structure consists of the agenda and other techniques that help a group stay focused on the task at hand. A meeting that gets off topic, has no agenda, or is too long needs more structure to keep it focused on its goal. Interaction is the give and take conversation that occurs when people collaborate; it is vital for the exchange of ideas. At the same time, a disorganized, out of control group that wastes time may have too much interaction or too much unfocused talk. One study suggests that people who communicate in groups and teams typically change topics about once a minute unless someone is helping them stay on track (Berg, 1967; Bormann & Bormann, 1976; Poole, 1983). If there is too much of either structure or interaction, the meeting can suffer.

Can a peer tutoring meeting have too much structure? Yes. If you have been to a meeting or group discussion that seemed more like a seminar than an interactive discussion, then there was too much structure. If the meeting is so controlled that one or two people do most of the talking, then you are not at a meeting, you are at a speech. The goal is to balance the amount of structure with group interaction. In an interactive group, there are fewer long utterances and more people are contributing. In a highly structured meeting, there is more control over who talks, about what, and for how long. The key is to find the right balance between structure and interaction.

Preparing for Meetings

Effective meetings don't just happen; the best way to have a good meeting is to prepare. Investing time in preparing for work before actually beginning the work will pay dividends, especially if you are leading the meeting. There are three key tasks in preparing for meetings, including first deciding whether you even need to hold a meeting. Second, if a meeting is needed you will need to determine what the meeting goals are and how to structure precisely what you will talk about to achieve the meeting goals. Third, and perhaps the most important task in preparing the meeting, is to develop the meeting agenda.

Determining Whether to Have a Meeting

To meet, or not to meet: That is the first question. If you are leading a peer tutoring team, one of your jobs is to determine whether a meeting is needed. The cardinal rule of meetings is this: *Meet only when you have a reason to meet*. You can accomplish quite a bit of collaborative work without meeting face-to-face. For example, if you just need to share information and need no commentary or inter-action, sending a memo or email message may suffice. One leader periodically sends out what he calls a "meeting in a memo" that summarizes key announce-ments, reports, or reminders. You may want to ponder whether a meeting is premature; if people are not prepared for the meeting, are not well informed, or there is too much tension and conflict, holding a meeting will only make things worse. Rather than calling a meeting, you may need to do some one-on-one work by sharing written information, delegating background work to an individ-ual, talking to people individually to manage interpersonal conflict, or inviting people to read existing policies and procedures before calling a meeting.

Determining the Meeting Goal

Every meeting should have a goal. If not, don't hold a meeting! Regardless of the task or project, most meeting goals boil down to achieving one or more of the following three outcomes: (1) sharing information, (2) discussing infor-mation, and (3) taking action. The first step in preparing for a meeting, espe-cially if you are leading the meeting, is to determine its goal or goals.

Sharing information

An information-sharing meeting is like a briefing or a series of short speeches. Many weekly staff meetings are primarily gatherings during which someone shares information with others. Although these information-giving sessions are called meetings, it really is not a meeting in the true sense of the word. There certainly are times when you want to share information live and in person with the peer tutoring team to emphasize its importance or to get a reaction from others such as explaining a change in policy, procedure, or center goals. If you want reactions to what you present make sure to budget time for discussion and reactions. Sometimes you may need to give information during the early part of the meeting and then move into discussion before taking action. However, if the goal is to explain a new policy and you want or expect minimal discussion, then you are presenting a briefing rather than holding a meeting. Briefings have an important function in business and professional settings; sometimes the purpose can be to simply see other team members once a week to get an update on projects and assess team-member needs, particularly in businesses with global divisions. Briefings differ from collaborative meetings. While there is value in the ritual of seeing other people on the team and enhancing relationships, if people think they are going to attend a meeting and it is really a speech or briefing, the participants may end up feeling frustrated rather than enlightened.

Discussing information

An information discussing meeting is one in which there is considerable interaction and give-and-take discussion. The goal is to gather and assess reactions to information, policies, or procedures. If the primary goal is to gather or discuss information, it is important not to let the meeting become a series of long-winded speeches. It is important when the goal is to discuss information to encourage all group members to participate in the conversation and share ideas, data, opinions, and information (Brodbeck, Kerschreiter, Mojzisch, & Schulz-Hardt, 2007; Dane & Pratt, 2007; de Vries, van den Hooff, & de Ridder, 2006; Henningsen & Henningsen, 2007; Reimer, Kuendig, Hoffrage, Park, & Hinz, 2007). There are ways to use structured conversation techniques to ensure that all members feel free to participate. Those strategies will be discussed later in the chapter.

Taking action

A meeting to take action often involves making a decision, solving a problem, or implementing a decision or solution. For example, developing a new policy to assess peer tutoring learning outcomes involves taking action. Prior to taking action, a team should gather, analyze, and discuss the information. A meeting could have a single agenda item of making a decision, but team members would have undoubtedly had prior conversations and have shared information and options. They would come to the meeting with the background needed to make the decision.

Many, if not most, peer tutoring meetings will have multiple goals. You may first have information presented, then discuss the information, and finally take some action based upon the meeting goal. If you are the meeting leader, before beginning to draft your agenda, you need to know the meeting goal or each of those steps may involve a separate meeting. As you prepare for a meeting, identify what you would like to have happen as a result of the meeting. A typical goal might be "At the end of this meeting we will have decided who we will hire for the new tutoring job," or "At the end of the meeting, we will have discussed and evaluated the plan for hosting a writing award celebration event." Without a specific goal, it is likely you will accomplish little.

Developing the Meeting Agenda

Once you have identified goals and determined what you need to talk about, it is time to develop an agenda. An agenda is the written list of issues, questions, and topics that serves as the primary tool to help you structure the order in which you talk about each topic. To develop an agenda, first consider all of the topics, issues, and questions you need to discuss to achieve your meeting goals. As you start to identify the various agenda items you do not need to worry about the order in which to place them. First identify what the agenda items are, and then arrange the topics and issues in a logical structure.

Consider organizing the agenda around your meeting goals. Use subheadings of information items, discussion items, and action items to signal to team members the goal of the discussion. If your meeting goal is to discuss the pros and cons of the new hiring policy, then your agenda would likely include such straight-forward questions as "What are the benefits of the new peer tutor selection policy?" and "What are the disadvantages of the new policy?" Before making final decisions about which items you will discuss, estimate how long you think the team will need to discuss each item. Most groups take more time than you think to talk about issues and ideas.

Developing an agenda is an art, not a science. There are several issues to consider as you prepare your agenda. For example, it is usually best to put your most important item first because usually what is introduced first takes the most time. Depending on your meeting goals, you may want to first string together several small issues so that you can dispense with them before getting into the meat of the meeting. One strategy is to place the most challenging issues for discussion in the middle of the meeting, thus giving the group a chance to get oriented at the beginning and ease out of the discussion at the end. Another strategy is to make your first agenda item something that will immediately involve all meeting members in active discussion. By placing a high priority item early in the meeting you take advantage of having people talk about an issue when they are fresher. Starting the meeting with announcements and routine reports may set a climate of passivity, and boredom is the usual product, although sometimes it is necessary to start with reports before discussing an issue. One option for beginning your meeting is to actively involve members in finalizing the agenda; ask them for reactions to how you have structured the discussion. Ask participants if they have other agenda items to include on the agenda in an effort to avoid digressions and surprise agenda additions later. It is usually best to avoid placing routine announcements and reports at the beginning of a meeting (Kayser, 1990; Romig & Romig, 1996). In addition to creating a climate of boredom, members may also be less sensitive to the time constraints at the beginning of a meeting; participants may be tempted to spend too much time reacting to routine reports. The precise order of your agenda depends on your goals and your knowledge of your meeting participants.

Always distribute an agenda to meeting participants before the meeting. Without an agenda or some knowledge of what will be discussed at the meeting, participants will not know how to prepare. In addition to asking for feedback about the meeting agenda before you begin the meeting, periodically ask meeting participants if the agenda is serving its purpose. Ask, "Are we still discussing useful information?" or "Is our agenda helping us achieve our meeting goals?" Of course, this assumes you have a clear goal of what you and your colleagues are trying to achieve in your meeting.

In addition to distributing copies of the agenda before the meeting and having copies of the agenda to distribute when you meet, it is sometimes useful to visually display the meeting agenda during the meeting. Having a common image to look at can help keep a group focused on its goal. Teams need a common space in which to collaborate; showing a visual image of the agenda provides that common space visually and helps to keep the group literally focused on the same agenda.

Conducting Meetings: How to Structure Meetings to Achieve Results

After you have decided that a meeting is needed, developed your goal(s), and prepared your agenda, you need to develop strategies to accomplish the tasks you have outlined. If your meeting goals include taking action on issues or proposals, you will likely be making decisions, solving problems, or developing creative approaches to issues, decisions or problems. In order to take appropriate action you will need to develop strategies to structure the discussion to achieve those outcomes.

Strategies for Meeting Facilitators

The essential task of a meeting facilitator is to manage the interaction in order to achieve the goals of the group. A meeting facilitator may be a different person than the leader, boss, or the supervisor of the team. A facilitator's job is to help manage the flow of conversation and keep the group on track. Research suggests that one of the key duties of a meeting facilitator is to ask questions that help the group uncover information, ideas, and strategies for making decisions and solving problems. Specifically, facilitators who can help achieve the following results enhance team processes (Witte, 2007):

- Ask questions that help the group identify information it needs at the beginning of team deliberations.
- Strive to get as many people on the team as possible to participate in the conversation.
- Make sure team members understand the comments and suggestions offered by other team members.
- Solicit high-quality, on-task, relevant contributions from team members.

The essential skills of a meeting facilitator are to be a gatekeeper, keep the team focused on the goal, monitor time, and when appropriate, use tools and techniques to help structure the interaction that occurs.

Be a gatekeeper

A gatekeeper encourages less-talkative members to participate and tries to limit lengthy contributions by other group members. A meeting leader should make sure to involve all meeting participants in the discussion. A meeting facilitator needs to be a skilled listener who is sensitive to both individual members' needs as well as the over-arching team goals and knows when to step in. Gatekeepers make such comments as, "Alice, we haven't heard your ideas yet. Won't you share your thoughts with us?" Or, "Mike thanks for sharing but I'd like to hear what others have to say." Polite, tactful invitations to talk or limit talk usually work. An unruly over-verbalizer may need a private talk to let him or her know that you would appreciate a more balanced discussion.

Focus on the goal

As emphasized earlier, team members need to understand the team goals. Once they do, the team's agenda for each meeting should provide a road map for moving toward those goals. A leader often has to keep the group on course. One of the most effective ways to stay focused on the goal is for the team leader, or even a team member, to periodically summarize what the team has accomplished and where the team is on its planned agenda. Such summaries help a group take stock of what it has done and what it has yet to accomplish. Research has found that the most experienced facilitators help orient the group toward the goal, help them adapt to what is happening in the group, and involve the group in developing the agenda for the meeting (Niederman & Volkema, 1990).

Monitor time

Another job of a meeting leader is to keep track of how much time has been spent on the planned agenda items, and how much time remains. Think of your agenda as a map, helping you plan where you want to go. Think of the clock as your gas gauge, telling you the amount of fuel you have to get where you want to go. In a meeting, just as on any car trip, you need to know where you are going and how much fuel you need to get you to your destination. If you are running out of fuel (time), you will either need to fill up the tank (budget more time) or recognize that you will not get where you want to go. Begin each meeting by asking how long members can meet. If you face two or three crucial agenda items, and one-third of your group has to leave in an hour, you will want to make certain to schedule important items early in the meeting.

Structure interaction

To ensure that all members participate in the discussion, it may be useful to have team members write responses before discussing them verbally. This helps a team structure their interaction and involves everyone in the process.

A key task of the meeting facilitator is to orchestrate meaningful interaction during the meeting so that all participants have the opportunity to give input. Structured methods of inviting involvement are effective in garnering contributions from all group members.

Tips for Leading Team Meetings

How to determine whether you need a meeting, developing meeting goals, and establishing an agenda are each key tasks of a meeting leader. The meeting leader is the person who calls the meeting, sets the agenda and usually facilitates the meeting. Also, a meeting leader needs to be especially sensitive to balancing meeting structure with interaction. Here, I provide an overview of the key procedural expectations of meeting leaders.

To be an effective meeting leader the leader should facilitate rather than dictate how the group will conduct the meeting. One study found that groups generated more and better ideas when team leaders simply listened and waited for team members to contribute ideas before stating their own ideas than they did when the leader spoke first (Roy, Gauvin, & Limayem, 1996). Different groups accept (or tolerate) different levels of directions from their designated leaders. One simple rule of thumb is this: *A group will generally allow a leader who emerges naturally from the group, or who leads a one-time-only ad hoc group, to be more directive.*

Beyond giving direction, certain tasks are generally expected of leaders. In general, meeting leaders are expected to do the following (Mosvick & Nelson, 1987):

- Call the group together, which may involve finding out when participants can meet.
- Call the meeting to order.
- Review the agenda. Ask if there are additional agenda items to discuss.
- Keep the meeting moving; go on to the next agenda item when a point has been thoroughly covered. Use effective facilitation and gatekeeping skills.
- Prepare a report (or delegate someone to prepare a report) after one or many meetings. Teams need a record of their progress. Many groups designate someone to be a secretary and prepare the minutes or summary of what occurred at the meeting.

You may spend more of your time in meetings being a meeting participant than a meeting leader. Roger Mosvick and Robert Nelson (1987), in their book *We've Got to Start Meeting Like This!*, identify six guidelines for becoming a competent meeting participant: organize your contributions; speak when your contribution is relevant; make one point at a time; speak clearly and forcefully; support your ideas with evidence; and listen to what others say.

Avoiding Groupthink: Encouraging Interaction

During peer tutoring team meetings, be cautious if all team members agree too quickly—your team may be experiencing groupthink instead of consensus. Groupthink occurs when team members seemingly agree, but they primarily just want to avoid conflict (Beebe & Masterson, 2015). On the surface it seems as if team members have reached consensus–but it is an illusion of agreement. Another way of describing groupthink is as an ineffective consensus; too little disagreement often reduces the quality of team decisions. If a team does not seriously examine the pros and cons of an idea it is likely that the quality of the decision will suffer (Klocke, 2007). Effective groups do experience conflict, and then productively seek to manage the conflict. When conflict occurs in the group the entire group may experience a feeling of dissonance or discomfort. Some group members may want to manage the dissonance by quickly agreeing, but a mature, well-functioning group realizes conflict is part of the process of collaborating in groups and teams (Matz & Wood, 2005).

What causes groupthink? Groupthink is most likely to occur when: (1) the team feels apathetic about its task, (2) team members don't expect to be successful, (3) one team member has very high credibility and team members tend to believe what he or she says, (4) one team member is very persuasive, and/or (5) team members do not usually challenge ideas; it is expected that team members will agree with one another (Shulz-Hardt, Brodbeck, Mojzisch, Kerschreiter, & Frey, 2006; Veiga, 1991). To overcome groupthink consider the following strategies (Janis, 1971): Encourage team members to be independent, critical thinkers; don't agree with someone just because he or she has high status; consider asking someone outside the group to evaluate the group's decisions; ask someone to be a "devil's advocate"—to look for disadvantages and problems that might occur with a suggested solution; and sometimes break into smaller groups to look at the pros and cons of an idea or issue.

Reaching Consensus: Managing Conflict

Consensus occurs when all group members support and are committed to a decision. To manage conflict and disagreement in order to reach consensus takes time and skill, but to reap the benefits of group and team deliberations, it is a useful goal, if time permits, to strive for team consensus on key issues and decisions.

There are several strategies that can help teams reach consensus. One of the best strategies to keep the team focused on its goal is to use the discussion tool called metadiscussion. Metadiscussion literally means "discussion about discussion." It refers to comments about the discussion process rather than the topic under consideration. A metadiscussion comment helps the group stop and reflect on what it is doing. It helps a group be mindful or aware of how it is operating. The fundamental communication principle of being aware is especially important when several people are talking (sometimes at the same time) and people are thinking about what they are saying rather than really listening to what others are saying (Gurtner, Tschan, Semmer, & Nagele, 2007). Metadiscussional statements include, "I'm not following this conversation. What is our goal?" Or, "Can someone summarize what we've accomplished so far?" Periodically, using metadiscussion statements can help keep the team on track and focused. For example, saying, "Peggy, I'm not sure I understand how your observation relates to our meeting goal," can help gently guide a team member back to the topic at hand.

One way to soften making comments in a meeting is to use "I" messages rather than "You" messages to bring the team back on track (Beebe & Masterson, 2015). An "I" message begins with the word "I" such as "I am not sure where we are in our discussion" or "I am lost here." A "You" message is a way of phrasing a message that makes others feel defensive. Here are examples of "You" messages: "You're not following the agenda" or "Your point doesn't make any sense." Metadiscussion is an exceptionally powerful skill because you can offer metadiscussional statements even if you are not the appointed leader.

A second general strategy is to listen carefully to the ideas of others. Work to clarify misunderstandings. Maintain eye contact with the speaker and give him or her your full attention. Using the active listening technique in which you sometimes paraphrase key ideas to ensure that you understand what someone is saying is another useful tool to help a team get unstuck when consensus seem elusive. Consensus is more likely to blossom when the team can find some areas of agreement rather than just hammering away at the most contentious issues. Team members who help promote a positive climate, express agreement, are open to new ideas, and look for ways to support other team members enhance the likelihood that consensus will occur (Sager & Gastil, 2006).

A third general strategy is to promote honest dialogue and discussion. A true consensus is more likely to occur if many ideas are shared and team members do not just give in to avoid conflict. Changing your mind to avoid conflict will likely result in groupthink. Some teams may be tempted to take a quick vote to settle issues. Although voting can be a useful way of seeing where team members stand on the issues, be wary of taking a vote too quickly before the team has had an opportunity to discuss the issues. Consensus is most likely to be genuine if the team has explored several alternatives, despite the time it takes to have these discussions (Sager & Gastil, 2006).

Conclusion

This chapter has presented essential principles and strategies for developing a peer tutoring team. Developing an effective team takes skill and training. Teamwork and collaboration does not just happen without careful preparation. Although peer tutoring is often a one-on-one task, developing a collaborative team can result in benefits for individual learners as well as help the peer tutoring team achieve its collective goals. The underlying assumption of this chapter is that peer tutoring centers will function more effectively if all members of the center not only feel like they are part of a team, but when they also communicate in ways that foster team collaboration to achieve a common goal.

References

Argyle, M. (1991). *Cooperation: The basics of sociability*. London, UK: Routledge.

Beebe, S. A., and Masterson, J. T. (2015). *Communicating in small groups: Principles and practices*. Boston: Pearson.

Berg, D. M. (1967). A descriptive analysis of the distribution and duration of themes discussed by task-oriented small groups. *Speech Monographs, 34*, 172–175.

Bonito, J. (2006). A longitudinal social relation analysis of participation in small groups. *Human Communication Research, 32*, 302–321.

Bormann, E. G., & Bormann, N. C. (1976). *Effective small group communication*. Minneapolis, MN: Burgess.

Brodbeck, F. C., & Greitemeyer, T. (2002). Effects of individual versus mixed individual and group experience in rule induction on group member learning and group performance. *Journal of Experimental Social Psychology, 36*, 621–648.

Brodbeck, F., Kerschreiter, R., Mojzisch, A., & Schulz-Hardt, S. (2007). Group decision making under conditions of distributed knowledge: The information asymmetries model. *Academy of Management Review, 32*(2), 459–479.

Chang, A., Bordia, P., & Duck, J. (2003). Punctuated equilibrium and linear progression: Toward a new understanding of group development. *Academy of Management Journal, 46*, 106–117.

Dane, E., & Pratt, M. (2007). Exploring intuition and its role in managerial decision making. *Academy of Management Review, 32*(1), 33–54.

de Vries, R., van den Hooff, B., & de Ridder, J. (2006). Explaining knowledge sharing—The role of team communication styles, job satisfaction, and performance beliefs. *Communication Research, 33*(2), 115–135.

Fisher, B. A. (1970). Decision emergence: Phases in group decision-making. *Speech Monographs, 37*, 60.

Furst, S., Reeves, M., Rosen, B., & Blackburn, R. S. (2004). Managing the life cycle of virtual teams. *Academy of Management Executive, 18*, 6–22.

Gersick, C. J. (1989). Time and transition in work teams: Toward a new model of group development. *Academy of Management Journal, 32*, 274–309.

Gersick, C. J., & Hackman, J. R. (1990). Habitual routines in task-performing groups. *Organizational behavior and human decision processes, 47*, 65–97.

Gurtner, A., Tschan, F., Semmer, N., & Nagele, C. (2007). Getting groups to develop good strategies: Effects of reflexivity interventions on team process, team performance, and shared mental models. *Organizational Behavior and Human Decision Processes, 102*, 127–142.

Halfhill, T., Sundstrom, E., Lahner, J., Calderone, W., & Nielsen, T. (2005). Group personality composition and group effectiveness—An integrative review of empirical research. *Small Group Research, 36*(1), 83–105.

Henningsen, D., & Henningsen, M. (2007). Do groups know what they don't know? Dealing with missing information in decision-making groups. *Communication Research, 34*(5), 507–525.

Hoegl, M. (2003). Goal setting and team performance in innovative projects: On the moderating role of teamwork quality. *Small Group Research, 34*, 3–19.

Hopthrow, T., & Hulbert, L. (2005). The effect of group decision making on cooperation in social dilemmas. *Group Processes & Intergroup Relations, 8*(1), 89–100.

Janis, I. L. (1971). Groupthink. *Psychology Today, 5*, 43–46, 74–76.

Johnson, S. K., Bettenhausen, K., & Gibbons, E. (2009). Realities of working in virtual teams: Affective and attitudinal outcomes of using computer-mediated communication. *Small Group Research 40*, 623–649.

Katzenbach, J. R., & Smith, D. K. (1993). *The wisdom of teams: Creating the high-performance organization*. New York, NY: Harper Collins.

Kayser, T. A. (1990). *Mining group gold*. El Segundo, CA: Serif Publishing.

Klocke, U. (2007). How to improve decision making in small groups—Effects of dissent and training interventions. *Small Group Research, 38*(3), 437–468.

Maier, N. R. F. (1967). Assets and liabilities in group problem solving: The need for an integrative function. *Psychological Review, 74*, 239–249.

Matz, D., & Wood, W. (2005). Cognitive dissonance in groups: The consequences of disagreement. *Journal of Personality and Social Psychology, 88*(1), 22–37.

Mierlo, H. V., Rutte, C., Kompier, M., & Kompier, H. (2005). Self-managing teamwork and psychological well-being: Review of a multilevel research domain. *Group Organization Management, 30*(2), 211–235.

Mosvick, R. K., & Nelson, R. B. (1987). *We've got to start meeting like this!* Glenview, IL: Scott, Foresman.

Niederman, F., & Volkema, R. J. (1990). The effects of facilitator characteristics on meeting preparation, set up, and implementation. *Small Group Research, 30*, 330–360.

Poole, M. S. (1983). Decision development in small groups III: A multiple sequence model of group decision development. *Communication Monographs, 50,* 321–341.

Reimer, T., Kuendig, S., Hoffrage, U., Park, E., & Hinz, V. (2007). Effects of the information environment on group discussions and decisions in the hidden-profile paradigm. *Communication Monographs, 74*(1), 1–28.

Rico, R., Sanchez-Manzanares, M., Gil, F., & Gibson, C. (2008). Team implicit coordination processes: A team knowledge-based approach. *Academy of Management Review, 33*(1), 163–184.

Romig, D. A., & Romig, L. L. J. (1996). *Breakthrough teamwork.* Chicago, IL: Irwin.

Roy, M. C., Gauvin, S., & Limayem, M. (1996). Electronic group brainstorming: The role of feedback on productivity. *Small Group Research, 27,* 21–47.

Sager, K., & Gastil, J. (2006). The origins and consequences of consensus decision making: A test of the social consensus model. *Southern Communication Journal, 71,* 1–24.

Scheidel, T. M., & Crowell, L. (1994). Idea development in small discussion groups. *Quarterly Journal of Speech, 50,* 140–45.

Scholtes, P. R., Joiner, B. L., & Streibel, B. J. (1996). *The team handbook.* Madison, WI: Joiner.

Shaw, M. (1981). *Group dynamics: The psychology of small group behavior.* New York, NY: McGraw Hill, 281.

Shimanoff, S. B. (1980). *Communication rules: Theory and research.* Beverly Hills, CA: SAGE..

Shulz-Hardt, S., Brodbeck, F. C., Mojzisch, A., Kerschreiter, R., & Frey, D. (2006). Group decision making in hidden profile situations: Dissent as a facilitator for decision quality. *Journal of Personality and Social Psychology, 91,* 1080–1093.

Stark, E., Shaw, J., & Duffy, M. (2007). Preference for group work, winning orientation, and social loafing behavior in groups. *Group & Organization Management, 32,* 699–723.

Strubler, D., & York, K. (2007). An explanatory study of the team characteristics model using organizational teams. *Small Group Research, 38,* 660–695.

Veiga, J. F. (1991). The frequency of self-limiting behavior in groups: A measure and an explanation. *Human Relations, 44,* 877–895.

Wheelan, S., Davidson, B., & Tilin, E. (2003). Group development across time: Reality or illusion? *Small Group Research, 334,* 223–245.

Wilke, H. A. M., & Meertens, R.W. (1994). *Group performance.* London, UK: Routledge.

Witte, E. (2007). Toward a group facilitations technique for project teams. *Group Processes & Intergroup Relations, 10,* 299–309.

Note

1. This chapter is based on information presented in Beebe, S. A. and Masterson, J. T. (2015). *Communicating in small groups: Principles and practices.* Boston: Pearson; and Beebe. S. A. and Mottet, T. P. (2013). *Business and professional communication: Principles and skills for leadership.* Boston: Pearson.

· 4 ·

MAKING SURE THE WORK IS
GOOD WORK

Communicating Ethics to Tutors

Jon A. Hess

The author thanks Dude Coudret and Zelda Smith for their
contributions to this paper

Few issues in peer tutoring are as important as ethical conduct by all parties involved in the process. While poor quality work may fail to realize the educational potential of the program, poor ethical actions can harm individuals and jeopardize the entire institution. With increased attention to a host of compliance issues, including Title IX and National Collegiate Athletic Association athletic regulations, the institutional risk from ethical lapses is significant. So, one of the first considerations in developing or implementing any peer tutoring program should be a means of ensuring that peer tutors work within necessary ethical parameters.

Given the importance of ethics in peer tutoring, surprisingly little has been written on the topic. In search of literature on peer teaching, Grice, Bird, and Dalton (1990) noted that of 660 articles and papers written from 1983–1990, only three had *ethics* in the title or abstract. The proportion of papers that focus on ethics has not improved much in the ensuing decades, and while books and articles on peer tutoring are bountiful, few offer guidance on achieving excellence in ethical conduct. This chapter draws both upon the limited writings on ethics in peer tutoring, and also the larger bodies of work on communicating ethical standards and developing ethical behavior in organizations to offer guidance to those supervising peer tutoring programs.

The term *good work* in the chapter title is drawn from the writing of Gardner, Csikszentmihalyi, and Damon (2001), who recognized that doing work expertly but not responsibly is skillful labor, but at best it is of little value to humanity, and more likely, it is outright detrimental. Our goal in mentoring students should be not just to help them develop professional expertise, but also to develop a conscience that enables them to understand and conceptualize their work in the context of the ethical role their service provides to their peers, their institution, and to humanity. And, the goal of tutoring supervisors should be to create an environment that shapes a natural path toward ethically commendable behavior.

Promoting Virtuous Behavior

We begin with a statement that sounds too obvious to be meaningful: Those supervising peer tutoring programs have a better chance of seeing ethical conduct if tutors are well-versed in the principles they are supposed to enact. But, as it turns out, this seemingly unprofound statement encapsulates several important points that guide the development of ethically commendable peer tutoring programs.

1. *Lack of attention is not an adequate plan.* Left without any guidance, peer tutors will naturally act ethically in many ways, just due to their general level of integrity. And, sometimes tutors will make good ethical choices just out of good luck. But, luck invariably runs out, and if there is no intentional ethical planning, significant ethical violations are a matter of *when*, not *if*.

2. *Tutors must possess requisite knowledge in order to act ethically.* Tutors must either have this knowledge before they encounter a situation in which they need to apply it, or at the least, they must recognize that they are facing an ethical decision and be able to obtain the information in time to use it.

3. *Clear expectations offer no assurance of compliance.* Clearly communicating ethical policies has value only insofar as tutors are motivated to comply. Simply telling tutors the expectations helps, but if the environment makes ethical behavior difficult, that clear message may do little good. So, it is not enough merely to set out expectations; supervisors also need to create an environment that facilitates ethical behavior.

It is also worth noting that there will always be cases in which tutors willfully violate the rules set before them. The best communication and planning cannot stop someone who makes a conscious decision to put some other interest over policy and morals. Thus, perfect ethical behavior is not a possibility. But, good planning on a supervisor's part can at least largely eliminate the inadvertent problems, and largely reduce ethical violations to a small number of cases of willful misconduct.

Communicating Ethical Expectations to Tutors

In an ideal world, tutors would always know the appropriate ethical standards at the time they were needed. This means that tutors need to have been sufficiently exposed to their ethical expectations such that they can easily make the right choice *in situ*. A written code of ethics is considered one of the best starting points for this advanced knowledge, and it will be the central focus of this chapter. However, it is inevitable that situations will arise in which tutors lack that information. Before examining codes of ethics in detail, it is worthwhile to address the issue of how students can make ethical decisions for cases in which the stated code fails to offer guidance.

In these cases, it is essential that tutors can easily and readily access the information they need to guide their decisions. This means they need to be able to ask someone who can give a qualified answer. In order for this process to work effectively, three conditions must be met. First, tutors need to recognize that they have encountered an ethical question for which they are lacking adequate information. Without the recognition of an ethical situation, people will proceed without giving the moral dimension of their behavior any thought. Thus, a significant part of ethical training for student tutors needs to be devoted to simply helping them identify ethical situations. Second, someone who can offer an answer needs to be accessible. If a tutor is working with a student the evening before an exam, the tutor cannot wait until the next day to get an answer to how to proceed with a particular challenge pertaining to that exam. Finally, tutors need to feel comfortable asking. Kerssen-Griep (2001) found that students who felt their instructors created a supportive environment were more inclined to express independent ideas than those in an environment they found threatening, and this effect holds true with tutors as well. Students need to have a good rapport with their supervisor or resource person, feel they can discuss issues in a supportive environment, and know they will not experience negative repercussions just from asking.

If these three conditions are met—recognition of a red flag, available resource, and comfortable rapport—then students are likely to seek out necessary ethical information when they lack it. Ideally, these cases will be the exception, and tutors will already know what to do when they encounter and recognize an ethical question. To offer advanced knowledge in the best possible manner, tutor supervisors need to communicate ethical expectations with good clarity, and in a way that will allow the students to retain the information. This task can pose some challenges, as we live in an age of information overload, and even ideas that are understood and retained in the short term are often lost in a flood of new information to which people are continually exposed. For this reason, a written code of ethics can be helpful, as it can be easy to access any time that people want to refresh their expertise. It should also be a mandatory part of initial and refresher training sessions.

Value and Role of Written Codes

Written codes of ethics are popular in the corporate setting, where 95% of both U.S. Fortune 100 and Global 100 corporations have formal codes (Sharbatoghlie, Mosleh, & Shokatian, 2013). Although some scholars are not completely sold on the potential that codes have for enhancing ethical behavior in the workplace (Cleek & Leonard, 1998), the strong majority of literature suggests that written codes are an essential component in a viable approach to corporate ethics. The general consensus among researchers is that written codes are a necessary, but not sufficient, element of a successful program to foster ethical behavior (Hopkins, 2013). Reflecting on the WorldCom scandal, Schwartz (2004) wrote, "Although having a code of ethics certainly may not have prevented the scandal, it is hard to imagine how ethics could be made an integral part of a company's business practices without at least adopting a code of ethics" (p. 234).

However, scholars studying corporate ethics have been clear that codes are only of value insofar as they are a foundation for other elements that are necessary in concert with codes to promote ethical behavior. Hopkins (2013) noted, "Codes of ethics and ethics and compliance programs do work—but only if supported by strong systems, which not only encourage compliance but deter misconduct through enforcement" (p. 45). Likewise, research by Hess (1994), Romani and Szkudlarek (2014), and many others suggest that codes of ethics have impact only when included in the presence of compliance programs, strong leadership, and a culture that supports ethical behavior. In short, codes are an essential foundation for making ethical expectations clear, but if left to stand by themselves, will not promote ethical behavior. Nonetheless, without the clear presentation of information they offer, the rest cannot function effectively. For this reason, we turn our attention to developing and implementing an effective code of ethics.

Developing a Code of Ethics for Peer Tutors

Qualities of a Good Code of Ethics

Form

An effective code of ethics has at least three qualities. First, it should be labeled as such. While the title might seem trivial, students often fail to make connections that are not explicitly stated, and a listing of some behaviors without identifying them as ethics runs the risk that some tutors may perceive the advice merely as suggestions and fail to see their moral importance. Second, while containing all essential content, it needs to be brief enough that people will read it. While one survey found that working professionals preferred thoroughness to brevity (Schwartz, 2004), recent research has shown that college students are less likely to read longer selections (Berrett, 2013). Thus, I recommend balancing completeness with conciseness.

Finally, writing in a code needs to be clear, unambiguous, and easy to understand. Research has demonstrated that people will interpret a code based on their own perspectives (Winkler, 2011). Although it is impossible to eliminate all variation in how people make sense of the world they encounter, writing a code in a manner that reduces the possible range of interpretation is important. Use of concrete language is one of the most effective tools in this pursuit. Johannesen (1988) recommended, "Vagueness and ambiguity should be minimized. Key terms in code provisions, especially abstract value-laden terms, could be clarified through further explanation and concrete illustration" (p. 60).

Content

Although we will turn our attention in the next section to specific content that might be included in a code of ethics for peer tutors, there are some qualities about content that are desirable, no matter what the specifics are. First, codes need to be as comprehensive as possible, covering all topics that are relevant to the job at hand. Second, they should offer both general principles along with known specifics. It is the combination of these two elements that is particularly powerful. A number of sources offer general principles for ethics and peer tutoring (discussed below), but these general principles by themselves are too abstract to be useful to student tutors. Specific guidance on the issues they will have to face is much more helpful. However, no one can anticipate all the specifics, so some general principles to offer ideas when tutors encounter novel situations are necessary. In general, a code focusing on specific issues but enriched with some general principles gives students specific mandates for all the known issues they should face and some general principles to offer ideas for unexpected issues.

In both specific issues and general principles it is essential to include examples, as they help increase comprehension. Examples are important enough that Schwartz (2004) noted, "The respondents made it clear that a code (or training based on the code) that lacks relevant examples would most likely remain ineffective" (p. 329).

Finally, the expectations in a code need to be realistic. If the code is seen as unrealistic or unattainable, workers do not see it as legitimate (Schwartz, 2004). As Johannesen (1988) put it, "Under ordinary circumstances the code should not require heroic virtue, extreme sacrifice, or doing right no matter what the obstacles. Rather it should be aimed at persons of ordinary conscientiousness and persons willing to following [sic] it on the condition that others do likewise" (p. 60).

Developing a Code of Ethics

Doing the Research

Writing an effective code of ethics involves three steps, beginning with doing background research. Consulting industry standards and existing codes of ethics, where available, is a good place to start. As of the writing of this chapter, a number of organizations offer ethical guidelines pertaining to tutoring and make ethics statements available on the Internet. Two prominent organizations include the National Tutoring Association (NTA) and the Association for the Tutoring Profession (ATP). These two organizations offer codes of ethics specific to tutoring and the issues tutors face in their work, with the NTA's code offering the most concrete guidance. The Council for the Advancement of Standards in Higher Education (CAS) has posted a Statement of Shared Ethical Principles that is relevant to tutoring, focusing on general underlying principles, rather than on specific applications. The College Reading and Learning Association (CRLA) also addresses ethics, although at the time of writing, the CRLA notes that it supports the ATP, and offers a reprint of their code of ethics. Balancing the general and specific, Ender and Newton (2000) propose twelve general principles illustrated with specific issues tutors face in their guidebook for peer educators, *Students Helping Students*. Taken together, these codes make a great starting point, as they introduce both general issues to consider, and specific concerns that tutors may face.

However, just looking at general industry-wide guidelines is not sufficient. Each school has its own history, culture, challenges, and goals. The latter point—institutional goals—often stem from mission-based concerns. Faith-based institutions, military schools, and schools with other aspirations for the manner in which they shape students' lives may wish to contextualize ethical guidance in terms of their larger mission, or may even have expectations specific to their institution that go beyond what a more general code of ethics might require. Thus, it is essential to write a code that is tailored to that particular institution. Discussing needs and desired ethical codes with the institution's academic and athletic leaders (the latter for their familiarity with National Collegiate Athletic Association regulation), legal team, and for faith-based institutions, clerical leaders, are essential for developing a complete picture of elements needed in the code.

Involve Those Who Will Use the Code

Once the topics that should be included in the code are assembled, it is important to get the people involved who will use it (Messmer, 2003). There are two reasons for this. First, it increases the fidelity of the message. By having tutors participate in drafting and editing, there are higher chances that the final document will make sense to them. Aspects ranging from word choice to examples have the chance to be interpreted and discussed, and elements of the writing that might have led to erroneous interpretations can be fixed. This process of clarifying is important, as misinterpretation of ethical codes is one common problem in compliance (Winkler, 2011). Second, having the people using the code involved in creating it is a form of consultation that gives them some ownership, and that buy-in can also foster better compliance (Stevens, 2008).

Revisit the Code

In our busy lives, once a code is written it is tempting to set it aside in favor of other current priorities. And in general, a well-developed and well-written code should stand the test of time fairly well. However, no code is perfectly written (especially in its first iteration) and even if such perfection were possible its validity would not last indefinitely, due to changing times. As technology, teaching methods, and external policy evolve, new ethical questions arise that must be addressed. Furthermore, even where a code seems fairly current with respect to the issues it addresses, a good code of ethics "should stimulate further discussion and reflection leading to possible modification or revision" (Johannesen, 1988, p. 60). The benefits of ongoing review and revision are twofold: They continue to improve the code, and they keep future tutors invested in it through their contributions. While a code does not need to be tinkered with constantly, review on reasonable intervals (perhaps every two or three years) is worth the time.

Topics to Consider for a Peer Tutoring Code of Ethics

A wide range of topics exist that supervisors should consider for inclusion in a peer tutoring code of ethics. There are an infinite array of ways to organize such topics. For ease of presentation, some of the elements that are worth considering are organized into five categories. These topics represent some more prevalent issues tutoring centers must address, but the list is not intended to be exhaustive. *The reader should consider this list as a starting point to stimulate thinking, rather than an ending point in the process of developing code content.* And, this organization scheme is by no means necessary, or even ideal. As specific users develop their own codes, they should choose content that applies to their institution and needs, and they should structure the information in whatever manner is most appropriate for the final content of their code.

The topics listed here were culled primarily from the NTA and ATP codes of ethics, Ender and Newton's (2000) ethical guidelines, and from the author's conversations with peer tutor supervisors. In order to avoid being too prescriptive, only topics are listed. Users should specify their own ethical guidelines about any of these topics that are included in their own code. Notice, too, that some of these topics could involve questions or actions that are not ethical in nature. Not every issue is an ethical issue. And, some items on here might be seen as less important (such as being on time for clients), such that they might unnecessarily bloat a code of ethics and distract from more important issues. The need to make decisions on issues such as these shows why each tutoring center needs to develop its own code of ethics.

Rules and Regulations

- Family Educational Rights and Privacy Act (FERPA) regulations
- Working with athletes—includes relevant NCAA regulations

- Confidentiality requirements
- Data security—for tests, record-keeping, etc.

Interaction with Clients

- Sexual harassment
- Discrimination
- Maintaining a professional, not personal, relationship
- Respecting students—individual dignity, learning abilities, cultural differences, etc.
- Being on time

Interaction with Supervisor and Other Tutors

- What and how information is reported to the supervisor
- Seeking assistance when needed

Tutoring Procedures

- What types of assistance are provided or not provided
- Keeping current in subject area and learning methods

Appropriate Faculty Behavior

- Not doing work for faculty that goes beyond tutoring

This last topic—appropriate faculty behavior—is one that may not initially occur to people unfamiliar with the peer tutoring field. However, those involved in the process will quickly learn that faculty may request or expect tutors to do work that goes beyond the bounds of their roles—proctoring exams, offering review sessions, and more. Peer tutors, with the support of their supervisors, need to recognize requests that are inappropriate for their roles and politely decline such invitations.

Implementation: Putting the Code into Action

As noted previously, copious research demonstrates that codes of ethics are an effective tool for conveying ethical standards, but they are only effective when used in conjunction with other methods. Left on its own, a code of ethics will be largely ineffective. Recommendations for making codes work effectively can be grouped into two chronological stages: initial presentation of ethical expectations and ongoing attention to ethics.

Establishing Ethics

Ideas that are presented first in a speech or meeting benefit the staff in two ways. First, they are more likely to be remembered due to primacy effects (Bligh, 2000), and second, they are perceived as more important due to their prominent placement in the agenda. If ethics are truly essential, then they should occupy an early and prominent role in the initial training of new tutors.

One approach to ethical training in industry that would be appropriate for use with peer tutors is to include a sign-off process, in which students sign a statement indicating that they have read and understood the code, and that they commit to adhering to those expectations. Signing such a statement increases awareness of the code and also creates a sense of responsibility among the users, who have now made the commitment to act accordingly. However, the message surrounding this process is important. The sign-off process needs to be couched as enhancing awareness instead of indicating lack of trust if it is to be positively received by users (Schwartz, 2004).

It is worth noting, as well, that presenting ethical expectations does not need to wait until the beginning of employment. Supervisors may find it valuable to introduce ethical issues during the interview process. Doing so can offer several benefits. It sends a clear message of the importance of ethics, it begins the training process right away, and most important, allows supervisors to consider job-relevant ethical characteristics of students (aptitude, analytical skills, enthusiasm) when making hiring decisions. A peer tutor candidate who shows disinterest in ethical matters or clear inability to make fundamental ethical distinctions is likely to be a liability if hired for that position. In contrast, a candidate who shows enthusiasm for considering and discussing ethical issues and an ability to develop insightful perspectives could be a role model for other tutors and a strong asset not only in her or his own work, but in shaping an ethically-grounded culture within the tutoring center.

A code cannot fulfill its potential if it is not readily accessible to its users. Placing a copy of the code of ethics in the front of any manuals or other training material student tutors receive makes the code available when needed, and it helps signal its importance. Better yet, posting the code in each room where tutors work is a visible reminder not just to the tutors but also to clients about the importance of ethical conduct. It not only makes the information readily available, but sends a reminder to all involved. Replacing such a poster annually allows supervisors to incorporate updates and keeps it from becoming a weathered relic that says "out of date and never used."

Finally, practice is a powerful way to help students understand the code of ethics while simultaneously starting to make ethical behavior habitual. This can be done during training through case studies or role plays. For the more adventurous supervisors, ethics can be combined with other quality control issues by sending in student confederates who present various challenges (including tests of ethics). While it is essential that student tutors know that they will receive some "test cases" as part of their training, sending in confederates can give the tutor experience in a "real" situation which can sharpen their understanding and ability to respond appropriately when confronted with an actual challenge instead of a hypothetical analysis.

Ongoing Relevance of Ethical Code

Supporting and Reinforcing

As has been previously noted, a code of ethics is a great way to clearly communicate basic ethical expectations, but its effectiveness depends on a variety of other factors: ongoing attention, a culture that supports ethical behavior, effective leadership, and in the corporate setting, an effective compliance program. Thus, if we are to assure that peer tutors' work is not just effective work, but is *good* work, the code needs to be used appropriately beyond its initial presentation.

Effective use of a code of ethics begins with ongoing support of that code from those in leadership positions. Hess (1994) and Schwartz (2004) found that employee perceptions that their leaders supported a code of ethics were essential to their belief that the code was important. Even the best-written code can instantaneously lose all authority if a tutor's supervisor makes a remark that dismisses the value of that code. One careless comment questioning the quality or importance of the code can undo all the work that went into creating it. And while lack of any attention to the ethical dimensions of the job is not as damning as a comment that undermines it, chronic inattention is corrosive as well.

In showing support for the code of ethics, supervisors need to reinforce the code's content periodically. Supervisors do not need to take their support of a code to an extreme and talk about ethics so much that tutors tire of hearing about it. But, commenting on ethical dimensions of the tutors' work when relevant, and occasionally reminding tutors about ethical issues are essential in supporting the code.

Motivating Tutors in Ethical Priorities

Finally, and perhaps unexpectedly, it is important not just to offer logical reasons for tutors to attend to their ethical guidelines, but also to offer motivational appeals that resonate on an emotional level. Ethics are typically treated in the domain of reason (but see Haidt, 2007, for a compelling argument that ethics extend well beyond reason), so people often tend to focus on reason whenever ethics are a concern. But the mind has two primary forces that control action—reason and emotion (Haidt, 2006). While reason ideally provides intelligent choices, emotion provides the strongest motivational force (Heath & Heath, 2010). Seeing and feeling something can lead to more powerful motivation than just thinking and analyzing. Reason and emotion sometimes clash, as happens when a dieter struggles to resist a tempting treat that will ruin the day's calorie count. But reason and emotion united offer a powerful force for action. Thus, to smooth a path for ethical action, supervisors need to include both elements in their approach to ethics.

How can supervisors appeal to the emotional processing systems of their tutors to promote compliance? First, it is important to distinguish the roles played by negative and positive emotions. Negative emotions motivate specific actions. For example, a stone in the shoe hurts, and the negative emotions that follow motivate a person to remove it. In contrast, positive emotions motivate creativity, flexibility, and ingenuity, but no specific actions (Fredrickson, 1998; Heath & Heath, 2010). So, people feeling positive emotions might be motivated to improve their mastery of an art or sport. Ideally, peer tutors should be motivated both to do a specific set of actions—avoid behavior that violates ethical policy—but also to ethically self-actualize, that is, to achieve greater optimization of ethical conduct. For that reason, a balanced appeal to both positive and negative emotions is optimal. But, it is also important that appeals to negative emotions work to support reasoning, rather than disable it, as many negative appeals have the tendency of doing (such as appeals to prejudice).

One of the more compelling emotional triggers is to visualize the consequences of ethically commendable or condemnable behavior. This can best be accomplished by sharing stories of ethical successes or violations. In one case, a tutor was fired because of what might seem at first glance like a miniscule violation of policy. After becoming frustrated from a lengthy session with an athlete who just could not understand, the tutor typed three words on the student's laptop. Even though three words are not many, that act constitutes an NCAA infraction. The incident had to be reported to the NCAA and the tutor removed from service. In contrast, a story of a positive outcome from ethically admirable behavior can offer an inspirational counterpart to inspire tutors to reach higher in their work.

In their work on inspiring change, Heath and Heath (2010) offer a range of other ideas that can help inspire the emotional power needed to promote and sustain desired behavior. Getting others to share their success stories can be compelling because of the powerful influence peer behavior has on one's behavior choices. In training or in regular meetings, asking tutors to share examples of how they acted with high ethical quality can help foster a culture of ethical decision-making.

Linking ethical actions to a person's identity is another strong force in shaping emotions and behavior. Heath and Heath (2010) note that subconsciously people often ask three questions that shape their actions: "Who am I? What kind of situation is this? What would someone like me do in this situation?" (p. 153, italics removed). To the degree that supervisors can help shape those perceptions with regard to tutoring ("I am the type of person who has integrity, and when confronted with this situation I rely on the code of ethics to make a good choice"), they can direct a student's behavior toward ethically praiseworthy behavior. A genuine focus on ethics during initial tutor training and consistently throughout the tutor's tenure at the tutoring center will help shape formation of ethical identity.

Conclusion

This chapter began with the warning that the damage done by unethical conduct can far exceed the damage done by poor quality tutoring. It is worth balancing that admonition with the recognition that actions of high ethical quality can be a powerful force for good in the lives of those impacted. In light of the great importance of getting ethics right, this chapter advocated using a written code of ethics as a tool to help guide tutors. In addition, because a written code by itself is likely to be only minimally effective, if at all, the chapter also focused on the context that makes that code work—actions in developing, using, and supporting a code.

Making ethics a foundation for a peer tutoring center might not be the approach that everyone first considers, but with a little planning it is not that difficult. More importantly, it is essential for the success of the center. The results of a firm ethical foundation will enhance the lives of those involved in the tutoring process on a daily basis and in a variety of ways. If attention to ethics prevents even one major incident, the extra effort exerted to embed ethics into the fabric of the work of the tutoring center may well have paid itself off in time and effort.

References

Berrett, D. (2013, May 10). Students may be reading plenty, but not for class. *Chronicle of Higher Education*, p. A6.

Bligh, D. A. (2000). *What's the use of lectures?* San Francisco, CA: Jossey-Bass.

Cleek, M. A., & Leonard, S. L. (1998). Can corporate codes of ethics influence behavior? *Journal of Business Ethics, 17*, 619–630.

Ender, S. C., & Newton, F. B. (2000). *Students helping students: A guide for peer educators on college campuses.* San Francisco, CA: Jossey-Bass.

Fredrickson, B. L. (1998). What good are positive emotions? *Review of General Psychology, 2*, 300–319.

Gardner, H., Csikszentmihalyi, M., & Damon, W. (2001). *Good work: When excellence and ethics meet.* New York, NY: Basic Books.

Grice, G. L., Bird, J. W., & Dalton, J. D. (1990, November). *The student as communication tutor: Ethical dilemmas and responsibilities.* Paper presented at the annual meeting of the National Communication Association, Chicago, IL.

Haidt, J. (2006). *The happiness hypothesis: Finding modern truth in ancient wisdom.* New York, NY: Basic Books.

Haidt, J. (2007). The new synthesis in moral psychology. *Science, 316*, 998–1001.

Heath, C., & Heath, D. (2010). *Switch: How to change things when change is hard.* New York, NY: Broadway Books.

Hess, J. A. (1994). Business as usual: Ethics as mundane behavior, and the case of Target Corporation. In J. A. Jaksa (Ed.), *Proceedings of the Third National Communication Ethics Conference* (pp. 53–67). Annandale, VA: Speech Communication Association.

Hopkins, S. L. (2013). How effective are ethics codes and programs? *Financial Executive, 29*(2), 42–45.

Johannesen, R. L. (1988). What should we teach about formal codes of ethics? *Journal of Mass Media Ethics, 3*, 59–64.

Kerssen-Griep, J. (2001). Teacher communication activities relevant to student motivation: Classroom facework and instructional communication competence. *Communication Education, 50*, 256–273.

Messmer, M. (2003). Does your company have a code of ethics? *Strategic Finance, 84*(10), 13–14.

Romani, L., & Szkudlarek, B. (2014). The struggles of the interculturalists: Professional ethical identity and early stages of codes of ethics development. *Journal of Business Ethics, 119*, 173–191.

Schwartz, M. S. (2004). Effective corporate codes of ethics: Perceptions of code users. *Journal of Business Ethics, 55*, 321–341.

Sharbatoghlie, A., Mosleh, M., & Shokatian, T. (2013). Exploring trends in the codes of ethics of the Fortune 100 and Global 100 corporations. *Journal of Management Development, 32*, 675–689.

Stevens, B. (2008). Corporate ethical codes: Effective instruments for influencing behavior. *Journal of Business Ethics, 78*, 601–609.

Winkler, I. (2011). The representation of social actors in corporate codes of ethics. How code language positions internal actors. *Journal of Business Ethics, 101*, 653–665.

MANAGING CONFLICT IN THE
PEER TUTORING CONTEXT

Jennifer L. Bevan and Jennifer H. Waldeck

This volume and prior literature have firmly established peer tutoring as a helpful resource for boosting student motivation and engagement, as well as enhancing critical cognitive and affective learning outcomes. These outcomes are important not only for student success, but also for institutional success, given that these factors are related to academic retention. As such, there is a renewed interest in peer tutoring, and many institutions are establishing or reinforcing their peer tutoring centers and programs.

However, for the tutoring to be effective, the peer tutor should receive training that prepares them in the skills and competencies needed for effective tutoring. Indeed, research points to the importance of tutor training and experience for positive cognitive and affective learning outcomes from the relationship. Tutors with accurate, in-depth training in the subject matter and instructional strategies have more constructive and positive tutoring relationships. These relationships tend to be characterized by fewer conflicts when compared with those of tutors with little experience or tutors with deficient, or even non-existent, training (Fuchs, Fuchs, Bentz, Phillips, & Hamlett, 1994).

However, even the most seasoned tutor with excellent preparation in training will face some form of conflict or other during their tutoring experience. Goodboy (2011) clearly states that although competent communication can prevent many conflicts associated with the learning experience, some conflict is "simply unavoidable" (p. 423). For a variety of reasons, peer tutoring inter-actions can be characterized by difficult interpersonal dynamics and conflict, which can diminish learning-related benefits. The instructional communi-cation literature documents a number of potential dysfunctional interaction patterns related to learning, and peer tutoring is no exception. For exam-ple, students may have lowered self-esteem related to the reasons for seeking tutoring, such as perceived deficiency, poor course performance, or instructor criticism (Miller, Topping, & Thurston, 2010). Low self-esteem and insecu-rity provide a weak foundation for constructive relationships, and may set the stage for defensiveness, unwillingness to accept advice from a peer (Waring, 2007), and possibly conflict as a result of these behaviors and attitudes.

Further, when students who seek tutoring do not perceive value from their efforts—i.e., do not see rapid visible gains in grades, positive reinforcement from the instructor, or enhanced understanding of the material as a result of tutoring—they may become frustrated with their tutor and the entire tutoring process, and the relationship can become tense, possibly leading to conflict. Additionally, but not incidentally, conflicts occur when the student misses appointments, fails to dependably fulfill commitments, or perceives lack of interest or effort from the other in the learning and performance improve-ment that tutoring is designed to facilitate (Gordon, 2005).

So, while peer tutoring is a valuable and effective way to promote student learning, it also has the potential to be challenging, potentially leading to conflict. The good news, however, is that there are a number of communica-tion strategies highlighted in the instructional and interpersonal communica-tion research literature for minimizing the likelihood of conflict, or mitigating its impact on the peer tutoring relationship. The primary objectives of this chapter, then, are to: (1) illustrate the potential for difficult interactions in the peer tutoring context, and promote awareness of the factors which may lead to conflict in peer tutoring relationships; (2) examine the unique nature of interpersonal conflict and dissent in the peer tutoring context; (3) apply the literature on interpersonal conflict interaction styles to peer tutoring relationships; and (4) offer practical suggestions for anticipating, minimizing, managing, and resolving conflicts in peer tutoring relationships.

Peer Tutoring as a Difficult Interaction

Broadly, the act of peer tutoring includes any interactions where students teach or coach one another (Evans & Moore, 2013). Peer tutoring is a potent and effective method for learning stimulation and improvement, as well as for empowering students (Burton, 2012), and is a social process that involves interpersonal bonding (Jones, 2001). The peer tutoring relationship, in many ways, reflects the rhetorical and relational approach to instructional communication (Myers, Atkinson, Ball, Goldman, Tindage, & Carton, Chapter 13 this volume).

Specifically, like effective instructors, effective peer tutors should be concerned with both content (rhetorical) goals related to the subject matter, as well as with establishing effective, competent communication relationships with recipients of tutoring to maximize its benefits. Although they studied teacher/student interactions, Frymier and Houser (2000) made the important argument that instructional relationships share many of the same characteristics as interpersonal ones, including going through the process of meeting, exchanging information, and developing and adjusting expectations for one another as well as for the relationship. Inherent in this, and any, type of human interaction is the potential for misunderstanding, unmet expectations, and conflict.

Complicating this already challenging relationship is its pseudo-hierarchical nature. Tutors may be older than the students they tutor (Evans & Moore, 2013), and by virtue of their position, have elevated status in the academic environment. Like an instructor facilitating a course, the tutor must set and maintain an agenda or plan for each tutoring session (Benwell & Stokoe, 2002).

However, peer tutors do not have the same level of legitimate, coercive, or reward power that instructors do. These forms of power (French & Raven, 1966) figure prominently in any type of relationship where social disparity or distance exists. More specifically, in the tutoring context, a tutor may stimulate perceptions of *coercive power* (the student feels that he/she will be punished by the tutor for not complying with requests); *legitimate power* (the student perceives the tutor as powerful simply because he/she has been designated in this role by an even more powerful third party, such as a professor or department chair); *expert power* (the student perceives the tutor to be a credible, competent expert on the topic); or *referent power* (student sees the tutor as someone he/she would like to be like, and wants that person to like him/her). Especially in the early stages of the tutoring relationship, peer tutors may lack important referent (i.e., relational) and expert influence (see Roach, 1991) because they are not perceived to have the same credibility as instructors. As a result, peer tutors may have difficulty gaining student compliance with their requests or suggestions that can be critical to managing the tutoring process and maximizing learning outcomes (see Kearney, Plax, Richmond, & McCroskey, 1985; Roach, 1991; Waldeck & Kearney, in press). Further, peer tutors lack formal institutional authority, which can aid in reducing students' stress and anxiety (Jones, 2001). In other words, tutors can help motivate students and enhance their self-esteem (Miller et al., 2010); however, students may not view their tutors as having the same credibility that course instructors do for reassuring students that they know what they are doing and that they can help students to improve.

We have chosen to label the complex power dynamic which exists in peer tutoring relationships a *pseudo-hierarchy* because, although status differences exist, the two students remain, fundamentally, peers. Grice, Blackburn, and Darby (1991) refer to this as a *near-peer* relationship. Thus, students and their peer tutors could find themselves engaging in "a subtle negotiation of a range of sometimes-conflicting identities" (Benwell & Stokoe, 2002, p. 450) when working with one another. When these role identities are not clearly and effectively negotiated, and social influence is not established, there is an increased likelihood of resistance and conflict.

Extensive research documents a range of resistance behaviors that students demonstrate when instructional authority figures (e.g., professors and graduate teaching assistants in secondary education, teachers and classroom aides in the earlier grades) ask them to do something in the instructional context that they are unwilling or unmotivated to do. Resistance behaviors include questioning, nagging, complaining, appealing to a higher authority, making disrespectful remarks, being late, and even verbal or online aggression (Burroughs, 2007; Dunleavy et al., 2008; Golish & Olson, 2000).

Many of the same behaviors are seen in the peer tutoring context. For example, students can be disruptive in their peer tutoring sessions, avoid or reject recommended behaviors, steer the discussion off-task, respond to questions with silence or ambivalence, challenge the stated agenda (Benwell & Stokoe, 2002), attempt to get the tutor to simply do whatever is needed for the student to earn a good grade (e.g., make the necessary edits or corrections for her, rather than coach the student on becoming proficient on how to do so by herself) (Dannels & Gaffney, 2012), miss or be tardy for appointments, demonstrate a lack of commitment or demotivation, and exhibit dominant behaviors (Kindler, Grant, Kulla, Poole, & Godolphin, 2009).

These disruptive behaviors can not only create tension within the tutoring relationship, but they can also become a distraction to learning. In peer group learning situations, Kindler et al.'s (2009) research specifically identified tension as a hindrance to learning. The peer tutors in Kindler et al.'s (2009) study described these tensions as "very challenging," so much so that most of their attempts to resolve them were unsuccessful. These outcomes are not only distressing to participants, but also dangerous in terms of student learning.

What are some ways that peer tutors respond when faced with a challenging student or difficult situation? One conversational analysis study found that peer tutors reacted to student disruptions with politeness strategies such as using humor, irony, avoidance, and mitigating or hedging statements, rather than explicitly enforcing their rightful authority (Benwell & Stokoe, 2002). In general, more competent communication skills are required of the tutor to implement passive management strategies, i.e., to avoid automatically getting embroiled in conflict, although implementing them is not always a failsafe solution.

Challenges, and the ensuing potential for conflict, exist in any tutoring session. Successful navigation of challenging situations requires solid tutor training. For example, Kindler et al. (2009) recommend that both students and peer tutors be trained in multiple interpersonal skills for working through dysfunctional interactions. Although difficult, learning to manage these interactions effectively can be beneficial to peer tutors. Wilson's (2012) survey of former peer tutors revealed that providing constructive criticism to students in difficult and diverse situations was a particularly useful skill that remained valuable to the tutors' personal and professional development after graduation. Thus, developing a repertoire of competent communication techniques for dealing with interpersonal conflict in peer tutoring relationships can both preserve the opportunity for student learning, and support the tutor's individual and professional growth.

With an understanding that peer tutoring relationships can be fertile ground for interpersonal conflict, we turn now to a more specific definition of conflict. Further, we will examine the nature of serial arguments, and how conflict and serial arguments are navigated using five distinct conflict styles.

Interpersonal Conflict and Serial Arguments

Many definitions of interpersonal conflict exist, but Wilmot and Hocker's (2013) description is often-used and informative. They define *interpersonal conflict* as "an expressed struggle between at least two interdependent parties who perceive incompatible goals, scarce resources, and interference from others in achieving their goals" (p. 13). Wilmot and Hocker further explain the five individual elements that combine to comprise their definition.

First, the notion that conflict is an *expressed struggle* means that one or both individuals must communicate about the existence of a disagreement via verbal and/or nonverbal messages. For instance, consider the case of a student who was referred to the communication skills center for peer tutoring by his instructor. The student lacked motivation, and exhibited a range of cognitive and affective performance problems. He lacked small talk skills, avoided eye contact with his tutor, and generally contributed little to the first meeting with the tutor. Over the course of several meetings, the tutor became frustrated that the student was chronically late, failed to complete assigned enrichment activities in between visits, gave one-word or unrelated answers to the tutor's questions, and generally had a poor attitude toward the course, tutoring, and the tutor, which was apparent through his verbal and nonverbal behavior. Through the lens of Wilmot and Hocker's (2013) definition, when the tutor confronted the student about his behavior, the struggle became an *expressed* one.

Second, that the parties are *interdependent* indicates that they mutually need and depend upon one another, and that the decisions that one makes affect the other in some way. In our example of the tutor and the unwilling, demotivated student, we can view their relationship as an interdependent one because the tutor's reputation as helpful and effective, as well as her own feelings of self-efficacy, is linked to the student's improvement. Simultaneously, the student's ability to correct his performance problems, improve his grade, earn his instructor's praise, acquire knowledge, and develop a good attitude toward the course are linked, to a large degree, to his interactions with the tutor.

Third, the presence of interpersonal conflict depends on *incompatible goals*, where the parties involved in the conflict seek to accomplish different or opposing objectives, or want the same thing, but cannot both have it. In our example, the tutor's and student's goals are incompatible because the student is unwilling to expend the effort required to carry out the tutor's recommendations. As a result, the tutor is unable to accomplish her rhetorical (i.e., course-related/content) and relational goals relevant to the tutoring arrangement.

The fourth element is *scarce resources*, which are tangible and intangible "things" that can provide aid or support, such as time or money. Students such as the one in our example might cite lack of time for studying, the pressures of competing demands such as internships, jobs, and social activities, the expense of materials like the textbook, or their inability or lack of self-efficacy as reasons why they cannot or will not succeed, despite tutoring. Additionally, self-esteem and power are two resources that are frequently perceived as scarce during interpersonal conflicts (Wilmot & Hocker, 2013). In our example, due to the pseudo-hierarchical nature of the relationship, the tutor became frustrated with her lack of power and inability to influence the student in any meaningful way. Although the student may, on one level, feel like he is "winning" at resisting the tutor, any self-esteem or self-efficacy problems will remain as he continues his pattern of poor performance in the course.

Fifth, the *interference from others* element involves viewing the presence of the other party in the conflict as getting in the way of, or blocking, what is sought or a preferred action. Our student perceived tutoring and the tutor as annoying inconveniences imposed upon him by his instructor that got in the way of his goal of simply coasting through the course and hopefully earning at least a "C" grade. The tutor viewed the ongoing, unresolved conflict about the student's lack of effort and commitment as a deterrent to her ability to be a good tutor and as taking valuable time from students who were truly interested in improving their performance through tutoring.

Although data focusing on conflict specifically in peer tutoring relationships are mostly absent in the literature, research on instructional relationships in general has documented an increased frequency of conflict-related behaviors, such as incivility and dissent, over the past two decades. We might expect to see that pattern evident in peer tutoring relationships, as well. For example, Burroughs (2007) found that about 30% of college students actively resist or openly reject recommended or required behaviors related to their courses and learning, leading to strained interpersonal dynamics between teachers and students both in and out of the classroom. Additionally, such behavior creates conflict among peers. Students perceive peers who resist, challenge, and disrupt instructional activities negatively and as a barrier to their own learning in classroom and group situations (Bjorklund & Rehling, 2010).

When an interpersonal conflict continues into subsequent interactions, as it did in our peer tutoring example, it becomes a *serial argument*. A serial argument is defined as an unresolved, ongoing conflict about a single topic or issue. This serial argument is linked by multiple (that is, at least two) argument episodes where the individuals involved continue to disagree about that particular issue.

Hample and Krueger (2011) investigated serial arguments in classrooms. Specifically, college students were asked to recall a serial argument that they took part in or witnessed, either at their university or when in high school. Together, the majority of these serial arguments had either not been resolved (20%) or had ended without agreement because the class concluded (37%). Only 12% of classroom serial arguments ended because they were mutually resolved. Further, as in prior studies, perceived resolvability was central to the classroom serial argument; namely, the greater the perceived resolvability, the more civilly (i.e., productively and appropriately) individuals treated one another, the more they used constructive communication, and the less they engaged in destructive communication during these arguments. These findings offer compelling preliminary evidence, then, that interpersonal conflict can be ongoing and unresolved in the education context, but that appropriate and effective communication can improve the likelihood that conflict will be adequately addressed.

Though serial arguments have not been studied specifically in the peer tutoring context, based on Hample and Krueger's (2011) findings, it is logical that an issue could emerge more than once between a peer tutor and a student and thus develop into a serial argument. For example, in the peer tutoring example just presented, the tutor had to discuss the problematic behavior multiple times with the student. Because the student responded with excuses, challenges, and defensiveness, the conflict became a serial argument episode. As with other contexts, including the classroom, in peer tutoring interactions where serial arguments arise, both parties should strive to use constructive messages (such as the compromise and collaboration conflict styles discussed below), and consider the perceived resolvability of the serial argument in order to make progress toward resolution.

Conflict Management Styles

Wilmot and Hocker's (2013) definition of conflict emphasizes the centrality of communication. As such, the ways that individuals in conflict communicate with one another is important to understand. Research by Rahim (1983) identified five *conflict management styles*, which are behavioral patterns that people tend to prefer using in different conflicts and with different individuals. Rahim's conflict management style typology has been applied to the study of conflict in a variety of relationships and situations, including the educational context.

For example, Cornille, Pestle, and Vanwy (1990) examined teachers' conflict styles in interactions with parents and colleagues; Colsman and Wulfurt (2002) studied students' conflict styles as predictors of maladaptive behaviors in school such as fighting and substance abuse, as well as academic achievement; and Somech (2008) measured conflict styles in a study of conflict management in elementary school teaching and administrative teams.

According to Rahim (1983), the five conflict management styles reflect a communicator's position on two related dimensions: (1) the extent to which there is concern for oneself and what one seeks to accomplish in the conflict; and (2) the amount of concern for the other person and how much an individual wants to help the other party accomplish his or her goals. The first conflict management style is *avoidance*, where one or both parties in the conflict have low concern for both themselves and for the other person. Individuals engaging in the avoidance conflict management style hope that if they ignore the issue, it will simply disappear. Specific examples of this conflict style include being evasive about the issue, changing the topic, denying that there is a conflict, physically or psychologically withdrawing from the conflict, and using humor to deflect discussing the issue.

Conflict avoidance can be helpful in some instances, such as when one or both parties want to take a step away from a heated discussion to cool off. However, always seeking to avoid conflict can be detrimental to the individual and to the relationship, and in instructional contexts, to the resolution of problems that may impede learning. Thus, avoidance is not a preferred conflict management style in most circumstances. Accordingly, in their study of student conflict styles, Colsman and Wulfurt (2002) found no meaningful relationship between use of the avoidant style and academic achievement.

With the *competition/dominating* conflict management style, the individual has a high concern for self and a low concern for the other party in the conflict. This is the style that many immediately think of when they imagine what a conflict looks like. Because the goal for someone using the competitive/dominating style is to win—often at any cost—his or her communication is likely to be threatening and forceful. The competitive/dominating style is characterized by challenging messages, and can include aggression, sarcasm, intimidation, and hostile behaviors. Consistently using this dominating conflict style is associated with decreased relationship quality in close relationships in the vast majority of research studies (e.g., Cramer, 2002; Gottman & Krokoff, 1989).

Specifically, in instructional settings, contentious student communication behavior consistent with this style has been found to predict physical fighting, rudeness toward authority figures, and lowered academic achievement (Colsman & Wulfurt, 2002). Goodboy and Bolkan (2013) found that dominating, competitive conflict behavior may lead to the most maladaptive expressions of dissent among students, which involve student attempts to ruin an instructor's reputation. Additionally, students with this conflict management style will vent and complain to others, and nag or even bully the instructor to make changes.

In contrast to the competitive/dominating style, the *accommodation* style is characterized by a low concern for oneself and a high concern for the other party. Here, an individual who prefers this style will strive to have the other person get what they want, and forgo pursuing any of their own conflict goals. Specific communicative examples of accommodation include giving in to others' requests or demands, being reluctant to express one's own opinions, and nonverbal behaviors such as avoiding eye contact, looking away, and speaking at a soft, low volume. In interpersonal relationships such as friendships or marriage, when an issue of disagreement is not central to you, but is very important to the other person, the accommodating style could be a viable option. Because accommodating means putting the other person's goals above your own, this style is another one to avoid using on a consistent basis; otherwise, you run the risk of always letting the other person "win" and never getting what you want out of the conflict.

This dynamic may unfold a bit differently in instructional relationships, however. Inherent to the instructional setting is a fundamental power imbalance, where some degree of student submission to authority figures is typically necessary for academic success (Plax, 2008). In order to maximize positive instructional outcomes, students must perceive the requests and recommendations of teachers, administrators, coaches, and peer tutors as worthwhile. And, these figures must competently communicate in ways such that students are motivated to do things they may not want to do. Not surprisingly, then, student conflict management styles that emphasize cooperation and accommodation are associated with higher academic achievement than competitive and contentious ones (Colsman & Wulfurt, 2002). Similarly, teachers' prosocial communication (which emphasizes cooperation, behaving in ways that benefit others, showing kindness and consideration, and communicating respectfully toward students) is found to lead to heightened motivation, student compliance, and learning (Rodriguez, Plax, & Kearney, 1996).

Rahim's (1983) fourth conflict management style, *compromise*, reflects a moderate concern for both parties in the conflict. In other words, individuals who prefer this style have some gains and some losses in their conflict, because a fair, acceptable resolution for both parties is the goal. Employing the compromise style in conflict can involve negotiating back and forth, brainstorming solutions that take both individuals' goals into account, suggesting trade-offs, and prioritizing which goals are ranked as being most to least important.

Often, compromise will be the best potential solution for everyone involved in the conflict, and it is for this reason that it is a preferred style to use in conflict. For example, in formal conflict mediation situations, compromise between the parties is often the best way to reach a formal settlement that everyone can agree upon. In instructional settings, we see compromise when teachers extend deadlines, offer students the opportunity to revise and resubmit work, or personalize the learning experience for individual students by offering alternative assignments to introverted students who prefer working alone to working groups, and selecting teaching approaches based on individual learner needs (Waldeck, 2007; Weimer, 2014).

The final conflict management style, *collaboration*, is the most preferred, but also the most difficult to accomplish. Collaboration involves a high concern for both parties in the conflict, and a win/win situation is thus the ultimate goal. This win/win goal means that both individuals accomplish all of their conflict goals and fully support the resolution that is reached. Specific examples of collaboration include each party offering disclosures and descriptions of their thoughts, feelings, and preferences and expressing openness and support through verbal and nonverbal communication. Feeling fully satisfied with a conflict outcome is rare for one individual, let alone both, making this a challenging and demanding style to actually achieve. However, it is also a preferred conflict management style because both individuals can walk away from the conflict completely supporting the outcome that was reached.

In educational contexts, this productive approach to tension is frequently seen in intense, close working relationships such as mentoring (Waldeck, 2007) and when instructors communicate in confirming (Ellis, 2004), caring (Comadena, Hunt, & Simonds, 2007), and prosocial ways (Tibbles, Richmond, McCroskey, & Weber, 2008). In addition to teacher behaviors that contribute to collaboration, research has demonstrated the importance of students' orientation to prosocial, collaborative communication, as well (Barringer & McCroskey, 2000).

This work points to the relational and community nature of learning experiences. For true collaboration to occur, all parties must be heavily invested in the learning process and product. Specifically, Edwards, Edwards, Torrens, and Beck (2011) found that student motivation and learning were highest in classrooms that were characterized by collaborative communication and perceptions of community, and by extension, low levels of destructive conflict. When parties have a collaborative style, conflict can be healthy and productive. Goodboy and Bolkan (2013) found that students who have a collaborative conflict style will still engage in instructional dissent in an attempt to get their needs met, but do so in appropriate and effective ways (e.g., approach an instructor in an effort to remedy a problem, correct their own behavior, or negotiate a solution to a problem). These findings underscore the point that conflict in general, and dissent in particular, are not necessarily always negative forms of instructional communication.

Conflict Styles in the Peer Tutoring Context

A number of these conflict management styles can also logically arise in the peer tutoring interaction, to either the benefit or detriment of the relationship and the learning outcomes of tutoring. The most common conflict management style that seems to occur between peer tutors and learners is collaboration. Indeed, peer tutoring is a specific form of collaborative learning, "in which participants are assumed to negotiate meaning on a regular basis either in small groups or in fixed pairs and in which one peer clearly takes a supportive role as peer tutor" (De Smet, Van Keer, & Valcke, 2009, p. 87). When peer tutors use a collaborative approach, their intellectual maturity increases (Jones, 2001). Crinon and Marin (2010) also found that the practice of collaborative revising, where elementary school students reviewed and edited their writing based on peer tutors' suggestions and explanations, resulted in the inclusion of more relevant content and increased understanding, compared to groups where collaborative revising was not used. In this context, collaborative conflict resolution is appropriate, as the *modus operandi* is to collaborate during a peer tutoring session, and it would logically follow that the tutoring session structures the interactants to work on resolving these conflicts in the same way, through collaboration by default. But different personalities and situations will bring about the use of other conflict management styles as well.

The avoidance, accommodation, and competitive/dominating conflict resolution styles can also be evident in peer tutoring interactions. The silence, ambivalence, humor, and avoidance responses that peer tutors sometimes have to student disruptiveness are elements of the avoidance conflict style, and the mitigation/hedging (e.g., "we should probably also cover..." or "this is sort of important") peer tutoring response (Benwell & Stokoe, 2002) is an example of the accommodating style. The criticisms, challenges, and dominant behaviors noted by Benwell and Stokoe (2002), Dannels and Gaffney (2012) and Kindler et al. (2009) reflect the dominating conflict management style. Recall that, generally, this style is unproductive in instructional settings in terms of learning and relational goals. Thus, although data regarding the frequency and specific nature of peer tutoring conflicts are unavailable to date, we can logically infer from the study of conflict management styles in other instructional and organizational settings that tutors and students exhibit all five aspects of Rahim's conflict styles in their interactions, with a range of positive and negative outcomes.

Implications for Practice

Then, what communication behaviors in particular promote greater positivity and less conflict surrounding the learning experience? Decades of research in instructional contexts have consistently demonstrated that students' positive attitudes and cognitive learning are a function of a number of antecedent behaviors most often practiced by teachers, but these behaviors can be employed by peer tutors, as well. Rodriguez et al. (1996) established that when instructional authority figures behave in particular ways, student affect or liking for the course and subject matter is heightened (and by extension, conflict associated with learning diminished), and cognitive gains follow. The following behaviors are recommended for increasing positivity and decreasing the likelihood of conflict in instructional settings.

Nonverbal immediacy

Defined as physical and/or psychological closeness, this series of behaviors signals relational perceptions of approach, friendliness, warmth, and interpersonal closeness. Nonverbal behaviors indicative of immediacy include positive head nods, smiling, eye contact, vocal expressiveness, direct and relaxed body posture, overall body movements, and physical gestures. Without exception, the research on teacher immediacy has established a substantial and positive association with student compliance and affect toward the teacher, education, and course content. Further, nonverbal immediacy is related to openness and motivation in difficult manager/subordinate conversations (Kay & Christophel, 1995), and may help to deescalate conflicts in progress (T. S. Jones & Remland, 1993). Thus, peer tutor training should include extensive focus on learning, developing, and routinely practicing nonverbal immediacy behaviors during tutoring to diminish the likelihood of destructive, dysfunctional conflict and serial arguments.

Source credibility

Defined as believability (McCroskey, 1998), credibility encompasses perceptions of trust or character, competence, and caring. Source credibility in instruction is particularly important for outcomes such as student motivation, enjoyment, and engagement (Martin, Chesebro, & Mottet, 1997; Myers & Martin, 2006; Pogue & AhYun, 2006). When students find their peer tutors knowledgeable about the content, trustworthy and honest, and concerned about their learning, we should not be surprised to find that they will comply with tutor recommendations and that conflict will be minimized, and more easily managed, when it does occur. Thus, peer tutors must be selected on the basis of their expertise in the subject matter (competence); however, this is an insufficient condition for effective tutoring. They must also possess or develop the ability to verbally communicate to students that they care about them, be relatable (rather than emphasizing status differences), and deliver responsive and assertive feedback (Teven, 2001). Further, they must be reliable and honest in their communication and activities with students (McCroskey, Holdridge, & Toomb, 1974).

Confirmation

Yet another instructional communication strategy is available to peer tutors that will minimize the likelihood of conflict or mitigate the effects of inevitable conflict: confirmation is defined as messages that endorse, recognize, and acknowledge learners as valuable and significant (Ellis, 2000). Tutors can confirm students by using encouraging questions and responding to them with interest and openness, using a variety of techniques to ensure student understanding of material, and avoiding rude or embarrassing comments directed to students. Teachers who engage in frequent confirming communication experience fewer conflicts with students and less dissent in their classrooms than teachers who are less confirming. Furthermore, students of teachers with confirming communication patterns experience lowered communication apprehension and heightened willingness to communicate (Ellis, 2004; Turman & Schrodt, 2006). Reduced communication apprehension has numerous important learning benefits, but also contributes to more productive and satisfying conflict, and relationship duration (Loveless, Powers, & Jordan, 2008).

Instructional management skills

To avoid or resolve conflicts related to students' misunderstanding of the tutors' expectations, tutors should cultivate and practice effective instructional management skills. Structured activities, clear instructions, using prompts and asking good questions, and maintaining momentum of tutoring sessions can serve to engage students and keep them on task, and minimize confusion, distraction, and misunderstanding (Woolfolk, 2001).

Conclusion

As in the case of any human relationship, peer tutoring has the potential for dysfunctional patterns like conflict and serial arguments. Though the peer tutoring communication context is frequently one of collaboration and negotiation, it can also be one where tutored students question or resist the influence and suggestions of their tutors. However, communication research from the interpersonal and instructional contexts offers extensive guidance and advice on how to maximize the benefits of tutoring so that they outweigh potentially negative outcomes.

Academic departments should not launch peer tutoring programs without careful planning and study of how to effectively select and train tutors. Good grades or other indicators of strong performance in the course or major are necessary, but insufficient, conditions for excellent tutors. Additionally, in order to minimize conflict and effectively deal with that which is unavoidable, student tutors should be selected on the basis of their communication competence. Systematic training and ongoing performance review should then focus on peer tutors' ability to demonstrate nonverbal immediacy, all three dimensions of credibility (competence, caring, and trustworthiness), confirming communication, instructional management skills, and effective negotiation of conflicts using the styles described in this chapter. By doing so, peer tutoring can fulfill its function as a potent method for learning stimulation and improvement, as well as an effective way to empower students to succeed academically.

References

Barringer, D. K., & McCroskey, J. C. (2000). Immediacy in the classroom: Student immediacy. *Communication Education, 49*, 178–186.

Benwell, B., & Stokoe, E. H. (2002). Constructing discussion tasks in university tutorials: Shifting dynamics and identities. *Discourse Studies, 4*, 429–453.

Bjorklund, W. L., & Rehling, D. L. (2010). Student perceptions of classroom incivility. *College Teaching, 58*, 15–18.

Burroughs, N. F. (2007). A reinvestigation of the relationship of teacher nonverbal immediacy and student compliance-resistance with learning. *Communication Education, 56*, 453–475.

Burton, B. (2012). Peer teaching as a strategy for conflict management and student re-engagement in schools. *Australian Education Research, 39*, 45–58.

Colsman, M., & Wulfurt, E. (2002). Conflict resolution style as an indicator of adolescents' substance abuse and other problem behaviors. *Addictive Behaviors, 27*, 633–648.

Comadena, M. E., Hunt, S. K., & Simonds, C. J. (2007). The effects of teacher clarity, nonverbal immediacy, and caring on student motivation, affective and cognitive learning. *Communication Research Reports, 24*, 241–248.

Cornille, T. A., Pestle, R. E., & Vanwy, R. W. (1990). Teachers' conflict management styles with peers and students' parents. *International Journal of Conflict Management, 10*, 69–79.

Cramer, D. (2002). Linking conflict management behaviours and relational satisfaction: The intervening role of conflict outcome satisfaction. *Journal of Social and Personal Relationships, 19*, 425–432.

Crinon, J., & Marin, B. (2010). The role of peer feedback in learning to write explanatory texts: Why the tutors learn the most. *Language Awareness, 19*, 111–128.

Dannels, D. P., & Gaffney, A. L. H. (2012). The blind leading the blind? An ethnographic heuristic for communication centers. In E. L. Yook & W. Atkins-Sayre (Eds.), *Communication centers and oral communication programs in higher education: Advantages, challenges, and new directions* (pp. 87–112). Lanham, MD: Lexington Books.

De Smet, M., Van Keer, H., & Valcke, M. (2009). Cross-age peer tutors in asynschronous discussion groups: A study of the evolution in tutor support. *Instructional Science, 37*, 87–105.

Dunleavy, K. N., Martin, M. M., Brann, M., Booth-Butterfield, M., Myers, S. A., & Weber, K. (2008). Student nagging behavior in the college classroom. *Communication Education, 57*, 1–19.

Edwards, C., Edwards, A., Torrens, A., & Beck, A. (2011). Confirmation and community: The relationships among teacher confirmation, classroom community, student motivation, and learning. *Online Journal of Communication & Media Technologies, 1*, 17–43.

Ellis, K. (2000). Perceived teacher confirmation: The development and validation of an instrument and two studies of the relationship to cognitive and affective learning. *Human Communication Research, 26*, 264–291.

Ellis, K. (2004). The impact of perceived teacher confirmation on receiver apprehension, motivation, and learning. *Communication Education, 53*, 1–20.

Evans, M. J., & Moore, J. S. (2013). Peer tutoring with the aid of the internet. *British Journal of Educational Technology, 44*, 144–155.

French, J. R. P., & Raven, B. (1966). The bases for social power. In D. Cartwright (Ed.), *Studies in social power* (pp. 150–167). Ann Arbor: University of Michigan Press.

Frymier, A. B., & Houser, M. L. (2000). The teacher-student relationship as an interpersonal relationship. *Communication Education, 49*, 207–219.

Fuchs, L. S., Fuchs, D., Bentz, J., Phillips, N. B., & Hamlett, C. L. (1994). The nature of student interactions during peer tutoring with and without prior training and experience. *American Educational Research Journal, 31*, 75–103.

Golish, T. D., & Olson, L. N. (2000). Students' use of power in the classroom: An investigation of student power, teacher power, and teacher immediacy. *Communication Quarterly, 48*, 293–310.

Goodboy, A. K. (2011). The development and validation of the Instructional Dissent Scale. *Communication Education, 60*, 422–440.

Goodboy, A. K., & Bolkan, S. (2013). Instructional dissent as a function of student conflict styles. *Communication Research Reports, 30*, 259–263.

Gordon, E. E. (2005). *Peer tutoring: A teacher's resource guide*. Lanham, MD: Rowman & Littlefield.

Gottman, J. M., & Krokoff, L. J. (1989). Marital interaction and satisfaction: A longitudinal view. *Journal of Consulting and Clinical Psychology, 57*, 47–52.

Grice, G. L., Blackburn, S., & Darby, J. (1991, October). *Near-peer tutoring: Designing and implementing a student-staffed oral communication laboratory*. Spotlight paper presented at the meeting of the Texas Speech Communication Association, Lubbock.

Hample, D., & Krueger, B. (2011). Serial arguments in classrooms. *Communication Studies, 62*, 597–617.

Jones, C. (2001). The relationship between writing centers and improvement in writing ability: An assessment of the literature. *Education, 122*, 3–20.

Jones, T. S., & Remland, M. S. (1993). Nonverbal communication and conflict escalation: An attribution-based model. *International Journal of Conflict Management, 4*, 119–137.

Kay, B., & Christophel, D. M. (1995). The relationships among manager communication openness, nonverbal immediacy, and subordinate motivation. *Communication Research Reports, 12*, 200–205.

Kearney, P., Plax, T. G., Richmond, V. P., & McCroskey, J. C. (1985). Power in the classroom III: Teacher communication techniques and messages. *Communication Education, 34*, 19–28.

Kindler, P., Grant, C., Kulla, S., Poole, G., & Godolphin, W. (2009). Difficult incidents and tutor interventions in problem-based learning tutorials. *Medical Education, 43*, 866–873.

Loveless, M., Powers, W. G., & Jordan, W. (2008). Dating partner communication apprehension, self-disclosure, and the first big fight. *Human Communication, 11*, 231–239.

Martin, M. M., Chesebro, J. L., & Mottet, T. P. (1997). Students' perceptions of instructors' socio-communicative style and the influence on instructor credibility and situational motivation. *Communication Research Reports, 14,* 431–440.

McCroskey, J. C. (1998). *An introduction to communication in the classroom* (2nd ed.). Acton, MA: Tapestry.

McCroskey, J. C., Holdridge, W., & Toomb, J. (1974). An instrument for measuring the source credibility of basic speech communication instructors. *Speech Teacher, 23,* 26–33.

Miller, D., Topping, K., & Thurston, A. (2010). Peer tutoring in reading: The effects of role and organization on two dimensions of self-esteem. *British Journal of Educational Psychology, 80,* 417–433.

Myers, S. A., & Martin, M. M. (2006). Understanding the source: Teacher credibility and aggressive communication traits. In T. P. Mottet, V. P. Richmond, & J. C. McCroskey (Eds.), *Handbook of instructional communication: Rhetorical and relational perspectives* (pp. 67–85). Boston, MA: Pearson.

Plax, T. G. (2008). Classroom management techniques. In W. Donsbach (Ed.), *The international encyclopedia of communication.* Blackwell Reference Online. Retrieved from http://www .communicationencyclopedia.com/subscriber/tocnode?id=g9781405131995_yr2010_ chunk_g97814051319958_ss33-1

Pogue, L. L., & AhYun, K. (2006). The effect of teacher nonverbal immediacy and credibility on student motivation and affective learning. *Communication Education, 55,* 331–334.

Rahim, M. A. (1983). A measure of styles of handling interpersonal conflict. *Academy of Management Journal, 26,* 368–376.

Roach, K. D. (1991). Graduate student teaching assistants' use of behavior alteration techniques in the college classroom. *Communication Quarterly, 39,* 178–188.

Rodriguez, J. I., Plax, T. G., & Kearney, P. (1996). Clarifying the relationship between teacher nonverbal immediacy and student cognitive learning: Affective learning as the central causal mediator. *Communication Education, 45,* 293–305.

Somech, A. (2008). Managing conflict in school teams: The impact of task and goal interdependence on conflict management and team effectiveness. *Educational Administration Quarterly, 44,* 359–390.

Teven, J. J. (2001). The relationships among teacher characteristics and perceived caring. *Communication Education, 50,* 159–169.

Tibbles, D., Richmond, V. P., McCroskey, J. C., & Weber, K. (2008). Organizational orientations in an instructional setting. *Communication Education, 57,* 389–407.

Turman, P. D., & Schrodt, P. (2006). Student perceptions of teacher power as a function of perceived teacher confirmation. *Communication Education, 55,* 265–279.

Waldeck, J. H. (2007). Answering the question: Student perceptions of personalized education and the construct's relationship to learning outcomes. *Communication Education, 56,* 409–432.

Waldeck, J. H., & Kearney, P. (in press). Teacher influence and persuasion. In W. Donsbach (Ed.), *The international encyclopedia of communication.* Blackwell Reference Online.

Waring, H. Z. (2007). Complex advice acceptance as a resource for managing asymmetries. *Text & Talk, 27,* 107–137.

Weimer, M. (2014, April 9). Creating learning environments that help students stretch and grow as learners. *Faculty Focus: Teaching Professor Blog.* Retrieved from http://www .facultyfocus.com/articles/teaching-professor-blog/creating-learning-environments-help-students-stretch-grow-learners/

Wilmot, W. W., & Hocker, J. L. (2013). *Interpersonal conflict* (9th ed.). New York: McGraw Hill.

Wilson, S. (2012). The role becomes them: Examining communication center alumni experiences. In E. L. Yook & W. Atkins-Sayre (Eds.), *Communication centers and oral communication programs in higher education: Advantages, challenges, and new directions* (pp. 55–70). Lanham, MD: Lexington Books.

Woolfolk, A. (2001). *Educational psychology* (5th ed.). Boston, MA: Allyn and Bacon.

THEORY INTO PRACTICE

CASE 1

SUCCESSFULLY RUNNING A PEER-TO-PEER LEARNING SPACE

Kimberly M. Cuny

This piece describes how the author engages employees in order to develop a steward mentality among her tutors. She believes that emphasizing stewardship and satisfaction lead to a staff more willing to take on tasks and who have a stronger commitment to the center itself.

As the newly hired director of a speaking center in its second year at the University of North Carolina Greensboro, I was faced with the enormous task of establishing a strong center ethos on campus. In doing so I would have to recruit and train student staff, earn faculty buy in, educate the campus about our services, brand our support as being of high value to administrators, and put into place an organizational structure to support our work. The best thing I did as I prepared to step into the directing position was to attend a peer tutoring conference and to reflect on best practices for creating the right environment for training tutors. I left the conference with a genuine commitment to supporting our undergraduate peer consultants as *they did the work* of our learning space. My support, I felt, had to include the cultivation of an office/organizational culture of care. This care would extend beyond care for the speakers we enter into dialogue with; it had to include care for the peer consultants themselves. Looking back, I believe that the commitments to support and care are directly linked to the successful running of this particular peer-to-peer learning space.

I shared the commitments to supporting our student-staff and cultivating an ethic of care with our new graduate assistant on her first day of work. We quickly realized that the best way for us to do both was to step back and let the consultants do their work with an eye to identifying ways to help. We would look to implement new practices, policies, and paper forms in ways that avoided our being perceived as managing from the top down. Instead we would work shoulder-to-shoulder with our undergraduate consultants. We would seek their voices in solving problems and ask for feedback about operations. When we first addressed our peer educators we clearly communicated what we expected of them and identified what they could expect of us.

This support and care approach influenced our organizational communication. Our graduate assistant and I had extensive Friday afternoon meetings each week. During the meetings we shared what we saw and experienced, and identified areas of potential tension. Next, we sought to discover ways that we could be a part of helping our student employees to resolve these issues. We were deliberate in our use of inclusive language when we spoke about our learning space and when we spoke to our peer consultants. We taught them to do the same. For example we would talk about "our services" and "our peer consultants" instead of saying "my consultants" or "my center." What was going on in this learning space was far bigger than any one person.

We sought to maintain a kind, friendly, and cooperative workplace where our peer consultants could develop their professionalism. Our potlucks, game nights, committee projects, and Friday lunch gatherings would lead to our peer consultants leaving candy and genuine expressions of appreciation (for the support they got from one another) in everyone's mailbox. Consultants would later refer to the whole staff as their "Speaking Center family" and email messages seeking shift coverage were signed "Speaking Center Lov." Our ethic of care practices quickly cultivated a community of practice.

We believed that support and care led to satisfied employees. More satisfaction led to more willingly taking on tasks, and stronger commitment to the Center itself. In a recent *Forbes Magazine* blog posting, contributor Roger Dean Duncan of Duncan Worldwide states that "commitment thrives in an atmosphere of mutual purpose, mutual respect, and high levels of physiological ownership. In other words, engagement. Workers are engaged when they feel part of decisions that affect them. When they feel trusted. When they feel free (safe) in speaking up about issues that matter" (2014, p. 2). Given this, we realize now that the particular choices we were making were actually achieving employee engagement.

Duncan goes on to say that engaged employees develop a steward mentality. Stewards do the right thing all of the time, are proactive, resourceful, willingly adapt fast when conditions change, and are assertive. We have further found that our most highly engaged employees, the peer managers, are extremely loyal. Our support and care efforts have certainly led to stewardship.

The time we spend on fostering employee engagement far outweighs the cost of employee disengagement. Deliberately supporting the students who do our work and fostering a genuine ethic of care is what we do right, and where our focus should be if our peer-to-peer learning space is to remain successful.

Reference

Duncan, R. D. (2014, August 2). Why employee satisfaction is the wrong metric. [Web log post]. Retrieved from http://www.forbes.com/sites/rodgerdeanduncan/2014/08/02/why-employee-satisfaction-is-the-wrong-metric/

CASE 2

TEACHING THE TUTOR TO REFLECT VIA THREE ROLES

Client, Participant, and Practitioner

Alison Fisher Bodkin

In this piece, the author describes a training approach of role-playing that is essential to the tutoring process for experiential learning. By assigning students to perform the three roles, and then presenting a self-reflection of each respective role, the center's training program exposes students to the various aspects of the center and cultivates awareness about the multitude of experiences to be had there.

Assignment Description

This internship is a part of a university communication center training program, which is offered as a class and spans a typical 15-week semester.

Students play three different roles: client, participant, and practitioner to experience peer tutoring from different perspectives. After each phase is completed, the student writes a reflection detailing the objectives and the effectiveness of each meeting. Finally, their reflections should pose questions or insights. By assigning students to perform the three roles, and then present a self-reflection of each respective role, the center's training program hopes to expose students to the various aspects of the center and to cultivate respect and awareness of the multitude of experiences to be had there.

The Phases

Within the first two weeks of the internship, students complete the client phase of this activity by making an appointment with a tutor at the center to work on a speech, interview, class presentation, or the like. After the client phase is the participant phase, which entails shadowing a tutor in a session with a client; the students are observers of the process—neither receiving the advice nor conducting the consultation. Finally, students move into the practitioner phase where they act in the capacity of a peer tutor. A faculty member at the center facilitates the session, allowing the student to take the lead as a practitioner and test-drive being a tutor.

After each appointment, students write a brief descriptive analysis providing the overview, reflection, and insight or questions. For the overview, students answer questions such as: What agenda items were set for the session? How were these goals negotiated? What questions did the consultant ask? What did the client seem to want, and how did he/she express such needs? What kinds of strategies were suggested or used? What was accomplished during the tutoring session? How did the session end? For the reflection, students discuss what they thought was effective or ineffective about the consultation. Be specific. Describe the tutor's communication style during the session. Describe evidence of the client's learning. Provide suggestions for the tutor to improve. In the tutor's opinion, was the observed session a representative example of typical consultations in the center? To focus on insights and questions, students should write about how their consultations inform the class discussions about effective tutoring, as well as raise any other questions that they have developed about tutoring or how our center operates.

Appraisal

This internship appeals to faculty and tutors-in-training at the center because it clearly represents the two essential roles played in the "work" done there—the roles of the tutor and the client. In my experience, students display the most empathy for both roles because they have experienced both of them. This helps potential tutors actualize their (1) tutoring philosophy by having them demonstrate it, not just theorize, (2) strengths and weaknesses as a tutor by having them explain what happened, what worked, and what didn't, (3) critical thinking skills by having students articulate the situated knowledge they acquire from each session in the project. Overall, this comprehensive project enables students to fully experience the different roles played at our communication center, as well as assess their abilities in the tutoring role. This project gives students the experience that they all seem to already desire—to be a tutor for our center.

CASE 3

USING CREATIVITY AND COOPERATION IN STAFF TRAINING

Erin Ellis

The author uses her experience as both a trainee and a staff trainer to make recommendations that are simple and enjoyable, yet effective. The activities typically take place at the beginning of each semester. Cooperative team building has been found to be effective in developing a creative and collaborative team spirit.

Training students to work as peer tutors can have tremendous benefits to both the tutor and the tutee. Troillett and McIntyre (2012) state that the training of undergraduate staff tutors should include experiential activities, informal shadowing, and self-directed training in order to maximize learning. I want to extend their recommendations for what makes a successful staff training event.

Our staff training events take place at the beginning of each semester (before the center opens) for returning consultants in order to promote community, learn of new policies/procedures, and engage in activities that promote team building. Many of the learning strategies, guided processes, and evaluation processes that occur during the semester-long training course usually aren't the focus of these training sessions but are rather the focus of the semester-long training class. In order to have a desirable outcome from this type of short training event, there are two other variables that play a part in its success.

First, the training exercises that bring the most satisfaction from staff members usually involve building or creating an object in small cohorts. Training activities such as building a tower out of marshmallows and toothpicks or creating a poster or video that represents their group are team experiential activities that can engage trainees, increase their self-confidence, and help them discuss with one another how the training content can be transferred from the session to the workplace (Beebe, Mottet, & Roach, 2004). The team aspect is emphasized here because it taps into the potential of many minds, promotes cohesion among staff, and creates team energy (Scearce, 2007); all of which play an important aspect in creating engaged and united tutors.

The activity should be non-competitive so that staff members concentrate on team building and execution rather than winning. The small groups should average around five people and should be assigned according to either their group role type (test would be taken beforehand), role in the organization, or based on people they normally don't interact with. This way, groups can become more balanced and give the staff a chance to work with those they normally do not. Competitive activities can result in more passion and energy during the event, but often leave people feeling defeated, angry, or displaying unsportsmanship like behaviors. If competitive activities are the only route you see possible for a training event, consider giving a small reward to all parties involved, not just the winners.

The second recommendation for successful training actually has nothing to do with the activity itself or the environment. The second, often overlooked, component of a successful training event has to do with community building and having a sense of belonging within a group of people. The best way to build community in a small organization is with food. Littlejohn (2009) points out that there is an acknowledgment of the power of food to send messages, but the narrative qualities—captured in discourse and behavior—contribute to its meaning-making properties. Coffee, donuts, cookies, or pizza; no matter what the food may be, it is often the stimulus for a conversation to begin. Whether it is the hypnotizing aroma or the culinary artistic design, food stimulates the mind to share feelings and experiences people might have in that moment, or in previous times they have interacted with a particular dish. Food can not only start conversations, it can initiate relationship building with other staff members who might not typically interact. For example, as a trainer, you might think of buying three different types of pizzas, and have the staff sit at the table with the kind of pizza they like most (cheese, pepperoni, veggie). After eating their pizza, each table would form a group and come up with a unique group name. They would then engage in an activity or training session while in those small groups. The group name and experience of sharing a common love of something can create a sense of community when they see one another, either at work or around campus. They might not remember every person's name, but what they will remember is that they were in the "cheese pizza" group.

There are many ways to train staff members to become effective peer tutors. My aim is to extend the existing literature to include small group activities that are collaborative instead of competitive, and to incorporate food into training events. These recommendations are based on my years of experience as both a trainee and a trainer.

References

Beebe, S. A., Mottet, T. P., & Roach, D. K. (2004). *Training and development: Enhancing communication and leadership skills*. Boston, MA: Pearson Education, Inc.

Littlejohn, S. (2009). *The rhetoric of food narratives: Ideology and influence in American culture* (Unpublished doctoral dissertation). University of North Carolina at Greensboro, Greensboro, NC.

Scearce, C. (2007). *122 ways to build teams* (2nd ed.). Thousand Oaks, CA: Corwin Press.

Troillett, R., & McIntyre, K. A. (2012). Best practices in communication center training and training assessment. In E. L. Yook & W. Atkins-Sayre (Eds.), *Communication centers and oral communication programs in higher education: Advantages, challenges, and new directions* (pp. 257–272). Lanham, MD: Lexington Books.

CASE 4

SPEAKERS LAB CODE OF CONDUCT

Butler University Speaking Lab Staff

In the field of communication centers, Butler University center directors have long been known for their work on ethics and the communication center. Although this case is an example of one particular type of peer tutoring center, there are aspects of the ethical code that can be applied to other centers, as well.

Professionalism

- Each member of the Speakers Lab staff should respect the privacy of each tutee. The staff will not share information about a tutee, details of a tutee's assignment, or the events of a session with anyone who is not affiliated with the Speakers Lab. Such discussion amongst the staff will occur only in a private setting.
- Tutors should not predict grades or guarantee a level of success to a tutee.
- Tutors should not assist a student in committing plagiarism by writing or explicitly rewording a tutee's speech.
- Tutors should not use amorous or suggestive words or actions toward a tutee.

- Tutors should not promote social gatherings, functions, or dates that are unrelated to the Speakers Lab during lab sessions.
- Tutors have the right to end a session and ask the tutee to leave if a situation in the lab becomes inappropriate or uncontrollable. In such a situation, the tutor should contact the director immediately.
- Tutors should uphold all standards and policies set forth by Butler University.

Responsible Coverage

- Tutors alone are responsible for his/her scheduled coverage hours.
- Tutors should be prompt and remain for the duration of all shifts.
- Tutors are responsible for finding a replacement when necessary, using the established protocol described by the Speakers Lab Policies.

Ethical Communication

Speakers Lab tutors have highlighted honesty, integrity, and respect as guiding principles for ethical communication in the Lab. From these principles, they have agreed upon the following codes of conduct:

- Tutors should communicate positive regard for tutees and other Lab staff members by listening and responding with appropriate feedback to others' ideas, concerns, and questions.
- Tutors should give undivided attention to the student during the entire lab session.
- Tutors should not speak ill of other members of the Lab, including fellow staff members and tutees, as everyone is deserving of mutual respect.
- Tutors should maintain objectivity during all Lab sessions, regardless of the tutor's personal and political opinions, religious beliefs, or past/present experiences with tutees.
- Tutors should provide honest critique.
- Tutors should give an accurate account of Lab-related matters.
- Tutors should not allow his/her personal circumstances to negatively influence the session and other Lab-related work.

CASE 5

SPEAKING CENTER CODE OF ETHICS

University of Southern Mississippi Speaking Center Staff

The University of Southern Mississippi Speaking Center shares an example of a code of ethics that has been found to be effective in providing guidance for their staff in conducting their daily business at the center. Originally created in a group exercise and updated yearly, this code addresses professionalism, client communication, co-workers interaction, and disciplinary commitment. This example can become the basis for creating an effective code of ethics that is appropriate for other peer tutoring centers.

As a group, we pledge to uphold the following standards with attention to the following categories:

Attention to Professionalism

- We will strive to be responsible, honest, friendly, positive, accountable, flexible, patient, forgiving, approachable, tactful, and respectful.
- We will create a supportive communication climate by communicating effectively, clearly, and listening to staff and clients.
- We will listen and think before responding and will not make assumptions.

- We will show dedication to the Center and act as an advocate for the Center at all times by being punctual and following through on all jobs.

Attention to Clients

- We will make clients our priority by remaining "audience-centered" while tutoring.
- We will greet clients and always show respect for their work.
- We will encourage critical thinking by asking quality questions, listening carefully, and giving our best efforts while tutoring.
- We will be willing and able to adapt during an appointment quickly and gracefully.

Attention to Co-Workers

- We will be supportive and encourage each other to succeed.
- We will help train and advise each other.
- We will share work and collaborate in order to help each other professionally progress.
- We will always respect each other.

Attention to Our Discipline

- We will be self-reflective and always strive to improve.
- We will be knowledgeable about best communication practices, tutoring pedagogy, and class requirements.
- We will use communication concepts to inform our peer tutoring.
- We will strive to continue to bolster the role that Communication Centers play in our larger discipline.

PART 2
UNDERSTANDING THE
NEEDS OF STUDENTS

· 6 ·

WORKING WITH DIVERSE CLIENTELE

Patricia R. Palmerton

It is clear that our institutions of higher education are becoming increasingly diverse. In 1990, 77.5% of undergraduate students enrolled in degree granting institutions were White, 20.6% were Black, 9.6% were Hispanic, 6.1% were Asian/Pacific Islander, and .08% were American Indian/Alaska Native. In 2010, 60.3% of students were White, 37.5% Black, 14.8% Hispanic, 14.1% Asian/Pacific Islander, and 1% American Indian/Alaska Native (Digest of Education Statistics, 2011). In 2008–09, over 671,000 students in the United States were international students, 3.7% of the student population (IIE Network, 2010). Students who are first generation Americans from immigrant families are increasingly becoming part of the higher education demographic. The challenges and opportunities for helping all students understand more about multicultural interactions are abundant.

These statistics raise issues for any of us who are charged with helping students, especially for peer tutoring centers. There are several diversity-related reasons that prompt students to come to a tutoring center for assistance. Some students may be struggling in a work group, where they are having difficulty with another group member, or where they feel that their contributions are being rejected or ignored, related in some vague way to being perceived as "different." Some students may struggle with following a particular format for speaking, or with expectations about essay structures that are inconsistent with their experience and sense of what is needed in order to be understood. Some may find that speaking up in a discussion-oriented class is a harrowing experience because their perspectives are so different or because, in their cultural background, speaking up (especially by offering opinions or points of view) is simply not done. Others may feel that when they speak up they are perceived as being aggressive and offensive and cannot understand why. Still others may have encountered stereotyped responses that they feel are racist or sexist.

Faculty feel vulnerable too, wanting to do the right thing, but unsure as to what that would be. Students look to faculty to learn effective ways to interact with others, whether as members of the dominant group, or as individuals in the minority (Bonilla & Palmerton, 2000; Fox, 2009). Yet faculty members often feel lost too, when it comes to addressing diversity concerns when they arise. The idea of encouraging dialogue in order to develop a broader sense of understanding is foreign to many faculty members. Not only do many feel incapable, there is a sense by many that it simply is not their job; they are there to teach their content, and issues of diversity are issues for someone else to tackle. In cases such as these, students may often have no other place to go than to support services like a tutoring center.

Students may also seek out the peer tutoring center to find a resolution to some of their cultural misunderstandings that translate into academic difficulties. Students from cultures that have different cultural norms such as high power distance or "face needs," as explained in detail further in this chapter, may find it exceedingly difficult to explicitly address a professor about difficulties with an assignment. This may be so not only because of concerns about self-face, but also because of concerns about offending the professor (other-face) by intimating that the professor is not teaching well (Goffman, 1959, 1963; Ting-Toomey & Oetzel, 2001). Students may also be terrified by a request/suggestion/demand from a professor to meet the professor in her/his office. The threat to face of just the request may result in the student avoiding the whole situation by dropping the course.

On the other hand, peer tutors are peers first and foremost. So when faculty are not available, or when faculty are themselves at a loss for how to guide students on personal and cultural matters, chances are that students will likely seek out peers to get answers to their problems. Whether required to go to a peer tutoring center or when seeking help on their own, students may also present cultural issues as they get assistance on the content subject matter.

Tutors are perceived by students to be on an intermediate level between a peer and instructor, somewhat more knowledgeable than the average peer, but also not as intimidating as a faculty member. Therefore, they may be likely to address some of their questions of diversity to a peer tutor.

Sharing the information in this chapter with peer tutors during training sessions will be important in understanding tutoring centers' diverse clientele, and this, in turn, will make both students more comfortable visiting the tutoring center and tutors more comfortable with and confident in the assistance that they provide students. More visits to the tutoring center will translate into better student academic outcomes, higher retention rates, and a more central role for the tutoring center as an important side-product.

Diversity Is Not Just about Culture

While I will focus my attention primarily on cultural difference, much of what I will discuss applies when considering perceived difference generally. Many of the issues that students bring when confronted with reactions to their perceived "difference" are related to interpretation, attributions of intent, differences in communication styles, and the impact upon the sense of self. There are unrelenting challenges that face many students in academe who are not members of the majority, whether that be related to race, ethnicity, disability, age, gender, sexual orientation, class, or any other social category that is or is not visible to others.

Whether due to ignorance or outright bigotry, students who are the recipients of cruel or insensitive remarks and attitudes must deal with them in some way—whether by absorbing them, attempting to ignore them (which is next to impossible), or answering them. The isolation felt by individuals who are not members of the majority can be paralyzing, angering, depressing, demoralizing, and demotivating. Privilege exists for those who are seen as being members of the dominant group, leaving others with the task of proving themselves worthy. There are multiple articles and stories about individuals who have encountered racist barriers, and the strategies that they have used to respond (see Bonilla, 2006; Bonilla & Palmerton, 2000; Fox, 2009; Fugimoto, 2002; Lim, Herrera-Sobek, & Padilla, 2000; Nance & Foeman, 2002). These experiences are real, and they are difficult.

Students come from varied backgrounds, have different senses of identity, and bring different traditions, cultural expectations, and communication styles to the tutoring session. Yet, many students encounter an academy where the assumption is that if we speak the same language, we have the same interpretive systems in place. In essence, in the academy, the assumption is that there is one way to understand communication, and one way to enact communication if it is to be judged as "competent." We do not, however, all say things in the same way, and that does not mean that those who do not conform are inadequate or incompetent.[1] Our task, then, is to help surface the assumptions within the academy, and help students understand how their own identity and traditions fit in relationship to the new skills and approaches they are learning and are expected to accomplish.

Socialization to the Academy

Peer tutors can help students from diverse backgrounds adjust to new cultural rules within an education system that may be different from their expectations. When students come to a university setting, they bring with them patterns of communication that have worked for them in the settings they have previously experienced. For some students, the expectations about talk in an academic setting are very different from the patterns of communication they ordinarily use. For example, expectations about whether one should speak up differ, as do orientations toward initiating interaction (see Carbaugh, 2002; Fox, 2009; Philips, 1983). Additionally, participating in discussion where one is expected to support one's opinions with evidence is not necessarily a common experience.

However, it is not enough for peer tutors to learn about these different interpretive systems within academe. Helping students to navigate their own identities by making them more aware of these differences is also important. The very struggles that students have with the demands of academe can also be an opportunity for them to discover the powerful insights they have to contribute, and the possibility of developing an ability to translate between and among many different kinds of understandings. More importantly, by surfacing the character of different communicative systems, we can help legitimize students' struggles as part of learning a new language.

Gloria Anzaldúa describes the exhaustion of constantly dealing with being the outsider, and uses four metaphors to provide insight into ways of dealing with the challenge to identity brought on by living in the "Borderlands": the island, where one deliberately isolates oneself; the drawbridge, where one allows for some connection with others without giving up the safety of the island; the bridge, where one is mediating among self and cultures constantly; and the sandbar, where retreat and renewal is possible in a fluid way, recognizing constantly shifting and changing concerns (Foss, Foss, & Griffin, 1999). She argues that to come to terms with the challenges to identity experienced by dealing with the responses to difference, one needs to develop what she calls a "mestiza consciousness." This is a consciousness of self and of other, without the privileging of one over the other. It is a "both-and" sense, recognizing the contributions of all. This consciousness tolerates ambiguity and contradictions, and must remain flexible in order to juggle the cultures. This is a "plural personality" where "nothing is thrust out, the good, the bad and the ugly, nothing rejected, nothing abandoned" (Anzaldúa, 1987 p. 87).

The goal is to break down dualities: we-they and us-them. This can only happen if we look unsparingly at the experiences each of us bring, the differences that exist, and the ways in which communication functions within these interpretive worlds. But one cannot do this all of the time. Complete isolation is not an answer, yet that is where many of our students find themselves, because they do not know how to recognize or deal with what they are experiencing. On the other hand, leaving the bridge open all the time is exhausting, with little room for renewal. Students need permission to put up the drawbridge, or to welcome the tides covering the sandbar, and the exploration necessary to find the way again after the sands have shifted. Peer tutors can help to break that isolation by acting as a cultural "bridge" for cultural learning about expectations in U.S. academe. While this role may seem counter to the original role of the peer tutor of covering subject content only, it will pave the way for better adjustment by the student client in academia in general and to a smoother and more effective tutoring session in particular.

It is important that peer tutors and their student clients be aware that within academe, we are essentially enculturating students to a particular way of talking and thinking. The expectations we have about what comprises "competent communication" are embedded in a style of talk, with its own rules and characteristics. By encouraging these characteristics, this style, we are not only privileging that style of talk, but also the ways of thinking associated with that talk. The connection between talking and thinking is so fundamental that students are often judged for flaws in thinking because of the patterns of communication they use. Members of the academy are likely to consider communication patterns that do not conform to the academic standard as inferior, bad, lazy, or indicative of an inability to think clearly.

Lisa Delpit (1988) argues that in socializing students to academic discourse we are providing them with access to "codes of power" within our society. Being able to communicate in ways that conform to the dominant culture is a requirement for success. Nevertheless, in the experiences of many of our students, the communication styles and patterns to which we are socializing our students in the academy are not the only functional communication styles, nor are they the most functional in every circumstance. Even in the academy there are different styles from one discipline to the next. When working with students who hail from multiple backgrounds, we are encountering students socialized to functional communication styles within a context that we do not always realize nor understand. Students are also often unaware that there are any contextual differences. As a result, students socialized to communicate in ways that do not conform to the standard power structure of our society may find our demand that they conform to our preferred communication styles very unsettling. At the very least, students are likely to question their own capabilities as they struggle to learn this new language. Some students resist, without necessarily knowing why, as they feel their very essence is under attack. For these students, conforming to the academic code is a betrayal of their own culture, ways of thinking, and sense of identity.

Anzaldúa (1987) talks about the sense of being in a cultural Borderlands— of being torn between ways, where having to choose one way of talking and being means betraying a part of herself. No matter which way one goes, there is always that sense of betrayal of some part of oneself (see also Yep, 2002). These are issues of identity. The experiences many students have when learning the ways of academe place them firmly in these cultural Borderlands.

I worked closely with one Ojibwe student who struggled with the expectation that arguments follow a linear structure. He felt that he lost too much when he tried to express himself in the Western linear form. Where is the context, he wondered, that really helps someone understand the essence of what he was saying? How could anyone really understand without that context? The linear form eliminated that richness; the *whole* meaning simply could not be expressed. I have worked with others where the expectation to have a thesis statement flies in the face of the need to protect both self face and other face. Highly contextual indirect argument allows for all to gain a more complete understanding, without putting anyone on the spot. The Western linear form increases vulnerability and the potential for offense also increases exponentially. For these students, resistance to the academic style is embedded in the knowledge that what we are asking them to do is inadequate for what they want to express and how they need to express it—our style simply will not do the job. As one individual expressed to me, "It's not getting at 'real'" (Palmerton & Bushyhead, 1994).[2]

Fox (2009) discusses the experience of some African American students who interpret a "heated exchange" as indicating that students care. Politeness, respectful listening, or backing off when encountering direct confrontation is seen as showing a "lack of investment" (p. 77). Other students, encouraged to engage in "heated exchanges," may be traumatized because those who argue animatedly and emotionally seem self-centered, uncaring, and disrespectful.

Given these differences, students may be confused about various expectations for academic behavior. Students may bring concerns about how others perceive them, or about how others react to them to the peer tutor. When students are guided to understand the fact that there are different communication styles, they can begin to understand the interplay of behavior and interpretation. This gives them a choice, by being able to realize that they are working on expanding their repertoire of behaviors, rather than replacing what they know.

Ultimately our goal is to help these students achieve the ability to code-switch (or shift their language to match their audience), while knowing how and why they are doing so. This is a matter of building rhetorical flexibility. Rather than a betrayal, they can become translators, able to cross these rule boundaries as needed. As students come to realize their ability to translate, they also realize that by having learned how to code-switch, they bring something that other students will not have.

Cultural Difference

There are many books on intercultural communication, providing useful insights for anyone working across many different cultures. Helpful books include Schoem, Frankel, Zuniga, & Lewis (1995); Martin, Nakayama, & Flores (2002); and Requejo and Graham (2008). Fox (2009) is especially helpful in thinking about race and approaches to talking about race. Especially useful concepts to consider for the peer tutoring context are individualism and collectivism, cultural expectations about direct communication and indirect communication styles, and different orientations toward social power and the deference required (power-distance). Each of these elements can be associated with a particular cultural background, even looking at variations along a continuum based on predominant cultural orientation (Requejo & Graham, 2008).

Obviously, one of the dangers of making a connection between culture and communication style is making the assumption that all students with a particular cultural background (or gender, class, age, etc.) will display certain characteristics. Nevertheless, when working with students from diverse backgrounds, it is useful to be aware of cultural differences that may exist, as the differences in expectations that are associated with different cultural orientations can contribute to the kinds of difficulties that students face in academe. Raising these issues into awareness is one of the first steps toward helping students understand cultural expectations.

While I do not intend to provide an in-depth look at these concepts, it is useful to have a quick refresher, as these characteristics or orientations may provide insights into the kinds of issues faced by students in the academy. Using this information for content learning during peer tutor training, or to create handouts for students to become more aware of these issues of cultural difference, will be helpful not only to the tutors in conducting their tutoring sessions effectively, but also to students who visit the peer tutoring center.

Individualism and Collectivism

One of the most common ways of thinking about cultural difference is in examining orientations toward self and others (Hall & Hall, 2002; Hofstede, 2002). The dominant cultural orientation in the United States is individualistic (Requejo & Graham, 2008; Ting-Toomey & Oetzel, 2001), and our educational systems largely reward individualistic behavior. Individualism emphasizes individual identity over group identity, and individual rights over group obligations. Communication involves assertion of personal opinion, personal emotion, and a focus on individual accountability. Self-initiative is valued and rewarded. Face concerns, that is, concerns about perceived self-worth, tend to be focused on one's own face rather than concern over impact on someone else's sense of face (Goffman, 1959, 1963; Gudykunst & Ting-Toomey, 1988). Most U.S. educational systems are highly individualistic.

Individuals with a more collectivistic orientation emphasize group identity over individual wants and desires (Gudykunst & Ting-Toomey, 1988; Hofstede, 2002). Within group harmony is highly valued, and communication patterns focus on maintaining in-group relational harmony and conflict avoidance. Personal emotional expression is limited. There is a high concern for maintaining and protecting face, both self-face and other-face (Ting-Toomey & Oetzel, 2001). Students with a more collectivistic orientation may be torn between family (including extended family) obligations and academic obligations, and it is likely that family obligations will take priority. To discuss these pressures with an outsider is to betray the harmony of the community, which increases the isolation of the individual within the academic community. Peer tutors should be especially aware of the role of face in interactions with students from different cultural backgrounds. Students may find it difficult to discuss obligations they feel from others, out of a need to protect other-face. Being aware of face needs can help tutors look for what may be unspoken, but that still has a negative impact on academic performance.

Power Distance

Power distance refers to different cultural expectations about power and status, and how one should interact with others based upon their position in society (Hofstede, 2002; Requejo & Graham, 2008). Collectivistic societies tend to have high power distance—that is, members accept uneven distributions of power. Lower power individuals do not expect to be consulted about decisions. The higher status individual is not to be questioned. Forms of address are more formal, and students may be quite uncomfortable if a professor asks to be called by his or her first name. Credibility is status-based. The expectation is that rewards and punishments will be based on age, rank, status, title, and seniority. Students with a high power-distance orientation often find it difficult to approach a professor for help, as asking for help can be interpreted as insulting to the professor (he or she was not doing his/her job or the help would not be needed).

Conversely, individuals with a low power-distance orientation expect that people will be treated equally. All members of a group should be part of decision-making—the "democratic" ideal. Rewards and punishments will be equitable, based on performance. Students with a low power-distance orientation will be more likely to visit a professor during office hours, ask questions, and even challenge the professor at times. This orientation can be very unsettling for a student or a professor with a high power-distance orientation. I worked with one professor from an Asian-Pacific culture who felt that if students asked questions in her class they were challenging her authority. On a campus where class discussion and student participation are valued, students were angered by what appeared to be this professor's unwillingness to respond to their concerns. These misunderstandings resulted in a destructive negative spiral that was emotionally devastating.

Direct and Indirect Communication Styles

The communication style one uses is related to culture and values (Gudykunst & Ting-Toomey, 1988). Direct messages are explicit messages. The content of the message clearly expresses the speaker's intentions, opinions, needs, and/or desires. Direct messages are precise and straightforward. The speaker states his or her point clearly, typically without hedging. In the United States, phrases such as "don't beat around the bush" or "get to the point" are indicative of the expectation that speakers use a direct style.

Indirect messages embody the speaker's intentions, needs, desires, and opinions, but they are embedded in the *context* of the message. Someone not socialized to indirect communication styles may be oblivious to the messages being sent by the other, and to the interpretations of his or her own messages by someone socialized to indirect communication. When there is a clash or direct/indirect messaging, neither party feels understood, nor understands (Tannen, 1986).

Indirect styles tend to be associated with those cultures characterized by a priority on harmony, on not calling attention to oneself, and on not being self-centered (Gudykunst & Ting-Toomey, 1988). These tend to be more collectivist cultures, that is, those more communitarian in orientation. Tannen (1986, 2001) argues that many woman are socialized to use the indirect style, where the focus is on the relationship as opposed to self. Individuals are expected to attend to the needs of others, without others having to put themselves into the position of appearing to put their own needs ahead of others' needs (which would be self-centered, and not supportive of the community, or the relationship). Group harmony is achieved and relationships maintained through imprecise and ambiguous verbal behavior (Gudykunst & Ting-Toomey, 1988).

Tutors should be aware that the direct and indirect styles can be easily misinterpreted, including when they are interacting with their clients. Their own directness may be perceived as "rude" and "pushy" rather than as "honest" and "straightforward." Students may also complain to tutors that they are not being heard or their ideas are rejected, either in class, or as members of groups in which they are members. If they are using an indirect style among others who are more direct, they may be perceived as "manipulative," "passive-aggressive" or "wishy-washy" rather than as intended, as "polite" and "considerate." Tutors may also make these kinds of judgments, if they are not aware of these kinds of differences.

The point for our purposes is that students are often completely unaware of cultural style. Yet, they may be encountering difficulties, particularly in group situations or in interpersonal interactions (for, example, with a professor), where their style may be clashing with others. Bringing style issues into awareness may allow students to become more flexible, expanding their interpretive repertoire. It also helps remind students that their interpretations are not necessarily the only possible interpretations of the communication and messages in an episode.

Guidelines for Tutoring Culturally Diverse Clientele

Encouraging dialogue during a tutoring session is crucial, yet it is not easy. First, students (and peer tutors) must feel safe. Students can be taught ground rules that they can use to establish boundaries and to help foster helpful discussion about cultural differences. Bonilla (2014) argues that ground rules help all "take ownership for creating an environment conducive to learning about cultural competence" (p. 2). He offers five guidelines for engaging culturally diverse students. Although these guidelines were originally intended for the classroom context, they can also be used during peer tutor training to help tutors lay the groundwork for effective tutoring sessions, and are adapted here for the peer tutoring situation.

1. Share experience: talk about your own experience rather than speaking for an entire group of people. As Bonilla (2014) says, "This brings all our experiences into the room and also invites diverse perspectives from peers who often find themselves on the fringe" (p. 2)
2. Participate: share your own experiences while at the same time allowing your clients to participate. If you tend to talk a lot, focus on listening to your client instead. You are attempting to build common ground with your client.
3. Respect Confidentiality: While it is important for everyone to take away ideas and concepts and discuss them with others, individual experiences and personal stories are the property of the individuals who shared them, and need to be kept confidential.
4. Listening Respectfully: Encourage others to talk by listening first. If someone says something that you find offensive or distasteful, or with

which you disagree, it is important to say so and be open to discussing the different perspectives. Bonilla (2014) emphasizes that "[i]t is also important to remember that the human being behind that question or comment deserves our respect, even when we disagree with what they are saying" (p. 2).

5. Avoid "Zaps": This is related to respect. "Zaps" are put-downs, including jokes and sarcasm that may seem innocent, but that essentially tell the other that they are wrong, strange, off base, or even a bad person. "Zaps" effectively shut off communication, and "discourage open and honest exchange of ideas" (Bonilla, 2014, p. 2).

By implementing these ground rules when tutoring, the student client will feel more comfortable about opening up to the peer tutor about both the content issues with which the student is wrestling, as well as the struggles arising from cultural misunderstandings during his/her academic endeavors.

Once the appropriate communication environment has been established through the ground rules discussed above, there are more specific guidelines for conferencing with students suggested by Fox (2009). She suggests what she calls a modified LARA method (Listen, Affirm, Respond, Add). While these are guidelines for engaging students in conversations about race and diversity, they also apply well to the context of peer tutoring, especially when the student is from a different cultural background. Adapting the LARA method to peer tutoring: First, "Listen to the students' frustrations and points of view. Let them spill. Just having someone listen can relieve tension and make students more open and willing to question their own views" (Fox, p. 134). Any discussion of stylistic or cultural differences can challenge senses of identity and raise defenses. Listening lets the other know that their concerns are being taken as valid. Next, "Affirm the student's feelings and experiences: Commiserate, if necessary, with their position, even if you feel it's inappropriate or immature" (Fox, p. 134). As a tutor, it is important to find elements in the work of the students that you can agree with and support. Ideas are personal, and how one responds to those ideas can feel like a threat. By looking for some idea, or value, or fear that you can affirm, you show acceptance of the individual. As Fox emphasizes, sincerity is crucial. The next step is to Respond to the argument or concerns that the student raises without directly confronting the student with how he or she may be in error. Explore options, explaining your perspective while letting the student be the final decision-maker about how he or she will go forward. Finally, Add any additional information that can help clarify and reassure the student. Reassure students that their own cultural style is not wrong, but that what they are learning is a kind of language that they will now have the option to use in situations that call for it.

LARA is a method that can be used in peer tutor training, with an acronym that is easy to remember. It is a simple but effective method that can be helpful in engaging student clients. Implementing these guidelines can help student clients to feel affirmed and supported, while their questions are being clarified. If students feel more accepted they are more likely to be open to the suggestions and directives that will help them learn.

An important side-product is that the tutors themselves have access to a rich source of cultural learning, and learning about the self. Dace and McPhail (2002) argue for cultivating "implicature"—extending empathy from psychological understanding to "acknowledging that self and other are never separate and distinct, but are always interdependent and interrelated" (p. 350). It is a "'dialogic' experience of otherness" (p. 350), where one discovers self through understanding the experiences of other (see also Zúñiga & Nagda, 1995).

The challenge of embracing a new role of becoming a cultural bridge for culturally diverse students can also personally benefit peer tutors. A distinct advantage for peer tutors who learn to address issues related to cultural diversity in their tutoring sessions is that they themselves become skilled translators. Not only do they learn about themselves and others, but they develop skills valued by employers in an increasingly global society. Being able to handle communication in a multicultural context can make the difference between productive and successful working relationships and those that are painful and difficult for all (Aritz & Walker, 2010; Charles, 2007; Horwitz, 2005; Jameson, 2007; Sinclair, Laskowitz, & Sinclair, 2000).

Conclusion

Clearly, one individual in one support center cannot change the culture of an institution, or of academe. However, by beginning the process of unwrapping and demystifying the characteristics of difference and the interpretive dynamics associated with how we negotiate meaning through communication, the dialogue is started. It can make all the difference in the world to an individual to learn that he or she is not crazy or stupid, and that the struggles they feel are not because they are not capable, but because they are learning a new language and new ways of interacting that will prepare them to function in multiple contexts. We are reframing experiences for students by helping them not only to expand their communication repertoire by learning the communication codes that will help them succeed, but also by affirming their own senses of identity within the larger community.

Those working in support networks or tutoring centers are in a unique position to do this work. It takes courage and on-going openness and learning. All of us doing this work make many mistakes along the way. It is well worth it, however, when the face of a student lights up with comprehension that the struggles they are experiencing are understandable. When students realize that they need not abandon who they are as they learn additional ways of thinking and communicating, that is when we know that our own struggle to understand, learn, and communicate about difference matters.

References

Anzaldúa, G. (1987). *Borderlands: The new mestiza=La frontera.* San Francisco, CA: Spinsters/ Aunt Lute.

Aritz, J., & Walker, R. C. (2010). Cognitive organization and identity maintenance in multicultural teams: A discourse analysis of decision-making meetings. *Journal of Business Communication, 47,* 20–41.

Basso, K. H. (1992), "Speaking with Names": Language and landscape among the Western Apache. In G. E. Marcus (Ed.), *Rereading cultural anthropology* (pp. 220–251). Durham, NC: Duke University Press.

Bonilla, J. F. (2006). "Are you here to move the piano?": A Latino reflects on twenty years in the academy. In C. Stanley (Ed.), *Faculty of color teaching in predominantly White institutions* (pp. 68–79). Bolton, MA: Anker Publishing.

Bonilla, J. F. (2014 March). *Five lenses for educating for assessing cultural competence.* Presentation, Hamline University, St. Paul, MN.

Bonilla, J. F., Lindeman, L., & Taylor, N. (2012) Educating for and assessing cultural competence. In K. Norman Major & S. Goode (Eds.), *Cultural competency for public administrators* (pp. 294–309). Armonk, NY: M. E. Sharpe.

Bonilla, J. F., & Palmerton, P. R. (2000). Hamline faculty and student voices: Race, ethnicity, & gender in the classroom. *The Hamline Review, 24,* 72–94.

Carbaugh, D. (2002). "I can't do that!" but I "can actually see around corners": American Indian students and the study of public "communication." In J. N. Martin, T. K. Nakayama, & L. A. Flores (Eds.), *Readings in intercultural communication: Experiences and contexts* (2nd ed., pp. 138–149). Boston, MA: McGraw Hill.

Charles, M. (2007). Language matters in global communication: Article based on ORA lecture, October 2006. *Journal of Business Communication, 44,* 260–282.

Dace, K. L., & McPhail, M. L. (2002). Crossing the color line: From empathy to implicature in intercultural communication. In J. N. Martin, T. K. Nakayama, & L. A. Flores (Eds.), *Readings in intercultural communication: Experiences and contexts* (2nd ed., pp. 344–350). Boston, MA: McGraw Hill.

Delpit, L. (1988). The silenced dialogue: Power and ideology in educating other people's children. *Harvard Educational Review, 58,* 280–298.

Digest of Education Statistics. (2011). *"Fall enrollment in colleges and universities" surveys, 1976 and 1980, integrated postsecondary education data system (IPEDS), "Fall Enrollment Survey" (IPEDS-EF.90); and IPEDS Spring 2001 through Spring 2011, enrollment component.* National Center for Education Statistics, U.S. Department of Education, Higher Education General Information Survey (HEGIS). Retrieved from: http://nces.ed.gov/programs/digest/d11/tables/dt11_237.asp

Foss, K. A., Foss, S. K., & Griffin, C. L. (1999). *Feminist rhetorical theories.* Thousand Oaks, CA: SAGE.

Fox, H. (2009). *When race breaks out: Conversations about race and racism in college classrooms* (Rev. ed.). New York, NY: Peter Lang.

Fugimoto, E. (2002). South Korean adoptees growing up in White America: Negotiating race and culture. In J. N. Martin, T. K. Nakayama, & L. A. Flores (Eds.), *Readings in intercultural communication: Experiences and contexts* (2nd ed.) (pp. 265–275). Boston, MA: McGraw Hill.

Goffman, E. (1959). *The presentation of self in everyday life.* Garden City, NY: Doubleday Anchor Books.

Goffman, E. (1963). *Stigma: Notes on the management of the spoiled identity.* New York, NY: Simon & Schuster Inc.

Gudykunst, W. B., & Ting-Toomey, S. (1988). *Culture and interpersonal communication.* Newbury Park, CA: SAGE.

Hall, E. T., & Hall, M. R. (2002). Key concepts: Underlying structure of culture. In J. N. Martin, T. K. Nakayama, & L. A. Flores (Eds.), *Readings in intercultural communication: Experiences and contexts* (2nd ed., pp. 165–172). Boston, MA: McGraw Hill.

Hofstede, G. (2002). I, we, they. In J. N. Martin, T. K. Nakayama, & L. A. Flores (Eds.), *Readings in intercultural communication: Experiences and contexts* (2nd ed., pp. 289–301). Boston, MA: McGraw Hill.

Horwitz, S. K. (2005). The compositional impact of team diversity on performance: Theoretical considerations. *Human Resource Development Review, 4,* 219–245.

IIE Network (Institute of International Education) (2010). *Open Doors Data Tables.* Retrieved from: http://opendoors.iienetwork.org/?p=150810

Jameson, D. A. (2007). Reconceptualizing cultural identity and its role in intercultural business communication. *Journal of Business Communication, 44,* 199–235.

Lim, S., Herrera-Sobek, M., & Padilla, G. M. (2000). *Power, race, and gender in academe: Strangers in the tower?* New York, NY: Modern Language Association.

Martin, J. N., Nakayama, T. K., & Flores, L. A. (Eds.). (2002). *Readings in intercultural communication: Experiences and contexts* (2nd ed.). Boston, MA: McGraw Hill.

Nance, T. A., & Foeman, A. K. (2002). On being biracial in the United States. In J. N. Martin, T. K. Nakayama, & L. A. Flores (Eds.), *Readings in intercultural communication: Experiences and contexts* (2nd ed., pp. 35–43). Boston, MA: McGraw Hill.

Palmerton, P. R., & Bushyhead, Y. (1994, April). *"It's Not Getting At Real:" Exploring Alternative Approaches to Critical Thinking.* Paper presented at the annual meeting of the Central States Communication Association, Oklahoma City, OK.

Philips, S. U. (1983). *The invisible culture: Communication in classroom and community on the Warm Springs Indian reservation*. Prospect Heights, IL: Waveland.

Requejo, W. H., & Graham, J. L. (2008). *Global negotiation: The new rules*. New York, NY: Palgrave Macmillan.

Schoem, D., Frankel, L., Zuniga, X., & Lewis, E. A. (Eds.). (1995). *Multicultural teaching in the university*. Westport, CT: Praeger.

Sinclair, G., Laskowitz, K., & Sinclair, J. (2000). Gender differences in teams: Recognizing the proper level of assertiveness. *Journal of Engineering Technology, 17*, 48–51.

Tannen, D. (1986). *That's not what I meant! How conversational style makes or breaks relationships*. New York, NY: Ballentine.

Tannen, D. (2001). *You just don't understand: Women and men in conversation*. New York, NY: Quill.

Ting-Toomey, S., & Oetzel, J. G. (2001). *Managing intercultural conflict effectively*. Thousand Oaks, CA: SAGE.

Yep, G. A. (2002). My three cultures: Navigating the multicultural identity landscape. In J. N. Martin, T. K. Nakayama, & L. A. Flores (Eds.), *Readings in intercultural communication: Experiences and contexts* (2nd ed., pp. 60–66). Boston, MA: McGraw Hill.

Zúñiga, X., & Nagda, B. A. (1995). Dialogue groups: An innovative approach to multicultural learning. In D. Schoem, L. Frankel, X. Zúñiga, & E. A. Lewis (Eds.), *Multicultural teaching in the university* (pp. 233–248). Westport, CT: Praeger.

Notes

1. My focus in this chapter is primarily on cultural and ethnic difference, examining the communication variables that contribute to the difficulties that students may have when interacting in the classroom and peer tutoring centers. I would emphasize that there are different ways to examine diversity in educational settings, including social identity theory, examinations of social justice and oppression, social identity development, and managerial and organizational development. See Bonilla, Lindeman, & Taylor (2012).

2. Another example of contextually addressing an issue or problem can be found in a fascinating account of problem-solving by Keith H. Basso (1992).

· 7 ·

LEARNING STYLES

Rounding the Cycle of Learning in the Context of Peer Tutoring

Carl J. Brown, Michael L. King, and Steven J. Venette

Peer tutoring offers both tutees and tutors a unique learning opportunity. Tutees have the opportunity to learn in a one-on-one, peer-focused setting often resulting in greater understanding than a traditional classroom setting (Chi, Siler, & Jeong, 2004). Tutors have the opportunity to learn by sharing knowledge with others, and by practicing the application of a unique skillset (Topping, 1996). Effective communication is central to the learning experienced by both parties (Person, Kreuz, Zwaan, & Graesser, 1995). In order to achieve effective communication during tutor-tutee interactions, tutors should be trained to adapt to a variety of situations and personalities (Graesser & Person, 1994; Troillett & McIntyre, 2012). Additionally, tutors should be trained to use multiple tutoring styles to effectively connect and communicate with tutees (Roscoe & Chi, 2007). Even when extensive training is provided, tutors consistently inaccurately assess students' levels of comprehension during consultations (Graesser & Person, 1994). One reason for these inaccurate assessments is the tutor's failure to adapt his or her tutoring style to the tutee's learning style. For this reason, tutor training should include learning style literature aimed at enabling tutors to round the cycle of learning styles (Kolb, 1984). Rounding this cycle, or using multiple tutoring styles that align with each learning style preference, will increase the likelihood of making a meaningful connection with an individual tutee. Attending to multiple learning styles and employing various tutoring tactics should result in increased comprehension and ultimately more effective consultations.

The central premise of this chapter is that tutors prefer to teach to their own preferred learning styles. In order to understand and investigate this claim, learning style and tutoring style literature is reviewed. Next, a tutor style quiz created for this research is described and the results of its application are detailed. Finally, implications of the results and practical ways to implement new approaches to tutor training are discussed.

Learning Styles

The expansive body of research addressing learning style theory supports the popular notion that individual learners have a predisposition for a particular style of learning (Cassidy, 2004). Of the various learning theories that fill the literature, the Experiential Learning Theory (ELT) has been lauded as "enormously influential in education, medicine and management training" (Coffield, Moseley, Hall, & Ecclestone, 2004, p. 61). David Kolb's ELT is based upon a variety of disciplines and early 20th century theorists including John Dewey, Kurt Lewing, and Jean Piaget (Kolb, 1984). From this theoretical basis, Kolb (1984) identified that learning is not the result of cognition or perception alone. Rather, learning "involves the integrated functioning of the total organism—thinking, feeling, perceiving, and behaving" (p. 31). Additional benefits of the ELT are that it avoids the major critique of learning style scholarship—that such knowledge inappropriately stereotypes learners (Coffield et al., 2004)—by claiming that while people have a preferred style of learning, they learn best by rounding the cycle of learning. In other words, even though people have preferred ways of learning, optimal learning will occur when presented in a variety of ways.

According to the ELT (Kolb, 1984), learning is motivated by the satisfaction of, or movement between, two sets of dialectically opposed modes: concrete experience (feeling) versus abstract conceptualization (thinking); and reflective observation (observing) versus active experimentation (doing). Movement from mode to mode provides "synergetic transactions" (Kolb & Kolb, 2005, p. 2) that integrate the knowledge created from past experiences with new experiences. Thus, in the framework of the ELT, learning is the continual creation of knowledge through interaction with one's environment and resolutions of dialectical tensions (Kolb, 1984). In other words, by moving from one mode to another, learners are completely immersed in the subject area as they think, feel, perceive, and act within the experience.

As people pass from one pole to another, they pass over each learning dimension formed by the intersecting continuums: diverging, assimilating, converging, and accommodating (Kolb, 1984; Kolb & Kolb, 2005). Figure 7.1 shows a visual representation of the four learning styles, as well as preferred learning activities.

Divergent learners prefer both feeling and observing and they also desire to know how information is important to them. These learners prefer to talk through new ideas with tutors and understand the big picture of how ideas relate to their lives. Assimilative learners prefer both observing and thinking while desiring a traditional lecture-style format of learning. These learners may prefer the inclusion of critical thinking questions during consultations, but may be a challenge for tutors as they enjoy learning alone. Convergent learners prefer both thinking and doing and seek out ways to see direct real-life application of the presented ideas. These learners may prefer the inclusion of brief activities or experiments with tutors during consultations. Finally, accommodative learners prefer feeling and doing and will likely prefer group interactions and collaborative discussions. One method used to identify individuals' learning style preference is by administering Kolb's Learning Style Inventory (LSI) (Kolb, 1976).

The LSI was designed to verify the theorized relationships in the ELT and to identify one's learning preferences (Kolb, 1976, 1984). The inventory consists of 12 sentence beginnings (e.g., "I learn best when ...") each with four possible sentence endings reflecting separate learning modes. Respondents rank order each option in terms of their personal learning preference.

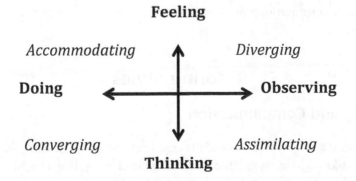

Figure 7.1. Learning Styles and Activities.

Using Kolb's scoring procedures one can identify his or her modal preference (feeling, observing, thinking, or doing) and dialectical pole (preference for feeling/thinking or observing/doing).

Despite the solid theoretical foundation, some scholars (e.g., De Ciantis & Kirton, 1996; Sternberg & Grigorenko, 2001) have challenged the instrument's validity and scoring procedures. Using Kolb's ideas as a theoretical foundation Deanna Sellnow (2005, 2008) and colleagues (Venette, 2014) created a measure that addresses several of these validity concerns, thus introducing the Learning Style Quiz (LSQ) as a more accurate alternative to Kolb's LSI.

The LSQ presents several changes from Kolb's LSI. One important change is a reconceptualization of the Experiential Learning Model (ELM). The LSQ views the ELM's modes as separate and additional learning preferences. With more specificity of learning preferences, comes a new scoring system: the Venette Teaching and Learning Style Calculator (VTLSC) (Venette, 2014). The scoring system used in the LSQ reduces previously unclassifiable (i.e., tied) scores and measures respondents' style intensity as well. Ultimately, the VTLSC assigns a specific value for each learning style on a scale from 1 to 5. An intensity of 1 indicates a weak preference for a particular learning style whereas a 5 indicates a strong preference. Measuring and understanding learning preference intensities are important. Individuals with weak preferences are more likely to adapt to other styles than those with strong preferences. It is likely that the intensity of a particular preference will dictate an individual's ability to use and appreciate a variety of learning styles.

The evolution of understanding learning style preferences and intensities makes it possible to now accurately assess individuals' learning preferences. However, before now, accurately and quantifiably assessing tutoring styles was not possible. Before discussing these assessments, it is important to understand the role that communication plays in tutoring, as well as approaches to training tutors.

Tutoring Styles

Tutoring and Communication

Peer tutoring is a transformational process (Schwartzman & Ellis, 2011). This means that knowledge is created and shared understanding is achieved when a tutor and tutee collaborate. Effective dialogue between both parties is key to collaboration (Person et al., 1995). To facilitate this dialogue, tutors must ask questions frequently, listen empathically, and respond thoughtfully.

First, asking questions is crucial to successful tutoring consultations (Graesser & Person, 1994). Asking specific, individually crafted questions allows a tutor to understand the tutee's needs, challenges, and expectations. Asking a few useful questions produces a better understanding than asking multiple general questions. Once these questions are asked, tutors should listen to responses empathically (Cuny, Wilde, & Stephenson, 2012; Wilde, Cuny, & Vizzier, 2006). In this setting, empathic listening is characterized by a tutor refraining from judging the tutee, and by the tutor putting himself or herself in the position of the tutee. This listening style is similar to the empathic listening associated with therapist-client relationships (Rogers, 1975). Finally, tutors must respond to tutees in a thoughtful way that supports the transformational process (Schwartzman & Ellis, 2011). In other words, tutors should avoid responses that portray the tutor-tutee relationship as a service provider interaction. Instead, tutors should respond in ways that highlight the collaborative nature of the tutor-tutee relationship.

As one may assume, effectively asking questions, listening, and responding requires tutors be well trained before interacting with tutees. These forms of effective communication will enable tutors to better evaluate the learning style preference of tutees. However, achieving effective communication does not always occur naturally. Rather, tutors should be trained to be effective communicators.

Tutor Training

Extensive, effective, and consistent training is vital to producing a successful tutor (Graesser & Person, 1994; Troillett & McIntyre, 2012). In fact, careful training is what separates peer tutoring from other forms of peer collaboration (Harris, 1992). Different tutoring centers approach training in a variety of ways (Troillett & McIntyre, 2012). Reading tutoring literature, discussing the tutoring process, and role-playing are all methods that some tutoring centers employ to train staff members. However, a popular training technique is the use of shadowing or peer observation (Bell & Mladenovic, 2008). This training method includes an inexperienced tutor observing an experienced tutor during an actual consultation.

While peer observations offer many benefits to beginning tutors, potential drawbacks of this training style exist. On one hand, Sparks (1986) found that peer observation was a more effective approach to training than expert coaching or workshops. This finding is well aligned with Social Learning Theory's claim that individuals learn via observation, imitation, and modeling (Bandura, 1977). On the other hand, trainees may not be objective observers (Lomas & Nicholls, 2005). This means that if a trainee observes an ineffective tutoring style, they are likely to incorporate that ineffective behavior into their own approach to tutoring without questioning the trainer's behavior. For example, if a tutor observes a trainer who uses ineffective communication practices, a trainee may also use ineffective communication practices. Likewise, if a trainee observes a trainer who approaches all consultations without adjusting to the tutee, the trainee may also fail to make tutoring adjustments following their training. At this point it should be clear that proper training be conducted to ensure tutors use effective communication and select an appropriate tutoring style. The potential for ineffective training, thus ineffective consultations, necessitates the establishment of training standards that incorporate a variety of approaches to tutoring.

It is unwise to view peer tutoring as a universal process (Topping, 1996). Tutors interact with a variety of tutees working on a variety of topics and assignments. For this reason, an array of approaches and tools should be used during consultations (Roscoe & Chi, 2007). Explanations, examples, idea maps, illustrations, and other methods of sharing information and achieving understanding are useful during tutoring consultations. Which specific tools and methods to use likely depends on the dynamics of each individual tutor-tutee interaction. However, even with extensive training and the use of effective questions, listening skills, and responses, tutors consistently inaccurately interpret tutees' comprehension of consultation content (Graesser & Person, 1994). This inaccurate assessment poses a threat to the effectiveness of consultations. To increase the likelihood of connecting with each tutee and maximizing their learning experience, tutors should be trained to round the learning cycle (Kolb, 1984). While an experimental tutor training model grounded in Kolb's learning cycle exists (Beebe, Mottet, & Roach, 2004), its lessons are frequently used inappropriately by tutors during individual tutor-tutee interactions (Troillett & McIntyre, 2012). However, understanding this experimental training model, reviewed below, is central to understanding a tutor's preferred style.

Experimental Training Model

In 2004, Beebe, Mottet, and Roach created an experimental training model that incorporates Kolb's (1984) learning cycle. While the model has not gained traction in all tutoring centers, the model is frequently used to train tutors (Troillett & McIntyre, 2012). The model includes five steps: *telling, showing, inviting, encouraging,* and *correcting*. First, *telling* involves sharing information with new tutors that will help them be an effective tutor. This step aligns with Kolb's thinking stage of learning. Here, tutors process information, categorize and store new knowledge, and begin to plan to use this knowledge. Second, *showing* involves a trainer demonstrating tutoring behavior for a trainee. This step aligns with Kolb's watching stage as trainees observe trainers act as models. Third, *inviting* sees trainees shift from observers to participants. Here, tutors practice a skill through role-playing, simulations, or discussions. This step aligns with Kolb's doing stage. The fourth and fifth steps, *encouraging* and *correcting*, occur in unison. Here, trainers encourage positive or prototypical behavior and correct negative or deviant behavior. Combined, these final steps align with Kolb's feeling stage as trainees respond to feedback.

Troillett and McIntyre (2012) point out four benefits of using this training model. First, immediate feedback produced during the encouraging and correcting steps provide trainees with a clear understanding of what they are doing well and what needs to improve. Second, by rounding the learning cycle, all staff members are trained, in part, using their preferred learning style. Third, this model provides trainees with an interactive model of the behavior that is expected from them. As opposed to watching a video, observing a trainer allows trainees to ask questions or participate in discussions about the observed behavior. Finally, and most important to this research, learning to use tutoring styles that round the learning cycle during their training increases the ability of tutors to effectively work with tutees with a variety of preferred learning styles. However, effective training does not guarantee effective tutoring. Therefore, it is important to assess tutoring styles used and preferred by actual tutors.

Assessing Tutor Styles

Taken in its entirety, this review of learning styles, tutoring styles, and training approaches framed questions that the following study was designed to address. After we discuss the surveys used in this study, the data is analyzed to compare tutors' preferred learning style to their dominant tutoring style. If our assumption that these styles are similar is correct, we can presume that tutors prefer to teach to their preferred learning styles. The data is also used to measure respondents' intensity for their preferred styles, which will be used to glean the likelihood that tutors will use a variety of approaches with their tutees. Tutors with strong preferences may be unlikely to round the learning cycle, whereas those with weak preferences may be more likely to do so. Regardless of intensity for a preferred style, without the proper training, tutors will not be aware of learning style preferences. In order to educate them about rounding the cycle, tutors should be trained using a version of the Experimental Training Model. For this reason, it is important to address what potential approaches trainers might use to instruct tutors to round the learning cycle. Before any of these questions can be answered, we must understand preferred tutor styles.

Two surveys were used in this study. The latest 15-item version of Sellnow's (2005, 2008) LSQ was used to assess preferred learning styles. To assess preferred tutoring styles the LSQ items were modified to reflect the change in perspective. For example, LSQ items like, "I tend to learn best when I can ..." were altered to read, "When considering the needs of my tutee, I think that I am at my best when I ..." Analysis of this new 15-item survey found that reliability was low ($\alpha = .60$) and validity was questionable as a principle component analysis yielded a multi-factor solution. After a rotational modification, a six-item scale was found to be reliable ($\alpha = .72$), and valid (all items loaded on a single dimension). Then, the VTLSC (Venette, 2014) was used to calculate the preferred learning and teaching styles for each participant, as well as a measure of intensity of preferences for each style.

The tutor style quiz was administered to a sample of 42 college-aged tutors attending a national tutoring conference. Participants were both graduate and undergraduate tutors and were at least 18 years of age. Participants represented diverse backgrounds and came from 12 different colleges and universities across the United States. A proctor approached participants and verbally asked them to participate in this study by completing a paper copy of a brief survey (tutor style quiz). A convenience sampling approach was used and tutors who had gathered in a common area were selected for participation. Participants were told that the survey aimed to better understand the stylistic choices made by tutors and tutees. The proctor distributed surveys, instructed participants to freely ask any survey-related questions, allowed up to 20 minutes for participants to complete the surveys, and then collected them. No participants asked questions and all participants fully completed the survey.

Findings

Matching and Adjacent Styles

The central premise of this chapter is that tutors prefer to teach to their own preferred learning style. Of the 42 tutors who participated, ten (24%) had exactly the same preferred teaching and learning style. Moreover, 18 (43%) respondents' preferred teaching and learning styles were adjacent. Thus, 28 respondents (66%) had matching learning and teaching styles, or their preferred styles were adjacent to one another (Table 7.1). Interestingly, participants whose learning and tutoring styles matched or were adjacent fell into styles that generally indicate a preference for emotional connection over abstract thinking. In fact, twelve of the 15 people (80%) in this group have intense preferences that focus on feeling.

Table 7.1. Distributions of Participants Whose Learning and Teaching Styles Were the Same or Adjacent.

	Participants	Percent of Sample
Diverging (Between Feeling and Observing)	8	7.1
Observing	0	0
Assimilating (Between Observing and Thinking)	1	0
Thinking	0	0
Converging (Between Thinking and Doing)	3	0
Doing	5	4.8
Accommodating (Between Doing and Feeling)	5	4.8
Feeling	6	7.1
Total	28	66.6

Preference Intensity

Not only does the VTSLC (Venette, 2014) calculate the preferred learning and teaching styles for each participant, it also provides a measure of the intensity of preferences for each style. The tool rates intensity on a scale of 1 (weak preference) to 5 (very strong preference). Although more research is needed in this area, the supposition is that individuals with weak preferences are willing to adapt to other styles. Conversely, people with strong preferences are not only unlikely to adapt to a particular educational approach that does not address their educational predilections, but they are more likely to see those approaches as unimportant. For the purpose of this study, for both learning and tutoring styles, participants with an intensity score of one or two were considered fairly adaptable. Scores of three, four, and five were identified as high intensity, indicating a strong desire to approach education from their preferred perspective only.

The intensity results for people whose learning and teaching styles matched or were adjacent reveal that five participants appear to be flexible in both teaching and learning styles. Three had a strong learning style preference, but a weak tutoring preference. Seven participants had intense teaching styles, but more flexible approaches to learning. Finally, thirteen were found to have strong preferences for both. For this last group, eleven had preferences that focused on feeling over abstract conceptualization, consistent with the previous findings.

For participants whose preferred learning and teaching styles were not similar, four individuals had a strong learning style preference, but a weak tutoring style; conversely, six had strong teaching styles, but were weak on learning. Two were strong and two were weak on both. The distribution of these scores highlights a consistent finding: participants with intense preferences tended toward feeling-based styles over thinking-focused ones.

Conclusions

The results are consistent with the notion that tutors teach in a manner that would appeal to their preferred learning styles. For participants whose learning and teaching preferences were the same or similar, the distribution skewed heavily toward feeling. In fact, no "matching" individual was found to have a thinking-oriented preference. The tendency to prefer styles focused on feeling rather than thinking continued when the intensity of the preferences was also considered. What does this mean for tutors and those tasked with training them? Below are a few practical suggestions based on this research.

Matching and/or Adjacent Styles Are Common

The results suggest that it is common for a tutor to teach and learn in similar ways. In other words, tutors are likely to impose their preferred learning style on tutees they encounter in the respective tutoring centers. While future data should examine a larger sample of both tutors and tutees to evaluate preferred teaching and learning styles, tutors will likely encounter tutees who prefer a variety of learning styles. If tutors are unable to use a variety of teaching styles during consultations, they are unlikely to broadly connect with tutees in meaningful ways. This means that tutors will be most effective with tutees who share their preferred learning style, but least effective when the preferred learning style differs. Given the variety of students seeking assistance in tutoring centers, training tutors to be tutee-centered and to round the cycle of learning would improve the quality and effectiveness of consultations.

Tutors Prefer Feeling

Results generally suggest that tutors prefer a feeling-based teaching and learning style. This means that talking about ideas and open discussion are central to tutors' styles. While this may explain why individuals choose to become tutors, it does not mean that tutors who prefer feeling-based styles will be able to work effectively with tutees who prefer different styles. We value tutors who are able and willing to talk openly with a variety of students; however, even with the best of intentions and communication skills, tutors risk ineffective connections with tutees who are dissimilar. For this reason, tutors should be trained for style diversity.

Training for Style Diversity

Since we know that tutees will have a variety of preferred learning styles and results suggest that tutors are likely to have the same or adjacent teaching and learning styles, it is important to train tutors to round the learning cycle, or use a variety of tutoring strategies aimed at making meaningful connections with tutees. Designing or retrofitting training programs that incorporate relevant learning outcomes will provide the necessary foundation on which to direct the center's necessary training program (Keeling, 2006)

On-campus student employment opportunities such as those found in tutoring centers provide a meaningful and educationally rich out-of-class experience for students (Astin, 1993; Padgett & Grady, 2009). To capitalize on this opportunity, we recommend anchoring the employment experience with well crafted learning outcomes. One possible learning outcome could be, "After tutors go through the training program, they will be able to adequately describe each of the Kolb-inspired learning styles." A more advanced learning outcome could be, "After tutors go through the training program they will be able to effectively incorporate activities within a session that accesses multiple learning style preferences." The success of these learning objectives is best measured using a post-session assessment. An item on the assessment survey might read, "I feel my tutor explained the material to me in a manner consistent with my preferred learning style," or, "I feel my tutor used a variety of techniques to answer my questions."

Establishing learning objectives to meet these training goals will provide the necessary, intentional learning environment within work settings such as tutoring centers (Perozzi, Kappes, & Santucci, 2009). A more complete investigation and explanation of out-of-classroom learning and learning outcomes is beyond the scope of this chapter, however. Instead, we recommend referencing Richard Keeling's (2006) *Learning Reconsidered 2* for a clear and in-depth explanation of learning outcomes, their theoretical foundation, as well as suggestions for practical application in your tutoring center.

Once the learning objectives and outcomes are set, tutor training programs can incorporate the Experimental Training Model (ETM) (Beebe, Mottet, & Roach, 2004) to help tutors make meaningful connections with their tutees. As previously stated, this model includes five steps: *telling, showing, inviting, encouraging,* and *correcting.* Taken as a whole, the use of this model will allow tutors to diversify their teaching styles that should result in better connections with a diverse group of tutees. The use of this training model will benefit tutors in that it should result in 1) the ability to provide immediate feedback that provides trainees with a clear understanding of what they are doing well and what needs to improve, 2) training approaches that provide tutors with the opportunity to use their preferred learning styles, 3) an interactive model of the behaviors from which tutees will most likely benefit and, 4) the ability for tutors to understand teaching styles that round the learning cycle while increasing the ability of tutors to effectively work with tutees with a variety of preferred learning styles.

While the ETM is an excellent resource for center administrators, it may not be practical or possible for all trainers to readily develop and institute a novel training program for their tutors. A simplified approach to a training program that still incorporates the process set forth by Beebe, Mottet, and Roach (2004) could be to simply alter current training practices. For example, many training processes already focus on open communication between tutors and tutees, the use of critical thinking questions, and the use of activities during consultations. A more intentional application of the ETM could incorporate the following suggestions. First, trainers should consider covering the essential elements of effective communication during training sessions. For example, a tutor's ability to read, understand, and respond to a tutee's nonverbal signals of understanding or confusion could increase the likelihood of using an effective or ineffective teaching style. Second, effectively using critical thinking questions can increase effective tutoring sessions. While many tutees may use the advice provided by tutors, they may not understand why the advice was given. Asking critical thinking questions can better ensure that tutees understand why they are making certain choices about their assignments beyond the fact that they were told to make the choices. This understanding should result in a longer-term ability of the tutee to make better choices and create more effective academic work. Finally, the use of brief activities during consultations will allow tutees to use trial and error to advance their understanding of content. Seeing what works and what does not should allow tutees to better understand and select their future approaches to problem solving and completing assignments. These three additions to training will effectively allow tutors to round the learning cycle and make better connections with a variety of tutees.

This chapter has highlighted the fact that tutors frequently use their own preferred style of learning when tutoring peers. This can result in the problematic potential of creating a disconnect between tutors who have one learning style and tutees who have a different learning style. Research presented here suggests that it is, in fact, likely that tutors will use their own preferred learning styles during consultations. The issue with this approach to tutoring is that tutees are diverse and have a variety of learning styles that are unlikely to align with the learning style held by the tutor. For this reason, we advise that tutors be trained to round the learning cycle and appeal to a variety of learning styles. While training using the Experimental Training Model is ideal for facilitating the rounding of the learning cycle, it is not always practical to implement a novel training system in tutoring centers. For this reason, some simple yet effective adjustments to tutor training have been presented.

Regardless of the specific training used to increase the ability of tutors to round the learning cycle used in tutor training, it is crucial that this issue and an effective solution is shared with tutors. When tutors do not appeal to the preferred learning style of tutees, the probability of establishing a meaningful connection is lowered. Therefore it is critical that tutors are trained to appeal to preferred learning styles held by their diverse clientele. It is true that this training may be more intense than other, simpler, training styles. However, the benefits outweigh the costs. For this reason, we advise tutoring center administrators and trainers to incorporate learning style literature and knowledge into their training programs.

References

Astin, A. W. (1993). *What matters in college? Four critical years revisited.* San Francisco: Jossey-Bass.

Bandura, A. (1977). *Social learning theory.* New York, NY: General Learning Press.

Beebe, S. A., Mottet, T. P., & Roach, K. D. (2004). *Training and development: Enhancing communication and leadership skills.* Boston, MA: Anker Publishing Company, Inc.

Bell, A., & Mladenovic, R. (2008). The benefits of peer observation of teaching for tutor development. *Higher Education, 55*(6), 735–752.

Cassidy, S. (2004). Learning styles: An overview of theories, models, and measures. *Educational Psychology, 24*(4), 419–444.

Chi, M. T. H., Siler, S. A., & Jeong, H. (2004). Can tutors monitor students' understanding accurately? *Cognition and Instruction, 22*(3), 363–387.

Coffield, F., Moseley, D., Hall, E., & Ecclestone, K. (2004). *Learning styles and pedagogy in post-16 learning: A systematic and critical review.* London: Learning and Skills Development Agency.

Cuny, K. M., Wilde, S. M., & Stephenson, A. V. (2012). Using empathetic listening to build client relationships at the center. In E. L. Yook & W. Atkins-Sayre (Eds.), *Communication centers and oral communication programs in higher education: Advantages, challenges, and new directions* (pp. 249–256). Lanham, MD: Lexington Books.

De Ciantis, S. M., & Kirton, M. J. (1996). A psychometric reexamination of Kolb's experiential learning cycle construct: A separation of level, style and process. *Educational and Psychological Measurement, 56,* 809–820.

Graesser, A. C., & Person, N. K. (1994). Question asking during tutoring. *American Educational Research Journal, 31*(1), 104–137.

Harris, M. (1992). Collaboration is not collaboration is not collaboration: Writing center tutorials vs. peer-response groups. *College Composition and Communication, 43*(3), 369–383.

Keeling, R. P. (2006). *Learning reconsidered 2: A practical guide to implementing a campus-wide focus on the student experience.* Washington D.C.: ACPA.

Kolb, D. A. (1976). *The learning style inventory: Technical manual.* Boston, MA: McBer.

Kolb, D. A. (1984). *Experiential learning: Experience as the source of learning and development.* Englewood Cliffs, NJ: Prentice-Hall, Inc.

Kolb, A. Y., & Kolb, D. A. (2005). The Kolb Learning Style Inventory—version 3.1 2005 Technical specifications. Haygroup: Experience Based Learning Systems, Inc.

Lomas, L., & Nicholls, G. (2005). Enhancing teaching quality through peer review of teaching. *Quality in Higher Education, 11*(2), 137–149.

Padgett, R. D., & Grady, D. L. (2009). Student development and personal growth in employment. In B. Perozzi (Ed.), *Enhancing student learning through college employment* (pp. 31–43). Bloomington, ID: Association of College Unions International.

Perozzi, B., Kappes, J., & Santucci, D. (2009). Learning outcomes in student employment programs. In B. Perozzi (Ed.), *Enhancing student learning through college employment* (pp. 31–43). Bloomington, ID: Association of College Unions International.

Person, N. L., Kreuz, R. J., Zwaan, R. A., & Graesser, A. C. (1995). Pragmatics and pedagogy: Conversational rules and politeness strategies may inhibit effective tutoring. *Cognition and Instruction, 13*(2), 161–188.

Rogers, C. (1975). Empathic: An unappreciated way of being. *The Counseling Psychologist, 2,* 2–10.

Roscoe, R. D., & Chi, M. T. H. (2007). Understanding tutor learning: Knowledge-building and knowledge-telling in peer tutors' explanations and questions. *Review of Educational Research, 77*(4), 534–574.

Schwartzman, R., & Ellis, E. D. (2011). Catering to customers or cultivating communicators? Divergent educational roles of communication centers. *International Journal of Humanities and Social Science, 1*(17), 58–66.

Sellnow, D. D. (2005). *Confident public speaking* (2nd ed.). Belmont, CA: Thomson and Wadsworth.

Sellnow, D. D. (2008, April). *The 10 best practices of risk and crisis communication: Effects of information needs on message variables.* Paper presented at the Central States Communication Association Annual Convention, Madison, WI.

Sparks, G. M. (1986). The effectiveness of alternative training activities in changing teaching practices. *American Educational Research Journal, 23*(2), 217–225.

Sternberg, R. J., & Grigorenko, E. L. (2001). A capsule history of theory and research on styles. In R. Sternberg & L. Zhang (Eds.), *Perspectives on thinking, learning, and cognitive styles* (pp. 1–21). Mahwah, NJ: Lawrence Erlbaum Associates.

Topping, K. J. (1996). The effectiveness of peer tutoring in further and higher education: A typology and review of the literature. *Higher Education, 32*(3), 321–346.

Troillett, R., & McIntyre, K. A. (2012). Best practices in communication center training and training assessment. In E. L. Yook & W. Atkins-Sayre (Eds.), *Communication centers and oral communication programs in higher education: Advantages, challenges, and new directions* (pp. 257–272). Lanham, MD: Lexington Books.

Venette, S. J. (2014). Venette teaching and learning style calculator (Version 1.0) [Python-based syntax]. Available from steven.venette@usm.edu

Wilde, S. M., Cuny, K. M., & Vizzier, A. L. (2006). Peer-to-peer tutoring: A model for utilizing empathic listening to build client relationships in the communication center. *International Journal of Listening, 20,* 70–75.

· 8 ·

CONNECTING WITH THE FIRST YEAR STUDENT

William J. Seiler

One of the most serious challenges facing universities and colleges today is the dropout rate of students after the first year. While enrollments have been relatively stable, with approximately 20.4 million new students enrolling in colleges and universities each year (U.S. Department of Education, National Center for Education Statistics, 2011), the transition for many high school students to higher education is often a very stressful time that can take both a physical and psychological toll (Credé & Niehorster, 2012) on the students. According to Boujut and Bruchon-Schweitzer (2009), many of these students suffer from academic stress, depression, feelings of loneliness, and an inability to establish ongoing relationships with their peers—all of which can lead to higher dropout rates. As a result, it is estimated that approximately 20 to 33 percent of all entering first year students drop out either during or after their first year (U.S. News & World Report, 2014). The reasons for students dropping out vary, but include financial, academic, and health issues, poor social fit, family problems, loneliness, and distance from home.

According to Schlossberg (1981), adaptation and transition to college is a very complex process with many different factors; there is no simplistic formula to explain why one student remains in college while others do not. The transition to college for many first year students brings uncertainty and stress because they are moving from the known to the unknown. These students are experiencing unfamiliar and differing social and intellectual situations, which requires them to establish new relationships as well as learn the norms and expectations of their new environment (Christie & Dinham, 1991; Tinto, 1993; Wang, 2012, 2014).

Among the obstacles facing first year students is the significant challenge of making the academic adjustments that are necessary for success. Many of them struggle academically due to their low attendance and lack of communication with their professors during the transition (Nazione et al., 2011). These struggles and behaviors have led to low grades and higher dropout rates among first year students, according to Chen (2012).

One solution to helping reduce the dropout rate and improve academic performance of first year students is the use of peer tutors.[1] The purpose of this chapter is to provide peer tutors, and those who supervise peer tutors, with an understanding of the necessary principles and communication strategies needed to communicate effectively with first year students, as well as an explanation of the challenges that first year students confront in the classroom. The rationale is that understanding their challenges will help the peer tutors to empathize with them, which has been found to be an important factor in the tutoring process. To do so, this chapter covers information needed to understand the first year student and the most effective means of providing tutoring services for those students.

Understanding First Year Students

Peer tutors, in order to connect with first year students, need to understand that college is a gargantuan step for many first year students. First year students leave behind both what they know and the security of family for what they know little or nothing about (Benjamin, Earnest, Gruenewald, & Authur, 2007). Many of these students, especially those arriving at college directly after high school, encounter unfamiliar and often more demanding social and intellectual situations than what they are accustomed to, or what they had previously experienced. This change often involves a new community, a separation from established relationships, as well as learning the norms and behavioral expectations of their new environment (Christie & Dinham, 1991; Tinto, 1993).

Adjustment to college is the ability to focus "explicitly on the degree to which students are able to quickly and effectively adapt to the various challenges encountered in the new college environment" (Credé & Niehorster, 2012, p. 134). Baker and Siryk (1984) identified four different categories that first year students must adjust to in order to adapt to college life and be successful: academic, social, personal-emotional, and institutional adjustment. One of the toughest challenges facing first year students is academic adjustment, with many of them having difficulty with studying, attending classes, and especially with communicating with their professors (Nazione et al., 2011). In a study of perceptions of instructors, Wyatt, Saunders, and Zelmer (2005) found that only 31.5% of them felt that first year students were adequately prepared for university classes. It was also found that there was a correlation between academic performance during the first year of college and persistence (Mallette & Cabrera, 1991). Thus, academic adjustment by first year students is critical to staying in school.

Social adjustment is the extent to which first year students take part in social and campus activities. It is their ability to integrate themselves into the social environment and structures of the college (i.e., getting to know new people, creating new friendships, and involvement with new social settings) that helps them adjust (Baker & Siryk, 1984; Credé & Niehorster, 2012). Personal-emotional adjustment is the extent to which a first year student is able to adjust their physical and psychological reactions while making the transition into college life (i.e., loneliness, depression, drug use, or weight gain). Finally, institutional attachment, at times referred to as attachment (Berjerano, 2014), means how much "students identify with and have become emotionally attached to the university community" according to Credé and Niehorster (2012, p. 135). These four categories describe what is necessary for first year students to adjust to the environment in order to succeed.

Nazione et al. (2011) interviewed students who were in their second to fourth year, asking them what other challenges, besides academic, that they have faced in their first year. They discovered that the students had, in addition to the academic challenges, relationship challenges, work challenges (i.e., getting a job), other challenges related to work duties, changing majors in order to obtain a desired career, as well as financial challenges. It is clear that first year students confront a variety of challenges affecting their overall adjustment to college life.

As mentioned earlier, peer tutoring can be the means by which a connection can be created with first year students that leads to relationships with other students and instructors, leading to successful outcomes, including retention and degree completion. It is peer tutors who can make the connection with first year students to help them understand and deal with the various challenges they face in making the transition to college.

Peer Tutors and First Year Students with Diverse Backgrounds and Abilities

There is little doubt that today's students are facing more challenges than they have in the past and many educators are predicting that there will be even more challenges for first year students in the coming years (Cartledge & Kourea, 2008). With more at-risk, first generation, international, low income students, and students with disabilities entering colleges and universities than ever before, there are greater challenges for educators to increase these students' chances of success (Cartledge & Kourea, 2008). These students confront a number of obstacles to graduating from college. There is, however, sufficient evidence that peer tutoring can help to improve and enhance their chances of success (Carledge & Kourea, 2008).

First year students and students who may have special needs, such as students with English as a second language, students who are at risk, or students with disabilities, might especially benefit from peer tutoring. The key to the success of students with diverse backgrounds and abilities, as with all students, appears to be the ability to engage fully in the learning process. According to Braxton, Milem, and Sullivan (2000), if classroom activities can be structured to involve students with diverse needs in the learning process with their peers, this can help to improve student engagement and success. Success is attributed to the careful alignment of student learning needs and support via peer tutors. The closer the alignment, the better students with specific challenges will be able to translate the support of peer tutors into successful outcomes. Developing educational learning communities which link basic skills to course content has been shown to be particularly effective in meeting students' academic challenges (Engstrom & Tinto, 2008). For example, setting up learning communities in which experienced peer tutors have learned the basic skills to tutor students with similar backgrounds (such as ethnicity or cultural connections) can be helpful.

International students have a qualitatively different challenge in that they may be engaged learners, but by definition they may lack the cultural or language skills to succeed. Consequently, they may also benefit from peer tutoring. International students often require additional assistance understanding the culture and language, thus many universities pair international students with domestic students for academic and transitional assistance into their new and very different cultural environment. After interviewing 38 tutors, international tutees, and administrators, Lassegard (2008) found that while tutees tended to focus on interpersonal relationships, peer tutors were more concerned about how they were doing as a tutor. Thus, it is important for the peer tutor to recognize that their need to see themselves as successful should not overshadow the needs of those who they tutor, who may have relationship needs in acclimating to a foreign environment.

Thayer (2000) indicates that institutions must not forget that their retention strategies often only take into account the general campus populations of first year students, without accounting for those with special circumstances such as first-generation students, students with disabilities, and low-income students. The actions taken to improve retention by the institution, instructors, and peer-tutors should be broadened to include specific attention for students with special needs to increase their engagement in academe, thus increasing overall retention.

Peer Tutoring as an Effective Method of Instruction

Given this understanding of the first year student, it becomes clear that student success resources such as peer tutoring are critical. The transition to college life and students' future success is shaped by the amount and type of interactions that occur during the first year (Bejerano, 2014). This is especially important for those who might have difficulty establishing relationships and connecting to their instructors and peers. Thus, peer tutoring may be the means by which a connection can be made to first year students, leading to relationships with other students and instructors, leading to successful outcomes regarding retention and degree completion.

Peer tutoring is defined as a method by which one student tutors another student or students, who are peers. Anecdotal information suggests that students who have received peer tutoring are more comfortable receiving instruction and advice from a fellow student than from a professor or instructor, according to Cascio (2014). Today, peer tutoring has been widely used in a variety of instructional settings and situations. It is a method that offers many more potential advantages than disadvantages. The advantages occur for both peer tutors and their assigned partners.

Tutoring is one of purest forms of one-on-one contact with students. For many years, tutoring was only available to the elite and very wealthy in our society and was the main method of instruction. Because tutoring is a personable form of instruction, and it can be geared to meet the needs or specific limitations of individual students, its use should become a more widely accepted method of instruction.

A seminal meta-analysis of 52 different studies by Cohen, Kulik, and Kulik (1982) found that tutoring helped students perform better on examinations, compared to those who were not tutored. In addition, tutored students tend to express more positive attitudes toward learning, and there are even reported positive effects on those peers who did the tutoring (Cohen et al., 1982). It was also found that peer tutors learned more about the subject they were tutoring than when they themselves took the course (Cohen et al., 1982).

Some of the reported social benefits of peer tutoring suggest improved interpersonal functioning, higher self-esteem and self-efficacy, and a better attitude toward learning (Scruggs, Mastropieri, & Berkeley, 2014). While these outcomes have not been shown to be a consistent finding from research, these are common anecdotal findings by teachers who have implemented peer tutoring practices as part of their instructional approach. It has also been shown that, when peer tutoring has been effectively implemented, it can benefit not only students with diverse learning needs (such as students with various learning disabilities) but also students whose second language is English (Scruggs et al., 2014).

Meta-analysis conducted by Cohen et al. (1982) confirms what had been suspected all along about tutoring: that overall it benefits both the tutors and tutee on the cognitive level as well as on the affective level. There are disadvantages of course; but there are few disadvantages, if any, in terms of learning. The disadvantages stem around two issues: 1) tutoring could lead to more favorable treatment of some students over others and 2) the lack of training of tutors could lead to more harm than good (Cohen et al., 1982). Training and close monitoring by their supervisors may be required to ensure that peer tutors are treating all tutees fairly, and that all responsibilities and activities are carried out effectively.

Peer Tutoring: Advantages for Working with the First Year Student

Given the difficulty of peer tutoring and especially working with first year students, why would undergraduates choose to undertake this work? Fortunately, academic gains are quite clear and have been consistently found in peer tutoring programs for both peer tutors *and* tutees. For example, the social benefits of peer tutoring, which includes improved self-esteem and self-efficacy, better and more positive attitudes toward learning, and improved relationships between tutees and their instructors as the outcome of peer tutor intervention and assistance with first year students are commonly reported anecdotally by instructors (Ayaz, 2014; Kalkowski, 1995; Seiler, 2014). Research related to these general outcomes, however, has been rather inconsistent, partially because much of the research must be tempered somewhat because very few of the studies are done comparing peer tutors and instructor-led instructional approaches. According to Greenwood, Terry, Delquadri, Elliott, and Arreaga-Mayer (1995) the difficulty is clearly determining the specific contributions of the peer tutor and teacher in most of the empirical research that has been done. While students report that their attitude toward the subject matter in which they are being tutored and their attitude toward the peer tutor is more positive, instructors who have implemented a peer tutoring program find that their relationships with students, and especially first year students, has been generally positive (Greenwood et al., 1995).

Kalkowski (1995) found that improvements in academics, social behavior, peer relations, self-esteem, and attendance are benefits of peer tutoring. Kalkowski also found that tutees were less intimidated by peer tutors than by instructors. The study concluded that tutees felt less vulnerable in their questioning and exploring when working with peer tutors, which allowed for more higher-order thinking, and improved cognitive outcomes. Much of the claimed success of peer tutoring is made possible because higher amounts of direct individual attention are paid to first year students by peer tutors than traditional classroom instruction can provide.

According to Sandi Ayaz (2014), Executive Director of the National Tutoring Association, there is "one distinct outcome" (p. 1) from the research regarding peer tutoring: it is inexpensive and provides many benefits, not only to the students, but to tutors as well. Seiler (2014) interviewed 15 peer tutors and found the following benefits of using undergraduate peer tutors:

1. Peer tutors learn course materials more thoroughly. Peer tutors are exposed to the course's content multiple times and thus their own learning is reinforced. This learning occurs especially when the peer tutor explains concepts to their assigned student or students. While there is no empirical research supporting this conclusion, there is sufficient testimony from peer tutors stating that they believe they have learned and retained more than when they took the course.

2. The experience peer tutors gain from working with others is invaluable. Peer tutors report that the most rewarding aspect of their working with their students is the experience of being a teacher. This outcome is especially beneficial for those peer tutors who are planning to become teachers or professors.

3. Peer tutors find the experience to be satisfying. Peer tutors find that working with students resulted in satisfaction with learning not only about themselves, but also with what they learned about their assigned students. This is supported by the fact that approximately 30 percent of peer tutors request to be peer tutors a second time, and some will even request a third time.

Wilson (2012) adds to the list of benefits to peer tutors, including improving their ability to use constructive criticism, improving listening, developing flexibility, and improving self-confidence. These benefits gained by peer tutors, along with the benefits gained by the tutees, cannot and should not be ignored. The evidence, whether empirical or anecdotal, is certainly supportive of peer tutoring, especially with first year students. However, there still remains much to learn about how effective peer tutors are in working with first year students.

Recruiting and Selecting Peer-Tutors for First Year Students

The recruitment of interpersonally competent and academically sound tutors who can connect with first year students is critical to the success of any peer tutoring program. Thus, the careful selection of peer tutors is imperative because just one unmotivated or incompetent student tutor can require extra time and energy by the instructor to "undo" the harm, and even that one instance can ultimately hurt the overall credibility of any peer tutoring program. It is important that very specific guidelines be used in the selection process in order to ensure that students who are selected meet the competencies and responsibilities of being a peer tutor.

The goal here is connecting with first year students and ensuring, or at least attempting to ensure, their success as they transition to college life. A Carnegie Mellon (2002) study indicates that serving as teaching assistant (peer tutor) can be a source of personal pride and satisfaction to those chosen, and that unique responsibilities for peer tutors in helping first year students include not only helping them to make the adjustment to college life, but also assisting them in the learning process. The bottom line, according to the Carnegie Mellon report, is the quality of peer tutors' work and its ultimate impact and effect on the students with whom they work.

Peer tutoring in this chapter is about working with and connecting to first year students.

The recruiting of peer tutors requires that those selected are able to connect with students and to provide first year students with the necessary information to succeed. There is also a considerable body of research examining gender and race matching in peer tutoring relationships. The findings, however, according to Terrion and Leonard (2007)[2], are conflicting. The authors state that matching of gender and race depends on "contextual factors, such as the culture of the university, the structure of the tutoring program, and so on" (p. 153).

Thus, when selecting peer tutors, the selection process should take into consideration students who have had similar experiences or face similar challenges (i.e., class, race, gender, etc.). The selection and similarity of experience when matching peer tutors to the first year students can be important in meeting potential common social and academic issues they will face in their first year (Klohnen & Shanhong, 2003).

Communication skills are an important necessary prerequisite for selecting peer tutors. Mee-Lee & Bush (2003) found that both tutor and tutees ranked communicating well as one of the top ten desirable characteristics of peer tutors. It was ranked third only to "understanding and sympathetic" and "accessible." A peer tutor applicant should display effective communication skills, which includes listening, nonverbal behaviors, and the ability to empathize with others (Tindall & Black, 2009). In addition, peer tutors must be honest, constructive, supportive, and have the ability to express themselves in an open and clear fashion.

Other criteria for selecting peer tutors include having such characteristics as dependability, organizational skills, interest in working one-on-one, a sense of humor, patience, an ability to make others comfortable, and an ability to communicate on a personal level. According to Schmidt and Moust (1995) other important characteristics are the personal qualities of the peer tutor. One is the ability to communicate with their assigned students in an informal way, coupled with an empathic attitude that enables the tutor to encourage student learning by creating an open atmosphere in which ideas can be exchanged and facilitated. The other stresses the tutor's subject-matter knowledge as a determinant of learning. The data presented, according to Schmidt and Moust, suggest that what is needed is much of both.

Another criterion that requires close attention is the peer tutor's motives for tutoring, as it has the possibility of leading to unwanted tutoring results. Allen's (2003) research regarding the motivations for becoming a peer tutor found that tutors who are motivated for their own self-enhancement are more likely to provide support to students. In an earlier study, Allen, Poteet, and Russel (2000) found that peer tutors who had indicated a need for being recognized as being effective as a peer tutor were more likely to select tutees who may not have the best potential or abilities, but could benefit from peer tutors' support. Self-enhancement may be a strong motivation to be a peer tutor, but according to Awaya, McEwan, Heyler, Linsky, Lumd and Wakukawac (2003), too much motivation for self-enhancement or to assert authority and power often leads to diametrically opposite results: either being an effective or poor peer tutor. This is especially likely among peer tutors who set unreasonable expectations for their tutoring outcomes, which may not be a desired outcome for first year students.

There are two other criteria that Terrion and Leonard (2007) describe in their review that are necessary for peer tutors to possess in order to make an effective connection with first year tutees. The first is "enthusiasm" or "passion." Mee-Lee and Bush (2003) also found that enthusiasm was the most important peer tutor characteristic as perceived by tutees. Tutees, when ranking the characteristics they want in a peer tutor, ranked peer tutor enthusiasm higher than communication skills. However, it is interesting to note that peer tutors ranked enthusiasm fourth of the ten characteristics, while tutees ranked it number one. It is quite obvious that, from the tutees' perspective, peer tutor enthusiasm is what creates a strong relationship between peer tutors and tutees.

The second criterion is "empathy," according to Terrion and Leonard (2007), who found that being an empathic peer tutor was highlighted in 24% of the articles they reviewed. Empathy is often defined as being able to put yourself into another person's situation or shoes, i.e., "the intellectual identification with or vicarious experiencing of the feelings, thoughts, or attitudes of another—in other words, when we have the capacity to recognize and, to some extent, share feelings (e.g., happiness or sadness) that are experienced by another" (Seiler, Beall, & Mazer, 2014, pp. 149–150). In working with first year students, peer tutors who have had similar experiences, or a similar background to those they are tutoring, can better empathize and connect to their assigned students.

Peer Tutors and Communication

After selecting the right peer tutors, it is then important to focus on developing the right communication strategies. Effective communication by peer tutors is essential to form and develop relationships with first year students. There have been several approaches that have dominated instructional communication scholarship related to teacher-student communication and teacher-student relationships. Among them, two have emerged that seem to directly relate to peer-tutor communication and peer-tutor relationship development with first year students: rhetorical and relational. The rhetorical approach to teaching, according to McCroskey and McCroskey (2006), view "teachers' behaviors as causal influences of student learning," while relational researchers examine "the shared development of teacher-student relationships as causal influences of student learning" (p. 37). Most communication scholars center their research on the traditional teacher/student relationship while examining the relational and learning outcomes associated with this traditional relationship. Frymier and Houser (2000) contend that most traditional teacher-student relationships directly relate to other interpersonal relationships that occur in a variety of contexts. In this way, the relationship between peer tutors and peer tutees in their first year require similar developmental steps that practically every relationship requires, i.e., the initial meeting, exchanging information, and adjusting and developing expectations. Thus, understanding the development of interpersonal relationships, and the role of communication in this process, is important for peer tutor training.

Peer tutors, to connect with first year students and to help the first year student connect with their instructors, must understand the importance of communication that takes place both outside as well as inside the classroom. In their research, Dobransky and Frymier (2004) discovered that those who engaged in outside of the classroom communication with their instructors established better relationships with their instructors. Students who engaged in outside of classroom communication also had higher levels of intimacy, shared control, and trusted their instructors more when compared to those students who did not engage in outside classroom communication. It was determined that intimacy, control, and trust were related to affective learning, which is more likely to help first year students make the transition to college life a positive experience.

To understand the communication behaviors that contribute to interpersonal relationships inside and outside of the classroom, it is also important to understand specific student communication behaviors. Martin, Myers, and Mottet (1999) identify five underlying motives to explain why students communicate with their instructors: relational, functional, excuse, participation, and sycophancy. Those who use relational communication are trying to develop a personal relationship with their teachers. Students who use functional communication want to learn more about a course and its content. Students using participatory communication want to earn participation points. This is especially true if the instructor requires participation or assigns a grade based on participation. Excuse communication is when a student tries to rationalize being late or missing an assignment. Finally, students who use sycophant communication do so to gain favor, or to make a favorable impression on their instructors. Peer tutors can assist their assigned first year students by understanding how in-class instructor/student relationship communication can be interpreted or used in the classroom. Thus, peer tutors should become aware of the motives so they can help those they tutor create a relationship with their instructors that is beneficial and positive for both the tutee and the instructor.

Peer Tutor and Social Support for First Year Students

Finally, peer tutors also need to know how to provide social support for students. Burleson, Albrecht, Goldsmith, and Sarason (1994) state that "the presence of caring relationships and the experience of social support indisputably contributes to the quality of a person's life" (p. xi). This is probably the most challenging for peer tutors to grasp and to accomplish, while being especially important for tutoring first year students. Historically, social support researchers have taken three different approaches: sociological, psychological, and communicative approaches. Much of early research concentrated on the sociological approach which found that social ties led to better health (Burleson et al., 1994). The psychological approach took into consideration the quality and quantity as well as the structure of social networks. The research emphasized perceptions of support availability and satisfaction, which influenced perceived support and well-being. The communication approach, according to Burleson et al. (1994), centers on how individuals build relationships and seek and obtain social support via communication and interaction. Using this approach, social support researchers, according to Wang (2012), focus more on supportive messages, interactions, and relationships. All of these are important for peer tutors to connect to first year students.

While Wang's (2012) research concentrated on first-generation students' overall transition into college life and persistence to graduate, her findings are helpful and excellent advice for peer tutors in their efforts to connect to first year students: (1) first year students are unique in their backgrounds and no one approach works for all; (2) first year students need help in making the connection of what they learn in the classroom to what they experience outside of the classroom; (3) first year students should not be judged or stereotyped: they may just need help seeing their potential for success; and (4) first year students need resources and guidance to help them through the challenges they face as they progress through their first year. Also, peer tutors must be committed to their own personal improvement as tutors as they work with first year students.

Conclusion

Peer tutoring work with first year students requires dedication, commitment, and motivation for the relationship to succeed. Tutoring requires making a connection and creating a relationship that is professional, ethical, genuine, and caring for it to be effective. Making the transition from high school to college is quite difficult for many first year students. Given the significant dropout rates at many college and universities, employing peer tutors who understand and who may have experienced some of the same adjustment issues can make the transition easier, thereby increasing retention. Additionally, peer tutors who are effectively trained to work with first year students with diverse backgrounds including international students, students at risk, and students with disabilities are needed to ensure that those students feel they can succeed.

References

Allen, T. D. (2003). Mentoring others: A dispositional and motivational approach. *Journal of Vocational Behavior, 62,* 134–154.

Allen, T. D., Poteet, M. L., & Russel, J. E. (2000). Protégé selection by mentors: What makes the difference? *Journal of Organizational Behavior, 21,* 271–282.

Awaya, A., McEwan, H., Heyler, D., Linsky, S., Lumd, D., & Wakukawac, P. (2003). Mentoring as a journey. *Teaching and Teacher Education, 19,* 45–56.

Ayaz, S. (2014). *Importance of training peer tutors.* Retrieved from http://www.peertutoring resource.org/wp-content/uploads/2014/05/The-Need-to-Train-Peer-Tutors.pdf

Baker, R.W., & Siryk, B. (1984). Measuring adjustment to college. *Journal of Counseling Psychology, 31,* 179–189.

Benjamin, M., Earnest, K., Gruenewald, D., & Arthur, G. (2007). The first weeks of the first year. In E. L. Moore (Ed.), *Student affairs staff as teachers.* San Francisco, CA: Jossey-Bass.

Bejerano, A. R. (2014). *An examination of the role of social support, coping strategies, and individual characteristics in students' adaptation to college* (Unpublished doctoral dissertation). University of Nebraska-Lincoln, Lincoln, NE.

Boujut, E., & Bruchon-Schweitzer, M. (2009). A construction and validation of freshman stress questionnaire: An exploratory study. *Psychological Reports, 104,* 680–692.

Braxton, J. M., Milem, J. F., & Sullivan, A. S. (2000). The influence of active learning on the college student departure process: Towards revision of Tinto's theory. *Journal of Higher Education, 71,* 569–590.

Burleson, B. R., Albrecht, T. L., Goldsmith, D. J., & Sarason, I. G. (1994). Introduction: The communication of social support. In B. R. Burleson, T. L. Albrecht, & I. G. Sarason (Eds.), *Communication of social support* (pp. xi–xxx). Thousand Oaks, CA: SAGE.

Carnegie Mellon. (2002). *Obligations and expectations for undergraduate teaching assistants.* Pittsburg, PA: Eberly Center for Teaching Excellence.

Cartledge, G., & Kourea, L. (2008). Culturally responsive classrooms for culturally diverse students with and at risk for disabilities. *Exceptional Children, 74*(3), 351–371.

Cascio, C. (2014). What are some advantages & disadvantages of peer tutoring? *Demand Media Education Index* © Hearst Seattle Media, LLC.

Chen, R. (2012). Institutional characteristics and college student dropout risks: A multilevel event history analysis. *Research in Higher Education, 53*(5), 487–505.

Christie, N. G., & Dinham, S. M. (1991). Institutional and external influences on social integration in the freshman year. *Journal of Higher Education, 62*(4), 412–436.

Cohen, P. A., Kulik, J. A., & Kulik, C-L. C. (1982). Educational outcomes of peer tutoring: A meta-analysis of findings. *American Educational Research Journal, 19*(2), 237–248.

Credé, M., & Niehorster, S. (2012). Adjustment to college as measured by the student adaptation to college questionnaire: A quantitative review of its structure and relationships with correlates and consequences. *Educational Psychology Review, 24,* 133–165.

Dobransky, N., & Frymier, A. (2004). Developing teacher-student relationships through out of class communication. *Communication Quarterly, 52,* 211–223.

Engstrom, C. M., & Tinto, V. (2008) Learning better together: The impact of learning communities on the persistence of low-income students. *Opportunity Matters, 1*(1), 5–21.

Frymier, A. B., & Houser, M. L. (2000). The teacher-student relationship as an interpersonal relationship. *Communication Education, 49,* 207–219.

Greenwood, C. R., Terry, B., Delquadri, J. C., Elliott, M., & Arreaga-Mayer, C. (1995). *Class-Wide peer tutoring (CWPT): Effective teaching and research review.* Kansas City, KS: Juniper Gardens Children's Project.

Kalkowski, P. (1995). Peer and cross-age tutoring. *School Improvement Research Series, 18,* 1–27.

Klohnen, E., & Shanhong, L. (2003). Interpersonal attraction and personality: What is attractive-self similarity, ideal similarity, complementary, or attachment security? *Journal of Personality and Social Psychology, 85,* 709–722.

Lassegard, J. P. (2008). The effects of peer tutoring between domestic and international students: The tutor system at Japanese universities. *Higher Education Research & Development, 27*(4), 357–369.

Mallette, B. I., & Cabrera, A. F. (1991). Determinants of withdrawal behavior: An exploratory study. *Research in Higher Education, 32,* 179–194.

Martin, M. M., Myers, S. A., & Mottet, T. P. (1999). Students' motives for communicating with their instructors. *Communication Education, 48,* 155–164.

McCroskey, J. C., & McCroskey, L. L. (2006). Instructional communication: The historical perspective. In T. P. Mottet, V. P. Richmond, & J. C. McCroskey (Eds.), *Handbook of instructional communication: Rhetorical and relational perspectives.* Boston, MA: Allyn & Bacon.

Mee-Lee, L., & Bush, T. (2003) Student mentoring in higher education: Hong Kong Baptist University. *Mentoring & Tutoring, 11,* 263–271.

Nazionne, S., Laplante, C., Smith, S. W., Cornacchione, J., Russell, J., & Stohl, C. (2011). Memorable messages for navigating college life. *Journal of Applied Communication Research, 39,* 123–143.

Schlossberg, N. K. (1981). A model for analyzing human adaptation to transmission. *The Counseling Psychologist, 9*(2), 2–18.

Schmidt, H. G., & Moust, J. H. C. (1995). What makes a tutor effective? A structural equation modeling approach to learning in problem-based curricula. *Academic Medicine, 70,* 708–714.

Scruggs, T., Mastropieri, M., & Berkeley, S. (2014). *Peer tutoring strategies.* Retrieved from http://www.education.com/print/peertutoring/

Seiler, W. (2014). *Communication 109 peer instructor survey/assessment.* Unpublished Manuscript, Department of Communication Studies, University of Nebraska-Lincoln, Lincoln, NE.

Seiler, W., Beall, M., & Mazer, J. (2014). *Communication making connections* (9th ed.). Boston: Pearson.

Terrion, J. L., & Leonard, D. (2007). A taxonomy of the characteristics of student peer mentors in higher education: Findings from a literature review. *Mentoring & Tutoring, 15*, 149–164.

Thayer, P. (2000, May). Retaining first generation and low income students. *Opportunity Outlook, 2–8.*

Tindall, J. A., & Black, D. R. (2009). *Peer programs: An in-depth look at peer helping—planning, implementation, and administration* (2nd ed.). New York, NY: Routledge.

Tinto, V. (1993). *Leaving college: Rethinking the causes and cures of student attrition* (2nd ed.). Chicago, IL: University of Chicago.

United States Department of Education. (2011). *Fast facts.* National Center for Education Statistics. Retrieved from http://nces.ed.gov/fastfacts/

U.S. News & World Report. (2014). *Freshman retention rate* [Data file]. Retrieved from http://colleges.usnews.rankingsandreviews.com/best-colleges/rankings/regional-colleges-west/freshmen-least-most-likely-return

Wang, T. R. (2012). *Formational relational turning points in the transition to college: Understanding how communication events shape first-generation students' relationship with their college teachers* (Unpublished doctoral dissertation). University of Nebraska-Lincoln, Lincoln, NE.

Wang, T. R. (2014). Formational turning points in the transition to college: Understanding how communication events shape first-generation students' pedagogical and interpersonal relationships with their college teachers. *Communication Education, 63*, 63–82.

Wilson, S. (2012). The role becomes them: Examining communication center alumni experiences. In E. L. Yook & W. Atkins-Sayre (Eds.), *Communication centers and oral communication programs in higher education* (pp. 55–67). Lanham, MD: Lexington Books.

Wyatt, G., Saunders, D., & Zelmer, D. (2005) Academic preparation, effort and success: A comparison of student and faculty perceptions. *Educational Research Quarterly, 29*, 29–36.

Notes

1. In the research literature, peer mentor, peer instructor, and peer tutor are often used to mean the same thing with slightly different roles. In this chapter the term peer tutor is used exclusively to include peer mentor(s) and peer instructor(s).

2. Jenepher Lennoz Terrion and Dominique Leonard (2007) provided many of the terms that follow in this chapter. In addition, their review of research provided a source for some of the research that is cited as well. Their literature review was related to peer mentoring, but is extremely relevant to peer tutoring as well. See references section for complete citation.

· 9 ·

HELPING STUDENTS CONQUER
ANXIETY IN THE SESSION

Karen Kangas Dwyer

When students first come to a peer tutoring center, many bring anxiety with them. Not only are they anxious about giving their first speeches or taking their first exams, but also many are nervous about coming to a peer tutor or consultant for help. Some wonder if they can be helped. Some may experience such an overwhelming anxiety that they will have trouble completing a class without assistance (McCroskey, 2008), while others have previously dropped a course when their instructor encouraged them to get *treatment* (Proctor, Douglas, Garera-Izquierdo, & Wartman, 1994). Students need to be reassured, however, that they can be helped and that tutors or consultants are trained to offer them assistance. They cannot do their homework or write their speeches, but they can guide them through the many steps and processes to help them be successful in the work required for their classes.

Students need to hear that some anxiety, especially communication anxiety, is normal. There is no need for students to feel they are odd or alone in their apprehension. For example, communication research confirms that up to 70% of college students report anxiety about giving a presentation (Dwyer & Davidson, 2012a; McCroskey, 2000). That means that in every public speaking class of 25 students, it is likely that up to 17 of those students will feel anxious about giving a speech. Anxiety is common in other disciplines too. Up to

80 percent of community college students and 25 percent of four-year college students report suffering from math anxiety (Jones, 2001; Yeager, 2012), while writing anxiety is so prevalent on college campuses (Baez, 2005) that it has become a significant concern for university faculty (Cheng, 2004). Thus, students will begin to feel relief when they realize their assignment anxieties are experienced by many and, in fact, are considered normal.

The good news for anxious students is that peer tutoring centers can help them conquer much their anxiety. In fact, communication research shows that the more students visit a communication center, the more they report a reduction in their speech anxiety, an increase in their confidence in public speaking, and higher grades (Dwyer & Davidson, 2012b, 2014; Ellis, 1995; Jones, Hunt, Simonds, Comadena, & Baldwin, 2004).

The goal of this chapter is to advise tutors on how to help anxious students, based on established communication scholarship. Specifically, this chapter will provide tutors with possible causes of anxiety, as well as the approaches and techniques that might help students. Although the techniques are drawn primarily from communication research because treating speech anxiety is so well researched, most of the techniques have been found to be helpful for other types of tutoring, as well.

The Causes of Anxiety

Communication researchers have discovered several causes for speech or communication anxiety and it is often helpful for tutors and anxious students to understand the causes of the anxiety so they can take action to reduce it. Although the causes of speech anxiety may be specific to the communication context, many of the causes explain anxiety in other contexts, as well. Possible causes include: (1) reinforcement or learned responses, (2) worrisome thoughts, (3) performance orientation, (4) perceived lack of skills, (5) excessive activation or body chemistry, and (6) situational aspects of the event or the audience. This section will focus on each of these causes and include how tutoring centers can help.

Reinforcement or Learned Responses

Reinforcement theory points out that learned responses impact an individual's behavior and emotions (Levine, 1997). For example, students may have learned to be anxious from their many experiences in school or at home when they perceived consistent criticism, low grades, negative evaluation, laughter, or even punishment when they tried to give a speech, write a paper, or perform a calculation. From this they learned an anxiety response. If a student has repeatedly experienced negative feedback from a family member, friend, teacher, or other familiar person, he/she will develop an expectation of negative consequences and will try to avoid the situation. The same is true for public speaking, as well as for mathematics, foreign language, and composition (Furner & Duffy, 2002). When a student tries again to present a speech or complete a math problem set or use the same skill, she may feel anxiety because of the learned response to the given situation. Consequently, students often continue to experience the same anxiety response related to their first feelings of embarrassment or failure learned as a child or teenager. In addition, modeling the reactions of others can explain a learned anxiety response. For example, students can learn speech anxiety by observing a family member or other adult who considers giving a speech frightening. Students in classrooms with female teachers who model or display math anxiety can learn to be anxious about math (Beilock & Willingham, 2014). A peer tutoring center is an essential place for students to begin to learn new positive responses to stressful situations in order to successfully handle future assignments and thereby stop the old learned anxiety responses.

Worrisome Thoughts

Worries about negative evaluation or failure often drive anxiety. In fact, the most common cause of stage fright is the fear of negative evaluation (Desberg & Marsh, 1988). Speech anxiety commonly arises when students think they cannot meet the expectations of their audience or cannot measure up to what is required (Ayres, 1986). Students with writing anxiety often express a fear of negative judgment or high expectation they cannot meet (Cheng, 2004; Kreuth, 2012; Martinez, Kock, & Cass, 2011). Likewise, students who have fears about failing to learn another language, or failing to pass a test about mathematical concepts have similar concerns. If students believe they will fail, their minds often jump to irrational conclusions. They will continue to entertain thoughts about their inability to learn the skill or content, about how "bad" they are for not being able to do well, and about how foolish they may look while attempting to practice a skill. With a spiraling effect, anxiety escalates and nervous energy fills their minds and bodies when they head down that tunnel. Fortunately, tutors can help students change fearful and worrisome thoughts into positive coping statements. Students can learn new thoughts and new skills to help them succeed.

Performance Orientation

Another cause of speech anxiety—and one that could apply to other contexts—is a *performance orientation* (Motley, 2009). Related to worrisome thoughts of negative evaluation, a performance orientation involves high self-expectations about a performance. In the performance orientation, a student views public speaking as a situation that demands perfect, flawless oratorical skills, uses eloquent language, and relies on a formal, polished, brilliant delivery. The performance orientation misinterprets any audience as hypercritical and judgmental, almost like appearing before a set of judges for the Olympic games. These misconceptions about the formality and demands of a speaking situation and the need for a perfectly performed presentation will only increase anxiety and fear. In other situations, students might feel a similar pressure to develop a perfect first draft of a paper or receive a high grade on a first math test. Tutors and consultants can help students learn to view public speaking as a communication encounter that focuses on the message, relying on a natural delivery style used in everyday conversation. That reframing, in turn, helps reduce the performance anxiety. Likewise, an emphasis on drafts of papers (gradually leading to a stronger paper) or practice exams (where mistakes might be less stressful) help move students away from an over-emphasis on perfection and performance in other areas.

Perceived Lack of Skills

A fourth cause of anxiety is real or perceived lack of skills (Richmond & McCroskey, 1998). Individuals often feel anxious when they have not learned the skills for the situation or do not know how to perform a task. In a public speaking context, when students have not learned public speaking skills and do not know what to do or say, anxiety will likely increase. When it comes to math or writing, students with limited experience in these areas might feel anxious. Fortunately, tutors can help students feel more confident by confirming what students already know and by providing additional guidance. For example, tutors can reinforce the skills and information that students are already learning in their classes and show how that information can be used to successfully navigate assignments.

Excessive Activation or Body Chemistry

Another cause for presentation anxiety, as well as writing and math anxiety, can be related to a person's activation level or physical nervousness (Addison, Ayala, Hunter, Behnke, & Sawyer, 2004; Ayres & Hopf, 1993; Cheng, 2004; McCroskey, Ralph, & Barrick, 1970). Research has shown that some people have a high reactivity or anxious arousal index that leads them to experience excessive activation easily (Addison et al., 2004; Behnke & Sawyer, 2001, 2004; Finn, Sawyer, & Behnke, 2009). In personality research, these personalities are called sensors and they are more aware of their physical nervousness than others (Dwyer & Cruz, 1998).

Students who are sensors report a lower tolerance for uncertainty and stress, and their bodies produce stress-related chemicals that cause a quickened nervous response (Dwyer & Cruz, 1998). To avoid the feelings of excessive physical reactions such as trembling hands and feet, dry mouth, nausea, blushing, tense muscles, pounding or rapid heartbeat, temporary memory loss, wavering voice, shortness of breath, or nervous gesturing, students will try to avoid classes where public communication or other performance is required. Even if anxiety is caused by excessive physiological activation or a body chemistry prone to activation, tutors can help students learn to alleviate those physiological sensations and develop a calming response.

Situational Aspects

There are also general situational aspects that contribute to increased anxiety in any situation; these include novelty, conspicuousness, and audience characteristics (Daly, Caughlin, & Stafford, 2009; Putwain, Woods, & Symes, 2010). The novelty of an unfamiliar situation, where a student does not know what to expect or how to act, will likely increase anxiety. Conspicuousness, where attention is focused on someone easily visible to many (e.g., a speaker standing in front of an audience) will contribute to anxiety. Audience characteristics such as size, status, similarity, expectations, and formality also contribute to situational anxiety. The larger the number of people in an audience, the higher the status of the audience, the more dissimilar an audience is in age, gender, education, or culture to a speaker, the more conspicuous a person feels, the more pressure the person feels to meet expectations, and the more novel the situation appears, the more anxiety the student will likely feel. But students can learn skills and apply anxiety-reduction techniques to help alleviate this anxiety.

General Tips for Tutors to Help Alleviate Students' Anxieties in the Session

Situational causes of anxiety are easiest to address in peer-to-peer tutoring. Students who experience anxiety report that guidance and structure can help them overcome the ambiguity and novelty of the assignments (Booth-Butterfield, 1986). Speech anxiety, math anxiety, and writing anxiety are all improved when students receive the guidance, clear direction, and process structure that helps them proceed on their assignments (Booth-Butterfield, 1986; Smith, 1984).

Structure

Apprehensive students often have trouble determining where to start on an assignment or how to get organized. They also find it difficult to envision the end product (Booth-Butterfield, 1986; Smith, 1984). Tutors can help students by offering them some task structure, such as showing them examples, templates, models, general outlines, or examples of what is expected. In this way students can begin to envision what they can do, what they need to do, and what the outcome might look like. They will tend to develop a positive self-efficacy or belief in their ability to succeed (Dwyer & Fus, 1999, 2002; Klassen, 2002; Martinez, Kock, & Cass, 2011).

Sometimes students are so anxious that they cannot express where they need help. Again the novelty of the situation and even the idea of the conspicuousness of a public speaking assignment flame anxiety so that students have trouble thinking about what they need. When they come to the peer tutoring center, they may not have considered what they need most or where they are struggling. Advising students to read over a classroom assignment and circle any code words or concepts that they find hard to grasp will be helpful to bring focus to the consultation. In addition, students can be asked to circle any steps where they have questions or need help. In this way, they are directing the structure and the process for the meeting. As they begin to go over their needs with the tutor, some of the anxiety related to ambiguity settles down.

Positive Reinforcement

Tutors need to give positive reinforcement to students in any consulting situation. Since the number one source of student anxiety is fear of negative evaluation, it is essential for tutors to offer feedback in a positive frame (Ayres, 1986). Tutors should try to use positive reinforcement that builds on something the student has done or said related to the assignment. Tutors might look for something that is going in the right direction and encourage the student to continue to build on that work or idea, while assuring them that they are capable of completing the assignment (Beilock & Willingham, 2014).

Perceived Caring

It is important for tutors to help the students know that they empathize with them, that they understand human anxiety based on many causes or challenges, and that they will be responsive to their needs. In communication research, perceived caring is related to student learning and student attitude toward a topic, a class, and an instructor (Teven, 2001). In a peer tutoring situation, perceived caring will help students feel less anxious about tackling a class assignment.

Perceived caring is based on student perception of a teacher's *empathy* (the capacity to view a situation from another's point of view or emotions), *understanding* (the ability to comprehend another person's feelings, ideas, or needs) and *responsiveness* (the attentiveness to another's concerns and the willingness to listen) (Teven, 2001; Teven & McCroskey, 1997). Perceived caring is expressed in immediacy behaviors, such as smiling, eye contact, open body position, a forward lean, occasional nodding, and using a person's name (Christophel, 1990; Gorham, 1988). Using a friendly voice and displaying immediacy behaviors to express empathy, understanding, and responsiveness are all ways tutors can help students become less anxious about a consultation and an assignment.

The Multidimensional Approach to Overcoming Anxiety

Understanding some of the causes for anxiety is helpful because it can assist tutors in remaining empathetic, understanding, and responsive to the students. One of the chief ways to help anxious students is to present the Multidimensional Approach that helps students analyze the source of their anxieties, and then self-select techniques to address their anxiety about public speaking (Dwyer, 2000, 2009, 2012). The approach relies on over sixty years of communication research that shows that the greatest reduction in public speaking anxiety is achieved when a combination of techniques are used (Allen, 1989; Allen, Hunter, & Donohue, 1989; Ayres, 1988; Ayres & Hopf, 1993; Fremouw & Zitter, 1978; Whitworth & Cochran, 1996). In addition, this approach guides students to select a technique that fits the source of the anxiety. This multidimensional or multimodal model has been taught in college classes as an educational guide to help individuals analyze their own anxieties and to self-select the most appropriate treatment techniques (O'Keefe, 1985). Thus, multidimensional assessment is really an educational guide that can be especially helpful to the instructor or tutor who is seeking to assist students manage their own anxieties (Lazarus, 2000).

The Multidimensional Approach emphasizes the importance of matching treatment techniques to a person's human personality dimensions. There are seven interactive personality dimensions to be considered in a multi-modal personal assessment involving anxiety (Lazarus, 1989, 1997). The dimensions and assessment can be remembered easily using the acronym BASICS:

B = BEHAVIOR (acts, habits, gestures, or lack of skills)

A = AFFECT (strong nervous feelings, negative emotions, or moods)

S = SENSATION (bodily shaking, dry mouth, pounding heart, sweating, nausea)

I = IMAGERY (negative mental pictures, imagining failure)

C = COGNITION (worrisome thoughts, negative self-talk, and irrational beliefs)

S = STRESS (overstressed lifestyle, including poor physical well-being, use of drugs or alcohol to cope, and minimal exercise combined with lack of interpersonal support or little positive interaction with others (Dwyer, 1998, 2005, 2012)

Tracking the Firing Order

To determine the personality dimensions involved in anxiety, an anxious student can go through the list and *track the firing order* of the dimensions involved in his/her anxiety (see Appendix A). "'Tracking the firing order' simply means pinpointing the personality dimension, where speech anxiety initiates and then looking for any sequence of dimensions that contribute to the anxiety" (Dwyer, 2009, 2012; Lazarus, 1989, 2000). This helps the student determine which anxiety-reduction techniques to choose and use. Once a student determines the dimension at the top of her firing order for anxiety, she can choose the techniques best suited to the initiating dimension or dimensions. In that way the source of the anxiety is targeted and an alleviation technique can be applied which results in the most reduction of anxiety (Dwyer, 2000, 2009; Lazarus, 1997, 2009).

Determining the best technique for reducing anxiety does not diminish the importance of learning more than one anxiety-reduction technique, but it shows where to begin and how to get at the root of the anxiety. For example, Colleen, age 21, shared: "When I have to give a speech, I suddenly *feel* my face turn bright red before it's my turn to get up. Then I *think*, 'Oh, this is terrible; my audience will see how nervous I am. I *picture* everyone laughing at me and then *fear* overwhelms me (Dwyer, 2009, 2012)." In Colleen's situation, speech anxiety begins in the sensation dimension (i.e., she physically feels her face turn bright red). The firing order or sequence of dimensions involved in Colleen's speech anxiety is (1) sensation (she physically feels), (2) cognition (she thinks), (3) imagery (she imagines), and (4) affect (she emotionally feels). The first technique for Colleen to practice and the one most effective for managing Colleen's speech anxiety will be the one targeted to the source of her problem—the sensation dimension.

Tracking the firing order can serve as a guide to help students determine which techniques will be most effective. Many students report that it helps them understand why one technique works better for one student, while another technique works better for still another student. The techniques that will work best for an individual will target the dimension at the top of their firing order—the one that fires first or initiates the anxiety.

Self-Select Techniques

After students determine the top of their firing order, they are ready to self-select anxiety-reduction techniques to match the dimensions of their firing order (see Table 9.1). Based upon the communication research, math anxiety research, and writing anxiety research focused on anxiety reduction-techniques, the following techniques would be matched to the BASICS dimensions.

Table 9.1. BASICS Personality Dimensions and Anxiety Reduction Techniques.

Dimension	Anxiety-Reduction Technique
Behavior (targets lack of skills)	Skills Training (Kelly & Keaten, 2009; Tooke & Lindstrom, 1998).
Affect (targets negative emotions)	Systematic Desensitization (McCroskey, 1972; Schneider & Nevid, 1993) and Diaphragmatic Breathing (Howe & Dwyer, 2007; Paul, Elam, & Verhulst, 2007).
Sensation (targets physical sensations)	Systematic Desensitization and Diaphragmatic Breathing
Imagery (targets negative imagery)	Visualization (Ayres, Hopf, Hazel, Sonandre, & Wongprasert, 2009) and Systematic Desensitization.
Cognition (targets negative thoughts)	Cognitive Restructuring (Fremouw & Scott, 1979; Salovey & Haar, 1990), COM Therapy (reducing a performance perspective; Motley, 2009), Positive Thought Training (Cheng, 2002), and Visualization.
Stress (targets stress, physical well-being, and social support)	Physical Exercise (Thomas, Dwyer, & Rose, 2001), Stress Reduction Programs (Rice, 1998/1987), Referral to a Physician or Counselor, and Interpersonal Support (via a workshop or class, especially designed to help reduce anxiety [Dwyer, 2005, 2012]).

A Personal Plan

Using the firing order and list of recommended techniques above, a student can craft a personal plan. The personal plan will start with using one of the techniques targeted to the top dimension, and then move on to techniques for the next two dimensions. For example, based on Colleen's experience described earlier in this chapter, Colleen would make a plan that includes her top three dimensions. Colleen would try to practice the (1) diaphragmatic breathing technique until she began to feel some anxiety reduction in her sensations before moving on the next technique, (2) cognitive restructuring for her cognitions or thoughts, and (3) visualization for her negative mental pictures.

Three Techniques

The anxiety-reduction techniques are presented in detail in other publications (Ayres & Hopf, 1993; Dwyer, 2005, 2009, 2012; Richmond & McCroskey,

1998). For this chapter, three anxiety-reduction techniques will be presented because they can apply to speech as well as to other commonly-cited student anxieties, including math or writing.

Cognitive Restructuring Technique

Cognitive restructuring is based on the premise that anxiety and nervousness are generated when individuals think negative irrational thoughts about themselves or their behaviors (Ellis, 2001; Meichenbaum, 1977). Cognitive restructuring targets the cognitive personality dimension, and the goal is to help anxious students change their thinking in order to change their nervous feelings.

This technique involves four steps that can significantly reduce nervousness and anxiety about public speaking: (1) Create a list of worries, fears and unproductive self-talk about the act that makes you nervous, (2) identify the worries as untrue/irrational and reword them into true statements and productive thoughts, (3) develop a list of coping statements that are the truth and can replace the unproductive thoughts, and (4) practice your new coping statements and memorize them until they replace the old unproductive thoughts. An example of steps 1 and 2 targeted to speech anxiety is summarized in the steps below.

Step one: List of worrisome, unproductive thoughts and Step two: Truth statements

Students can read through the following list of worrisome, unproductive thoughts and pay special attention to those that fit their fears list. As you read it, imagine how a peer tutor might adapt this technique for other kinds of anxiety.

- Unrealistic Self-Expectations and "Must" Thinking: I "must" be perfect. I "must" give a perfect speech or earn a "perfect grade." I "must" never make a mistake.
  The Truth: No one will ever be perfect in this life. We are all fallible humans who make mistakes. No one expects perfection from you. You only have to give your best effort.
- Excessive Fear of Disapproval: No one will like my presentation, performance, work or me. Everyone will be bored listening to me or

know more about the topic than me. The audience might think I'm stupid.

The Truth: Some will appreciate my ideas. I only need to prepare and offer what I can. If I have researched my topic, I will know more about the topic than many others. My enthusiasm and presentation will be contagious and interest others.

- Anticipating the Worst Outcome: I will never be a success. No one will like what I say or write. I will make mistakes and the audience will notice every mistake I make. I'll probably make a mistake or forget some part of the speech. I will be a failure.

The Truth: If I research, prepare and practice with an outline, I will have notes to guide me. If I make a mistake or forget a part, I can refer to my notes and keep going. Even the best speakers or writers make mistakes, correct themselves, and keep going.

- Believing the Audience Is Hypercritical: Everyone is judging every detail about me. If my audience sees me sweat, stumble, shake or blush, they will think I am a failure, and I will look like a fool. Everyone in the class is a better than I am.

The Truth: My audience is listening for helpful ideas. They are far less critical than I am. I feel nervousness from the inside. My audience cannot feel my heartbeat and will *not* notice the nervousness I feel. They are all students, just like me.

- Emotional Reasoning: I can feel my nervousness. It's going to be a terrible speech. I'm the only one who is this nervous. I'm going to get a bad grade.

The Truth: A little nervous activation is normal. Everyone experiences it. It can add to my keenness. It will *not* determine my outcome. Focusing on my task or message instead of nervousness will help nervous feelings to subside. Preparing, organizing, and practicing will help me get a good grade.

- Holding a Performance Perspective: I must become something other than I am to be a successful person or public speaker. Like all performances, public speaking demands perfect, formal, flawless, and eloquent oratorical skills.

The Truth: Public speaking is a communication encounter; it relies on communication skills that I use in everyday conversation. The focus is on helping the audience understand my message. I can be myself and use my natural conversational delivery.

*Step three: List of positive coping statements and truths
that help reduce anxiety*

The third step in cognitive restructuring is to create and memorize truthful coping statements to replace the negative self-statements, worrisome self-talk, and
unproductive thoughts. For example, see the following suggestions for examples
of positive coping statements that can replace many unproductive thoughts.

- Everyone experiences some degree of anxiety or nervousness when
  speaking in front of others. Feeling a bit of nervousness will not keep
  me from speaking. Such feelings are a sign that I am enthusiastic and
  "psyched up" to give my speech.
- Worry only agitates and demoralizes a person. I have no need to worry
  about my speech because I will contribute something by planning,
  researching, and sharing my ideas. Preparation and organization contribute most to earning a good grade.
- Audiences seldom notice nervousness; they can't feel my heart beat.
  Focusing on my fears or feelings of nervousness will only prevent me
  from concentrating on my presentation.
- No one is perfect or fully competent in all aspects of life. I do not have
  to be perfect or give a perfect speech/have a perfect exam. Like me,
  everyone in this class is learning and practicing new skills. I only have
  to give my best effort. Blaming myself for past shortcomings or failures
  will not foster my goals. Learning positive coping statements to replace
  unproductive thoughts and negative thinking will help reduce communication anxiety and nervousness.
- Even if I feel some anxiety, I will act as if I am not anxious. I will believe
  in myself and my goals. I will talk myself into being confident, not
  nervous.

Step four: Memorize and practice the coping statements

Students can develop a new mindful script to replace the worrisome unproductive thoughts by simply memorizing the coping statements and using them
to confront the old script of worrisome unproductive thoughts as they arise.
Students should memorize the coping statements that apply most to their
unproductive thoughts or create personal coping statements from a combination of positive coping statements. In summary, they will need to: (1) Read
through a personal list of coping statements every day or until they know it

by heart, (2) practice using the coping statements to confront and replace any worrisome thoughts, (3) be heartened as the process may take a few weeks of diligent practice to disconnect automatic worrisome, unproductive thoughts and to replace them with positive coping statements.

This cognitive restructuring technique has been applied successfully to help students who experience math anxiety (Hembree, 1990; Karimi & Venkatesan, 2009). Tutors can teach students how to do this using steps one and two, as described above, with a focus on math problems. In step three, all negative self-statements about math would be transformed into positive self-statements (Maloney & Beilock, 2012). In step four, students commit to memory the coping statements related to their unproductive thoughts about math. For example, the following statement, "Everyone can learn how to do differential equations but me" would be replaced with "I can learn how to do this particular problem" (Arem, 2009).

Diaphragmatic Breathing

One of the best ways to help students reduce tenseness and feel calm before giving a speech (Dwyer, 2012, 2013; Howe & Dwyer, 2007), taking a math test (Arem, 2009; Maloney & Beilock, 2012; Wilkinson, Buboltz, & Seemann, 2001), or performing any other stressful learning activity is to encourage them to practice diaphragmatic breathing which targets the sensation and affect personality dimensions. Diaphragmatic breathing is a technique or exercise distinguished by the abdomen rising as an individual slowly inhales and by the abdomen retracting as an individual slowly exhales (Greenberg, 2003). This deep abdominal breathing exercise is not just taking a few deep breaths, but is an exercise to practice daily for 5 minutes. It has helped many reduce anxiety, especially public speaking students (Howe & Dwyer, 2007). Just five minutes of this deep abdominal breathing can help reduce nervousness and bring on relaxation. It can be practiced either standing or sitting. A recording is often helpful to get started (Dwyer, 2013). Tutors can help students follow these steps:

1. First, scan your body and note if you are feeling any tenseness or anxiety.
2. Next, find your rib cage and place one hand directly below your rib cage (that is, on your abdomen).
3. Practice exhaling long breaths through your mouth making a *whoooo* sound, like the blowing wind. Count to six as you exhale and allow your abdomen to pull inward.

4. Now, inhale slowly and deeply through your nose, feeling your abdomen expand and your hand rise for a count of four. Your chest should barely move.
5. Pause slightly and smile for a count of four. Smiling releases endorphins (natural mood elevators) into your blood.
6. Then, exhale slowly and fully through your mouth, making the whoooo sound for a slow count of four.
7. Relax and take a few normal breaths. Tell your body to go loose and limp. Make an effort to let all tension drain away from every part of your body.
8. Continue taking at least ten to fifteen deep abdominal breaths with slow, full exhales in order to trigger relaxation.

Students should learn and practice diaphragmatic breathing every day for at least a few weeks before a stressful assignment. It will help reduce anxiety and nervousness.

Mental Rehearsal or Visualization

Mental rehearsal, also called visualization, is a *cognitive modification* technique that targets the imagery and cognitive personality dimensions (see Figure 9.1). This technique involves mentally rehearsing an activity before doing it. Many successful athletes have used it to help them reach their peak performance (Ayres & Hopf, 1990). Mental rehearsal helps students visualize success, increase concentration, and think positively instead of negatively about a presentation or other activity. In speechmaking, written exams, or math exams, for example, this technique should be practiced right before the activity starts. Mental rehearsal complements behavioral practice (i.e., practicing a speech aloud). It will prepare the mind for a positive and successful experience.

In the mid-1980s, the technique called *visualization* was found to help students decrease their anxiety levels in public speaking classes (Ayres & Hopf, 1989). Later, it was found to help students reduce writing apprehension (Ayres & Hopf, 1991). Several studies have shown that the technique is very helpful at reducing anxiety when students mentally rehearse a very positive and successful experience prior to giving a graded speech in class (Ayres & Hopf, 1985), performing a writing assignment (Ayres & Hopf, 1991), or taking a math test (Arem, 2009; Shobe, Brewin, & Carmack, 2005).

The easiest way to learn mental rehearsal is to practice the technique using a recording designed to help visualize an event in a positive light. It is helpful to use an MP3 file or CD (Dwyer, 2013) recorded for mental rehearsal to develop the positive visual script. A visualization practice will take about 5 to 10 minutes for it to be effective. See the Figure 9.1 below for student directions on how to create and practice a mental rehearsal for a classroom speech. A mental rehearsal plan can be created for a math test, writing a paper, or other anxiety-provoking tasks.

To begin a mental rehearsal practice, sit upright in a chair and try to become as comfortable as possible. Position your hands on your lap so they feel relaxed. Close your eyes and take at least three diaphragmatic breaths. Your abdomen will rise, not your chest. Next, begin to mentally picture the following scenes as the body relaxes completely. Students should visualize themselves performing the learning activity, using this order:

1. Getting out of bed on the day you will give a speech or take a big exam. You feel energized, confident, and say to yourself, "I am prepared to meet the challenges of the day"
2. Dressing in the clothes that are right for the day and noting your positive attitude
3. Engaging in the activities you usually do before you leave for your class
4. Driving and/or walking to the room where you will meet; practicing diaphragmatic breathing and reciting your positive coping statements as you go
5. Walking into a room filled with warm and friendly people who greet you
6. Taking your seat in the classroom, conversing very comfortably with others, and feeling confident
7. Waiting for class to begin while repeating your positive coping statements
8. Feeling very positive about your presentation or big exam
9. Delivering your presentation or starting your exam and feeling very confident
10. If it is a speech, see yourself step by step going through each part of the speech your practiced (e.g., presenting an attention-getter; establishing your credibility; previewing your speech and then presenting each main point with evidence such as examples, statistics, and quotations; speaking passionately and conversationally, with movement and gesturing; concluding your speech, summarizing main points, and using a memorable ending; fielding questions; and receiving applause and praise from your audience).
11. If it is a big exam, see yourself solving each problem over the areas you have practiced and prepared (e.g., opening the test booklet, reading the first question, understanding the problem, solving it with confidence, etc.)
12. Finally, see yourself returning to your seat feeling energy and gratification or see yourself walking out of the room with confidence knowing that you did your very best on the exam.

After you finish visualizing those scenes, return your thoughts to reality, take three diaphragmatic breaths, and then open your eyes. If you practice your activity and then practice the mental rehearsal technique to rehearse a positive presentation, test or other activity, you will make a giant step toward becoming confident and managing anxiety.

Figure 9.1. Mental Rehearsal/Visualization Directions (Dwyer, 2012).

Conclusion

This chapter has provided tutors with information about the causes of anxiety as well as the approach, tips, and techniques they can offer anxious students. Understanding the causes of anxiety can help tutors develop empathy for students and comprehend the challenges they face. This chapter also presented the multidimensional approach so that tutors can guide the anxious students to the source of their anxiety, determine their firing order, and then self-select techniques to make a personal plan for further reducing the anxiety. Finally, this chapter presented three techniques based in communication research that have been used with math and writing apprehension too: cognitive restructuring for the cognition personality dimension, diaphragmatic breathing for the sensation and affect dimensions, and mental rehearsal for the imagery and cognitive dimensions. These techniques help students conquer anxiety at their initiating sources. If students continue to report excessive anxiety in numerous situations, they may need encouragement to seek help from an on-campus counselor or medical professional who can offer in-depth anxiety-reduction therapy. Tutors and students need to remember, however, that multitudes of studies have confirmed that normal levels of anxiety can be conquered. Tutors can help in many ways by offering understanding and guidance to anxious students.

References

Addison, P., Ayala, J., Hunter, M., Behnke, R. R., & Sawyer, C. R. (2004). Body sensations of higher and lower anxiety sensitive speakers anticipating a public presentation. *Communication Research Reports, 21*, 284–290.

Allen, M. T. (1989). A comparison of self-report, observer, and physiological assessments of public speaking anxiety reduction techniques using meta-analysis. *Communication Studies, 40*, 127–139.

Allen, M., Hunter, J., & Donohue, W. (1989). Meta-analysis of self-report data on the effectiveness of public speaking anxiety treatment techniques. *Communication Education, 38*, 54–76.

Arem, C. (2009). *Conquering math anxiety*. Independence, KY: Cengage Learning.

Ayres, J. (1986). Perceptions of speaking ability: An explanation of stage fright. *Communication Education, 35*, 275–287.

Ayres, J. (1988). Antecedents of communication apprehension: A reaffirmation. *Communication Research Reports, 5*, 58–63.

Ayres, J., & Hopf, T. S. (1985). Visualization: A means of reducing speech anxiety. *Communication Education, 35*, 318–323.

Ayres, J., & Hopf, T. S. (1989). Is it more than extra-attention? *Communication Education, 38,* 1–5.

Ayres, J., & Hopf, T. S. (1990). The long-term effect of visualization in the classroom: A brief research report. *Communication Education, 39,* 74–78.

Ayres, J., & Hopf, T. (1991). Coping with writing apprehension. *Journal of Applied Communication Research, 19*(3), 186–196.

Ayres, J., & Hopf, T. S. (1993). *Coping with speech anxiety.* Norwood, NJ: Ablex.

Ayres, J., Hopf, T., Hazel, M. T., Sonandre, D. M., & Wongprasert, T. K. (2009). Visualization and performance visualization: Applications, evidence, and speculation. In J. A. Daly, J. C. McCroskey, J. Ayres, T. Hopf, D. Sonandre, & T. A. Wongprasert (Eds.), *Avoiding communication: Shyness, reticence, and communication apprehension* (pp. 375–394). Cresskill, NJ: Hampton Press.

Baez, T. (2005). Evidenced-based practice for anxiety disorders in college mental health. *Journal of College Student Psychotherapy, 20*(1), 33–48.

Behnke, R. R., & Sawyer, C. R. (2001). Public speaking arousal as a function of anticipatory activation and autonomic reactivity. *Communication Reports, 14,* 73–85.

Behnke, R. R., & Sawyer, C. R. (2004). Public speaking anxiety as a function of sensitization and habituation processes. *Communication Education, 53,* 164–173.

Beilock, S. L., & Willingham, D. T. (2014). Math anxiety: Can teachers help students reduce it? *American Educator, 38*(2), 28–32, 43.

Booth-Butterfield, M. (1986). Stifle or stimulate? The effects of communication task structure on apprehensive and non-apprehensive students. *Communication Education, 35,* 337–348.

Cheng, Y. S. (2002). Factors associated with foreign language writing anxiety. *Foreign Language Annals, 35*(6), 647–656.

Cheng, Y. S. (2004). A measure of second language anxiety: Scale development and preliminary validation. *Journal of Second Language Writing, 13*(4), 313–335.

Christophel, D. M. (1990). The relationships among teacher immediacy behaviors, student motivation, and learning. *Communication Education, 39,* 323–340.

Daly, J. G., Caughlin, J. P., & Stafford, L. (2009). Correlates and consequences of social-communicative anxiety. In J. A. Daly, J. C. McCroskey, J. Ayres, T. Hopf, D. Sonandre, & T. A. Wongprasert (Eds.), *Avoiding communication: Shyness, reticence, and communication apprehension* (pp. 23–52). Cresskill, NJ: Hampton Press.

Desberg, P., & Marsh, G. (1988). *Controlling stagefright: Presenting yourself to audiences from one to one thousand.* Oakland, CA: New Harbinger Publications.

Dwyer, K. (1998). Communication apprehension and learning style preference: Correlations and implications for teaching. *Communication Education, 47,* 101–114.

Dwyer, K. (2000). The multidimensional model: Teaching students to self-manage high communication apprehension by self-selecting treatments. *Communication Education, 49,* 72–81.

Dwyer, K. (2005). *Conquer your speech anxiety.* New York, NY: Wadsworth.

Dwyer, K. (2009). The multidimensional model for selecting interventions. In J. A. Daly, J. C. McCroskey, J. Ayres, T. Hopf, D. Sonandre, & T. A. Wongprasert (Eds.), *Avoiding communication: Shyness, reticence, and communication apprehension* (pp. 359–374). Cress-kill, NJ: Hampton Press.

Dwyer, K. (2012). *iConquer speech anxiety workbook.* Amazon: Createspace.

Dwyer, K. (2013). *iConquer speech anxiety: Techniques for reducing presentation or public speaking anxiety* [CD or MP3]. Amazon: Createspace.

Dwyer, K., & Cruz, A. (1998). Communication apprehension, personality, and grades in the basic course: Are there correlations. *Communication Research Reports, 15,* 436–444.

Dwyer, K. K., & Davidson, M. M. (2012a). Is public speaking really more feared than death? *Communication Research Reports, 29*(2), 99–107.

Dwyer, K. K., & Davidson, M. M. (2012b). Speech center support services, the basic course, & oral communication assessment. *Basic Communication Course Annual, 24,* 122–150.

Dwyer, K. K., & Davidson, M. M. (2014, November). *Forty years later: Public speaking is more feared than death, but not after taking a public speaking class.* Paper presented at the National Communication Association Annual Meeting, Chicago, IL.

Dwyer, K., & Fus, D. (1999). Communication apprehension, self-efficacy, and grades in the basic course: Correlations and implications. *Basic Communication Course Annual, 11,* 108–132.

Dwyer, K., & Fus, D. (2002). Perceptions of communication competence, self-efficacy, and trait communication apprehension: Is there an impact on basic course success? *Communication Research Reports, 19*(1), 29–37.

Ellis, A. (2001). *Overcoming destructive beliefs, feelings, and behaviors: New directions for Rational Emotive Behavior Therapy.* Amherst, NY: Prometheus Books.

Ellis, K. (1995). Apprehension, self-perceived competency, and teacher immediacy in the laboratory-supported public speaking course: Trends and relationships. *Communication Education, 44,* 64–77.

Finn, A. N., Sawyer, C. R., & Behnke, R. R. (2009). A model of anxious arousal for public speaking. *Communication Education, 58,* 417–432.

Fremouw, W. J., & Scott, M. D. (1979). Cognitive restructuring: An alternative method for the treatment of communication apprehension. *Communication Education, 28,* 129–133.

Fremouw, W. J., & Zitter, R. E. (1978). A comparison of skills training and cognitive restructuring-relaxation for the treatment of speech anxiety. *Behavior Therapy, 9,* 248–259.

Furner, J. M., & Duffy, M. L. (2002). Equity for all students in the new millennium: Disabling math anxiety. *Intervention in School & Clinic, 38*(2), 67–75.

Gorham, J. (1988). The relationship between verbal teacher immediacy behaviors and student learning. *Communication Education, 37,* 40–53.

Greenberg, J. S. (2003). *Comprehensive stress management.* New York: McGraw-Hill.

Hembree, R. (1990). The nature, effects, and relief of mathematics anxiety. *Journal for Research in Mathematics Education, 21*(1), 33–46.

Howe, M. M., & Dwyer, K. K. (2007). The influence of diaphragmatic breathing to reduce situational anxiety for basic course students. *The Basic Communication Course Annual, 19,* 104–137.

Jones, A. C., Hunt, S. K., Simonds, C. J., Comadena, M. E., & Baldwin, J. R. (2004). Speech laboratories: An exploratory examination of potential pedagogical effects on students. *Basic Communication Course Annual, 16*, 105–138.

Jones, W. (2001). Applying psychology to the teaching of basic math: A case study. *Inquiry, 6*(2), 60–65.

Karimi, A., & Venkatesan, S. (2009). Cognitive behavior group therapy in mathematics anxiety. *Journal of Indian Academy of Applied Psychology, 35*(2), 299–303.

Kelly, L., & Keaten, J. A. (2009). Skills training as a treatment for communication problems. In J. A. Daly, J. C. McCroskey, J. Ayres, T. Hopf, D. Sonandre, & T. A. Wongprasert (Eds.), *Avoiding communication: Shyness, reticence, and communication apprehension* (pp. 293–326). Cresskill, NJ: Hampton Press.

Klassen, R. (2002). Writing in early adolescence: A review of the role of self-efficacy beliefs. *Educational Psychology Review, 14*(2), 173–203.

Kreuth, N. (2012, October 10). Conquering writing anxiety. *Inside Higher Ed.* Retrieved from http://www.insidehighered.com

Lazarus, A. (1989). *The practice of multimodal therapy.* Baltimore, MD: John Hopkins University Press.

Lazarus, A. (1997). *Brief but comprehensive psychotherapy: The multimodal way.* New York: Springer.

Lazarus, A. A. (2000). Multimodal replenishment. *Professional Psychology: Research and Practice, 31*(1), 93.

Lazarus, A. A. (2009). Multimodal behavior therapy. *Cognitive behavior therapy,* 342–346.

Levine, P. A. (1997). *Waking the tiger.* Berkeley, CA: North Atlantic Books.

Maloney, E. A., & Beilock, S. L. (2012). Erratum: Math anxiety: Who has it, why it develops and how to guard against it. *Trends in Cognitive Sciences, 16*, 404–406.

Martinez, T., Kock, N., & Cass, J. (2011). Pain and pleasure in short essay writing: Factors predicting university students' writing anxiety and writing self-efficacy. *Journal of Adolescent & Adult Literacy 54*(5), 351–360.

McCroskey, J. C. (1972). The implementation of a large-scale program of systematic desensitization for communication apprehension. *Communication Education, 21*, 255–264.

McCroskey, J. C. (2000). *An introduction to rhetorical communication* (8th ed.). Englewood Cliffs, NJ: Prentice Hall.

McCroskey, J. C. (2008). Communication apprehension: What have we learned in the last four decades? *Human Communication, 12*(2), 157–171.

McCroskey, J. C., Ralph, D. C., & Barrick, J. E. (1970). The effect of systematic desensitization on speech anxiety. *Speech Teacher, 19*, 32–36.

Meichenbaum, D. (1977). *Cognitive-behavior modification.* New York, NY: Plenum.

Motley, M. T. (2009). COM therapy. In J. A. Daly, J. C. McCroskey, J. Ayres, T. Hopf, D. Sonandre, & T. A. Wongprasert (Eds.), *Avoiding communication: Shyness, reticence, and communication apprehension* (pp. 337–358). Cresskill, NJ: Hampton Press.

O'Keefe, E. (1985). Multimodal self-management: A holistic approach to teaching self-improvement. *The Journal of Humanistic Education and Development, 23*(4), 176–182.

Paul, G., Elam, B., & Verhulst, S. J. (2007). A longitudinal study of students' perceptions of using deep breathing meditation to reduce testing stresses. *Teaching and Learning in Medicine, 19*(3), 287–292.

Proctor II, R. F., Douglas, A., Garera-Izquierdo, T., & Wartman, S. L. (1994). Approach, avoidance & apprehension: Talking with high-CA students about getting help. *Communication Education, 43,* 312–321.

Putwain, D. W., Woods, K. A., & Symes, W. (2010). Personal and situational predictors of test anxiety of students in post-compulsory education. *British Journal of Educational Psychology, 80*(1), 137–160.

Rice, P. L. (1998). *Stress and health.* Pacific Grove, CA: Brooks/Cole Publishing Company. (Original work published 1987)

Richmond, V., & McCroskey, J. C. (1998). *Communication: Apprehension, avoidance, and effectiveness* (4th ed.). Scottsdale, AZ: Gorsuch Scarisbrick.

Salovey, P., & Haar, M. D. (1990). The efficacy of cognitive-behavior therapy and writing process training for alleviating writing anxiety. *Cognitive Therapy and Research, 14*(5), 513–526.

Schneider, W. J., & Nevid, J. S. (1993). Overcoming math anxiety: A comparison of stress inoculation training and systematic desensitization. *Journal of College Student Development, 34*(4), 283–288.

Shobe, E., Brewin, A., & Carmack, S. (2005). A simple visualization exercise for reducing test anxiety and improving performance on difficult math tests. *Journal of Worry and Affective Experience, 1*(1), 34–52.

Smith, M. W. (1984). *Reducing writing apprehension.* Urbana, IL: NCTE.

Teven, J. J. (2001). The relationships among teacher characteristics and perceived caring. *Communication Education, 50,* 159–169.

Teven, J. J., & McCroskey, J. C. (1997). The relationship of perceived teacher caring with student learning and teacher evaluation. *Communication Education, 46,* 1–9.

Thomas, J. T., Dwyer, K., & Rose, R. (2001, November). *Communication apprehension and exercise adherence: There is a relationship.* Paper presented at the annual meeting of the National Communication Association, Atlanta, GA.

Tooke, D. J., & Lindstrom, L. C. (1998). Effectiveness of a mathematics methods course in reducing math anxiety of pre-service elementary teachers. *School Science and Mathematics, 98*(3), 136–139.

Whitworth, R. H., & Cochran, C. (1996). Evaluation of integrated versus unitary treatments for reducing public speaking anxiety. *Communication Education, 45,* 306–314.

Wilkinson, L., Buboltz, W., & Seemann, E. (2001). Using breathing techniques to ease test anxiety. *Guidance & Counseling, 16*(3), 76–81.

Yeager, D. S. (2012 April). *Productive persistence: A practical theory of community college student success.* Paper presented at the annual meeting of the American Educational Research Association, Vancouver, Canada.

Appendix A

Tracking the Firing Order

To track your firing order, use the following assessment guide to help you determine where your specific anxiety begins (i.e., which dimension of your personality initiates your fear, anxiety, or nervousness).

1. Imagine a recent speaking experience or big exam or writing assignment (e.g., your instructor, employer, or boss has just told you that you must—be prepared soon—even within the next hour). With one of those scenarios in mind, try to pinpoint your initiating dimension(s). Try to rank order the dimensions that fire in your specific anxiety, using the descriptions below to guide you. Give special attention to ranking the top three dimensions.

RANK (1–6)

___a. Do you immediately think: "Having to give a speech (or write a paper or take an exam) will be awful. I can't do it! Everyone will laugh at me or think less of me. I could never please the audience. I will make a fool of myself." If irrational, negative, or unproductive thoughts are the first to fire, the top of your firing order is COGNITION.

___b. Do you immediately feel (physically) any of the following sensations (even before a thought seems to enter your mind): blushing, nausea or stomach tightness, heart palpitations, sweating, lightheadedness or other physiological reactions? If bodily sensations are the first to fire, the top of your firing order is SENSATION.

___c. Do you immediately and vividly visualize yourself in a scene where you have failed the audience, are the target of laugher or jeers, run from the room, or engage in any other negative activity? If negative mental pictures are the first to fire, the top of your firing order is IMAGERY.

___d. Do you feel (emotionally) upset, tense, anxious, or nervous? If emotional feelings of nervousness or anxiety are the first to fire, the top of your firing order is AFFECT.

___e. Do you immediately react with avoidant behaviors, such as procrastination or running from the situation? Do you avoid the situation because you think you have no skills? If avoidant behaviors related to lack of skills are the first to fire, then the top of your firing order is BEHAVIOR.

___f. Do you feel over-stressed in general so that giving a speech (or writing a paper or taking an exam) just adds one more stressful situation to your already stressful lifestyle? Do you get very little exercise, feel overworked, take drugs or alcohol to cope, eat poorly, or experience little social support? If stress in general, use of drugs, poor physical health, and lack of mutually supportive friendships fires first, the top of your firing order is STRESS.

2. List the firing order of the top three dimensions involved in your speech anxiety (ranked #1, #2, #3). (Used by permission, Dwyer, 2005, 2012)

· 1 0 ·

ONLINE COMMUNICATION
FOR THE SAVVY TUTOR

Catherine K. Wright

Over the past twenty years, the Internet has not only invaded our lives, but has completely changed the way we think, act, believe, and acknowledge communication. Computer-mediated communication (CMC), it can be argued, has changed the way we interact with each other, allowing a screen and keyboard to replace the face-to-face interactions that have existed for millennia. According to a Pew Internet Research article (Fox & Rainie, 2014), whereas only 14% of adults in the United States used the Internet in 1995, in 2014 that number rose to 87%, with 98% of 18–29-year-olds using their cell phone to gain online access. With this increasing dependence on technology, countless studies have been conducted about online interpersonal communication.

John December (1997) defines computer-mediated communication as "a process of human communication via computers, involving people, situated in particular contexts, engaging in processes to shape media for a variety of purposes" (para. 2). December's definition highlights the number of communication factors in online communication and this chapter aims to deliver a greater understanding of the richness and complexity that users encounter when taking their interpersonal communication into an online setting, especially in the context of peer tutoring.

Numerous educational portals (such as Blackboard and WebCT), chatrooms (AOL, Yahoo, MSN, etc.), and visual programs such as Skype or Oovoo have been used to conduct interpersonal communication via mediated means. In addition to these, education companies have added online learning portals such as Pearson's MyLab series, ALEKS through McGraw-Hill, and Plato. These opportunities have given rise to both synchronous and asynchronous communication, allowing people to use these tools at a time that is both convenient and useful. They have allowed people the opportunity to conduct business, further one's education, and maintain relationships effectively over long distances, leading to a variety of new possibilities that might not have been feasible due to geographic differences.

As educational institutions have realized the potential of educational portals such as Blackboard or WebCT, they have incorporated these elements into their curriculum. This chapter's focus is on how to effectively tutor in an online setting. In this setting, more than the conventional tutor-student relationship is at play. The tutor and student must also contend with the technological aspect of tutoring, and the changes in the interpersonal relationships mandated by synchronous and asynchronous communication. Thus, it is essential that there is an understanding of the complexity of both the interpersonal relationship between two people as well as the complexity of developing that relationship in an online-only forum.

Using two theories, Social Information Processing Theory by Walther (1992) and Uncertainty Reduction Theory by Berger and Calabrese (1975), this chapter will focus on how a peer tutor can effectively build an online relationship with students. The first theory focuses on that very communication setting and ways in which people strive to reduce uncertainty in their communication experiences. The second theory discusses how relationships are built when the face-to-face aspect of communication and non-verbal cues are removed.

In this way, the chapter will allow the reader to gain a stronger understanding of what interpersonal communication is, what computer-mediated communication is, how the peer tutor can use this information to create a stronger bond with the student learner, how they can create a relationship that allows them to use the online arena to effectively and efficiently convey information, and finally, how to overcome the inevitable technological challenges posed by using machines to conduct interpersonal communication.

Interpersonal Relationships While Tutoring

The tutor-student relationship is based on trust—trust that the tutor will give to the student all the information necessary to succeed and trust that the student will strive for improvement within the given field/area of study. Schmidt (2011) notes that there are many conundrums with the tutor-student relationship: "Both tutees and tutors ask themselves: is this a relationship or friendship, mentoring, or instruction? How formal is too formal? How close is too close? How personal is too personal?" (p. 46). There needs to be some interpersonal interaction, but it is not a friendship. Indeed in many ways it can be considered closer to a business partnership in which two people are seeking a profitable end result.

Vogel, Fresko, and Wertheim (2007) noted that tutoring is offered by a variety of people. It can be offered by "peers, by graduate students, by college faculty members, or by professional LD [Learning Disability] specialists" (p. 486). Just because someone has been trained in an educational area or is considered an expert in a subject matter, it does not automatically make them a competent tutor. Training tutors in communication skills such as active listening, interviewing (to probe for questions), and use of clear language is essential for a successful session. Peer tutors have been used for all age groups, including college, and the outcomes have been quite positive for both the tutor and the tutee (Roscoe & Chi, 2007). Roscoe and Chi (2007) explain that all students, especially the under-privileged, benefit from the one-on-one interaction. De Smet, Van Keer, and Valcke (2009) reinforced that peer tutors add important elements to learning such as modeling productive study skills, organizing their work habits, and encouraging interpersonal communication between student and teacher.

Whether or not we are discussing face-to-face or online communication, one of the most prominent features in the literature is the idea that effective communication is essential in a successful learning environment, whether as a primary instructor or as a peer tutor. In traditional teaching, the teacher is in the front of the room disseminating information, while the student sits at his/her desk, learning. Tutoring exists to bridge the gap between what the teacher is trying to explain that is not understood by the learner. A tutor's role is to help explain and reinforce the knowledge needed in order to master a subject or topic. Young (2006) explains that an instructor's role in an online setting involves "carefully designed, primarily written communication with the learners" (p. 73). Young continues by stating that "[A]n effective instructor can provide corrective feedback and encouragement, motivating the students to stay on task and to achieve the learning goals. Online learning should not be an isolated, independent activity but rather one in which students and instructors are partners in learning" (p. 73). An interpersonal relationship is essential in order for a tutor to help a student succeed.

Berger and Calabrese's (1975) Uncertainty Reduction Theory provides important context for understanding CMC. This communication theory states that when two people meet for the first time, the level of their uncertainty with the situation and with each other is high. What this means is that while humans have some understanding of what is culturally expected, they remain in a high state of anxiety or uncertainty until the other person responds in a reassuring manner. Thus, they are wary of each other and of the situation because they are uncertain of what the results will be. In the context of tutoring, when a tutor and student enter into an agreement, they must build a relationship from nothing. They do not know how the other will react, and are unsure if this relationship is the right one, or even a good one at that.

One of the most important aspects of this theory, and one that will certainly play strongly into the online/computer-mediated communication aspect of this chapter, is that relationships build slowly. It takes time to build trust. Building trust within the tutoring context is rendered more complex because, as Schmidt (2011) notes, "the role of a tutor is unique, and involves exhibiting the friendliness of a friend, the inspiration of a mentor, the strength of an authority figure, and the knowledge of an instructor. But a tutor is neither a friend, a mentor, an authority figure, nor an instructor" (p. 58). Relationship building is accomplished in various ways: through verbal and non-verbal means, seeking information, reciprocation of information, perceived similarity, and perception of "liking" the other. Given the complex nature of the tutor/tutee relationship, uncertainty reduction becomes of prime importance. If a student is unsure of a subject, their confidence in their ability to perform is probably low. There must be a trust that the person with whom the student is engaging can help them accomplish a learning goal. The student's uncertainty that this tutor can help, on both an interpersonal level and on an education level, remains high until such time as the tutor demonstrates his/her willingness and ability to help the student. Thus, the tutor's responsibility, in part, is to create an environment filled with trust.

According to Tait (2004), the role of a tutor is to enable learning within and beyond a course, encourage the development of discipline-specific understandings, and help students to master the content or knowledge-based elements of the course. In order for a tutor to be effective, some information must be shared with the student and the student is expected to reciprocate in the same fashion. During the exchange of information, trust is built and effective tutoring can begin. Albert Mehrabian (1967) found that face-to-face communication is broken down into three categories: non-verbal (over half), vocal, and facial (least) (p. 252). Thus, in a face-to-face situation between the tutor and the students, non-verbal cues will play an essential part of their communication interaction. This high dependence on non-verbal communication can imply that online relationships may be less effective than face-to-face relationships. However, online relationships can be very strong as non-verbal cues are replaced by others in the online setting. Relational communication is key and how both people define themselves within the relationship can be the basis for success or disaster.

There are numerous ways in which a tutor can strengthen a relationship using relational communication. As discussed above, establishing a relationship between tutor and student is essential. It is through this relationship that trust is built and work can be done. One of the most effective ways to create, build upon, and sustain a relationship is through empathetic listening. Empathic listening, as Cuny, Wilde, and Stephenson (2012) define it, "requires listeners to refrain from judging the speaker and instead advocates placing themselves in the speaker's position" (p. 250). This allows the tutor to engage with the student and encourages the student to state their concerns, opinions, and questions knowing they will be listened to in a positive way. In a face-to-face setting, students are able to ask teachers (or tutors) questions (Young, 2006). Tutors in return are able to note non-verbal cues that indicate confusion, understanding, frustration, or jubilation. Strong listening skills and a feeling of being valued are an important part of relational communication.

Building a relationship and establishing strong relational communication takes time and involves effort on the part of the tutor to gauge the student with whom he or she is working. Cobb (1998) found that "the effective tutors were skillful communicators and model listeners who ... knew how to converse with [the students]" (p. 99). Additionally, Yook (2006) noted that "the training of staff on effective listening skills can have a heuristic effect" because once tutors are trained in the art of listening, they can then model their behaviors during interactions with students and others" (p. 67). In this way, relational communication is reinforced.

Another important aspect of relational communication is knowing cultural expectations for non-verbal cues such as the inclusion or absence of eye contact. While this is specifically pointed at face-to-face communication, it might also include the online tutoring realm if a student-tutor pairing uses an online video program like Skype or Oovoo. Learning these cues, in workshops such as Yook (2006) noted above, builds a foundation of respect for others, which is also an essential part of communication.

Workshops are one way, according to Retna, Chong, and Cavana (2009) that a tutor can improve his/her communication and tutoring skills. They assert that when tutors are offered "a range of work-shops [that] specifically cater to tutors as a form of ongoing support on teaching and learning" that the workshops "instill teaching confidence … that will help them … engage students, communicate knowledge and provide constructive feedback for student improvement" (p. 252). There are communication skills that people can learn and upon which they can always improve. Workshops such as these foster the support necessary to create excellent tutors.

While active listening might be easier when done in a face-to-face setting, it is certainly possible to learn the skills of increasing perceptiveness in an online setting. The next section of this chapter discusses in more detail what online communication is and what it means for the tutor-student relationship.

Online Communication

For almost a full generation, people have engaged in numerous forms of online communication. Students under the age of 30 often entered elementary schools that had Internet access. As mentioned earlier, a majority of adults aged have Internet access, and almost all of this group access it through their smartphones (Fox & Rainie, 2014). People are increasingly familiar with the Internet, Internet searches, smart phones, and online applications such as chat rooms. Radicati and Buckley (2012) estimated that there were over 2.1 billion email users in 2012 and by the end of 2012, they estimated that 144 billion emails per day would be sent. The authors also noted that users expect their communication tools to be unified across platforms working with instant messaging, Web conferencing, and VoIP (Voice over Internet Protocol) as part of their packages. This is, most definitely, the age of online communicators. However, these technologies will likely still pose various challenges for the tutoring process.

One issue related to online tutoring is that the tutor and student will more than likely both be conversant in some Internet technology, such as email, smartphone usage, and Internet searches. However, they may come to the tutoring sessions with limited knowledge of the specific portal used for tutoring, and may have the erroneous expectation that they will be able to use the portal technology easily.

Additionally, there still exists a digital divide between those who have and those who do not have access to technology and the Internet. As of May 2013, Rainie (2013) estimated that only 70% of people in the United States have access to the Internet, with a significant number of those having broadband access. This same study agreed with previous research findings that non-White, lower-educated, lower-income people do not have the same access to the Internet. Thus the tutor and student alike may need to contend with issues of lack of technological knowledge and limited access to the Internet. In either situation, training and open communication are essential for a successful experience.

Burnett (2003) noted that there are concerns when transitioning from a face-to-face environment to a solely computer mediated one. In this case, the tutor needs to manage the length of contributions, the lack of paralinguistic cues, and the overload of responses forming multi-stranded conversations. However, she does note advantages of communicating in a chat room in that it provides a sense of immediacy and a written record of the conversations. This might be an option for many tutors, as sometimes it is necessary for a student to record the discussion in order to refer to that information at a later time.

Another issue arising from the online tutoring context is that many non-verbal cues available during face-to-face communication are not available in online communication. The theory that best fits our discussion of online communication and the need for tutors and students to recognize the differences between face-to-face communication and online communication is Social Information Processing Theory (SIP) by Walther (1992). This theory was built on the premise that we, as humans, seek social interaction with others and, in that process, we seek information.

As with Uncertainty Reduction Theory (Berger & Calabrese, 1975), Walther (1992) argues that people seek to reduce uncertainty in relationships. In face-to-face encounters, people rely heavily on non-verbal cues. In online relationships, these cues are substituted by others. The kinds of information we seek in a face-to-face encounter are similar to what we seek in computer-mediated communication encounters. As this kind of communication has evolved, we have adapted our communication skills to meet the needs of ourselves and others.

Verbal cues in an online context are those that communicators would add to a written conversation to replace the non-verbal cues. Non-verbal cues are those things people write that denote the way in which others should interpret their written language. For example, sarcasm is not easily conveyed through words only. Our non-verbal cues, such as the look on our face or the positioning of our body and tone of voice, can relay to another person our intent, such as sarcasm. In an online situation where non-verbal cues are not present, people might use these verbal cues. The language someone uses in the context can provide clues about that person and his/her intention at the time. With SIP, Walther (1992) posits that while the non-verbal cues that we rely on in a face-to-face encounter are missing, as noted above, people are able to adjust and adapt to this and are still able to create meaningful relationships by changing or re-interpreting "normal" social cues. We are still able to create impressions of others through several different means. Now, we are inveigled with countless opportunities for interpersonal communication online. The use of online communication is certainly more prevalent than Walther (1992) probably envisioned twenty years ago and the opportunities for expansion are endless.

The second way that Walther (1992) believes online communication is different from face-to-face communication, and yet is able to still be effective, is through the concept of "extended time." This is the rate at which people exchange information in an online setting. In CMC, the exchange rate is much slower than face-to-face. However, the rate of development does not necessarily impact the potential quality of that development. Information is being shared and, while it might be over a longer time, the same quality and quantity of information can be exchanged.

Another important aspect of time in CMC is the concept of synchronous and asynchronous time. Synchronous communication requires that all participants interact at the same time, but the medium can vary (Schwartzman, 2013). In this instance, a chat room or instant messaging provides a good example of synchronous communication. A tutor and student can agree to use AIM (AOL Instant Messaging) in order to chat about issues. Via phone, email, or some sort of other conversation, they agree to enter the chat room at a previously determined time. Thus, they are able to communicate together, synchronously. This synchronous chat enables them to ask questions and have questions answered, much like in a normal conversation. The caveat is that of course both parties must be in the same portal; it will not work if someone is logged into MSN's IM program and the other party is in AIM.

In some cases, people are not able, or willing, to engage in communication at the same time. This is known as asynchronous communication. Ishtaiwa and Abulibdeh (2012) defined asynchronous communication as "[taking] place when there is an interaction between instructors and students with intermittent time delay" (p. 142). Email is a good example of this form of communication. A tutor can email a student with an assignment or a question at 8:00 pm and the student may not check his/her email account until 11:00 pm that same evening. Once received, the student will have the option to respond to that email or to wait. An advantage is that the student can take his/her time to answer questions, but the disadvantage is that if the student needs clarification or other assistance, they would need to wait until the tutor answered his/her email at another time. Understanding these concepts can mean the success or failure of a simple communication interaction.

Additionally, the tutor and the student must come to an understanding of what these elements mean for their collaboration. If an educational portal like Blackboard is to be used, then it should be agreed upon that the tutor and student will only use that portal's technology. Expectations for synchronous or asynchronous online communication must be clarified, as must the expected lag time in reply. This agreement or understanding will streamline and enhance the relationship and its chances for success because it preempts the possibility of misunderstandings, which will in turn promote effective tutoring.

Effective Online Tutoring

So, how can a tutor be effective online? The answer is not simple, as we must consider numerous demographic differences such as age, technological capability, technology availability, and cultural differences. Butler (2010) discussed his involvement with the creation of an online learning portal for his school's students. He noted that "successful student connectivity and access has to be a priority in planning" or it is quite possible the online structure will crumble (p. 34).

As Schwartzman (2013) writes, "Communication scholars and practitioners may need to reconceive what a personal tutoring session means once the mentoring relationship incorporates interactions mediated through computers, smart phones, tablets, and other electronic devices" (p. 653). This chapter thus far has discussed interpersonal relationships and the complexities of online communication. The following section discusses face-to-face tutoring and the shift to online tutoring.

Face-to-Face Tutoring

There is no doubt that tutoring is very helpful. It has been prevalent through history, loved by royals and the wealthy as a means of educating their children. Kim (2013) noted that "social interaction is considered critical in learning and intellectual development" (p. 59). She continues by stating that peer interaction, along with teacher interaction aided students in retaining information. Retna, Chong, and Cavana (2009) maintained that "tutors play a very important role in the learning and teaching of undergraduate students in higher education" (p. 252) in that they can step in when a university class is too large for interpersonal communication to occur and the student feels lost. In these instances, "tutors supplement the activities of the faculty ... and help to engage students in individualised [sic] instructional opportunities" (p. 252).

Cooper (2012) argues that "objectives and pedagogical strategies are key attributes to foster an effective learning environment" (p. 200). There are many different ways that this can be accomplished, such as digitally with PowerPoint presentations, downloaded lecture notes, and video examples (Cooper). These elements, combined with the face-to-face presence of the tutor, allow the student a broader range of access to information than in years past. Additionally, as the interpersonal relationship builds, students feel more confident in themselves and are more receptive to learning, lessening their at-risk status.

Most higher education institutions have a tutoring or learning center designed to help students at risk. These centers are often part of a multi-faceted support system aimed at student retention. Tutoring, especially with at-risk students, has shown a marked improvement in graduation rates, as indicated in the following study. Rheinheimer, Grace-Odeleye, Francois, and Kusorgbor (2010) reported that when college students received tutoring, their academic performance, persistence in learning, retention and graduation rates all significantly improved. Additionally, they were 13.5 times more likely to graduate than those who did not receive tutoring. This study indicates the importance of building a relationship that not only focuses on the subject matter at hand, but also with the interpersonal relationship between the tutor and the student.

Given the importance of relationship building, it is not surprising that when initially engaging in a relationship, Boyd (2010) recommends that the tutor begin by "addressing issues of distance by creating a welcoming environment and taking account of open learning issues by trying to find out as much as possible about a student's motivation and level of prior learning" (p. 46). In this way, the tutor is creating a situation in which the student can see their relationship as team-related rather than as "better over lesser." This clarification of complementary and equal status is especially important for peer tutoring, as roles may be especially confusing in this context.

There are many different kinds of tutoring assistance available, such as online, face-to-face, in the classroom and at a specialty tutoring center. It may be that the tutor is engaging in a one-time only session where the student prefers to avoid building an interpersonal relationship. Or, a tutor might work in a peer tutoring center that is not structured to easily allow for interpersonal relationship development because they visit with students on a first-come, first-serve basis.

In either case, it will be important for the tutor to quickly recognize the interpersonal communication preferences of the student and allow the student to understand the situation as well. Knowledge of interpersonal communication and cues will aid both the tutor and the student's abilities to communicate their needs regarding the learning of the material. This, however, is something that would be best aided by extensive training of the tutor prior to engaging in the tutoring relationship.

Online Tutoring

Online tutoring has become more common in recent years, providing an alternative means for reaching learners. As Mammadov and Topçu (2014) write, "In recent years, a computer-mediated environment has become a vital part of the teacher and learning process" (p. 221). Cooper (2012) notes that "web-based learning environments bring something extra to learning situations because they are user-driven media" (p. 201), although Cooper draws from research that indicates that this greatly depends on the cognitive style of the student.

It is not only in the classroom that students interact and learn. Lin and Yang (2013) indicate that "students are predominantly living in a world of electronic text, spending a large proportion of their time reading and writing on computers" (p. 80). It should not be surprising, then, that to adapt to student needs tutoring has made the transition from solely a face-to-face activity to include an online modality.

Cooper (2012) argues that virtual learning offers students some advantages in that learning is nurtured in a different space than the traditional classroom. The online component has the advantage of being "flexible in terms of time" (Cooper, p. 209), enabling the student to balance their work and extracurricular activities with their tutoring or other outside-the-classroom learning environments.

The increasing prevalence of online tutoring has given rise to research about this new pedagogy. Schmidt (2011) stated that one of the issues reported in the literature is the problem that tutors are experts in their fields, but are not adequately trained to perform in an online setting or are filling a novel role. Thus, they are "often left to define for themselves" what that role might be (Schmidt, p. 45). Similarly, Schmidt notes that this same problem of role definition can plague the student seeking help. This uncertainty can be frustrating and confusing for both the tutor and the students.

When beginning an online tutoring relationship, it is essential for the tutor to have a fully defined sense of who he/she is and what the tutoring goals are in order to best teach the student the materials. Thus for a tutor to be effective online, they must first be confident about themselves and their ability to explain and share information in any setting. In order for the tutor to confidently engage the student in the online setting, effective training about online education or tutoring portals is in order.

One of the more exciting findings regarding online communication and tutoring was reported in research conducted by Peacock, Murray, Dean, Brown, and Girdler (2012). The authors found that when working in an online environment, tutors were challenged to "re-think the design of the learning environment, re-visit how they facilitated discourse and re-examine their communication skills especially with regard to feedback on student performance" (p. 1269). This enabled them to adjust and improve during a session as well as to improve their overall approach to tutoring.

The tutors also reported feeling challenged to use emergent technologies like Online Synchronous Learning Environments (OSLEs). OSLEs such as Blackboard Collaborate and Adobe Connect are web-based, computer-mediated communication programs, typically using video and audio. These are typically used through the student's existing school and offer the tutor the option of being able to place a name with the work. In this way, the student and the work become personalized to the tutor. The OSLEs provide an interactive, connected learning environment. Tutors considered the OSLE to be a more dynamic, interactive, personal, student-centric, and fun learning environment (Peacock et al., 2012).

Peacock et al. (2012) found the tutor's enthusiasm and commitment to using OSLEs remained throughout the study and most tutors were able to work around the technology. The OSLE was also used asynchronously as a reflective tool. This is an important aspect of online tutoring: while communication synchronously can be productive, sometimes the student needs the opportunity to let the information sink in. They need the opportunity to digest and process what they have learned and then come back to it with a fresh perspective.

Sometimes, however, students prefer their interactions (synchronous or asynchronous) with the tutors to remain anonymous, seeking information rather than relationships. McMahan (2011) discussed the preference of Asian students to use online services because of the anonymity it provides. His research, which has implications for tutoring, discovered that because Asian English as a second language (ESL) students "respond positively to computerized English instruction," this method worked for them (p. 10).

While some students may relish the lack of interpersonal relationship perceived in online tutoring sessions, others may conversely seek to establish or maintain a perceived interpersonal relationship. Schwartzman (2013) discussed the importance of creating a rich, warm, and inviting medium through which effective tutoring can be accomplished. A rich medium "such as face-to-face interaction, offers abundant sensory cues that create multiple layers of signification. Richer media allow a communicator to feel deeply immersed in a multidimensional communicative environment" (p. 655). However, this does not mean that less rich media, such as "text-based chats," do not have to be a less effective means of communication. It simply means that the tutor and student must be aware of the limitations of less-rich media and adjust accordingly.

Tools for Effective Online Tutoring

Now we look at the crux of this chapter: How can tutors be most effective when serving their students online? How can tutors take a less-rich environment, such as asynchronous and online textually-based communication, and create a rich environment? The attention now turns to how a tutor can most effectively create an environment in which student progress can flourish. What matters ultimately is what the student perceives as the most productive use of their time.

There are numerous ways in which the literature suggests this be accomplished. Below is a small synthesis of the literature to provide some background and guidance. Most importantly, it is intended to be heuristic, to spur other new ideas and recommendations, to create an opportunity for the tutor to synergistically use this information to create something better than listed here. Each student is different in his/her needs, so the ability to adjust and be creative is paramount for a tutor to be effective.

First, peer tutoring centers should have a set of guidelines, a peer tutoring "Bill of Rights" if you will, that delineates each person's expectations within the relationship. In this way, both the tutor and the student have a set of rules that can be followed. It is probable that something like this would lessen possibility of conflict that might arise between tutor and student.

Schmidt (2011) found four key tutor communication behaviors that could well serve as a basis for setting online behavior standards between the tutor and student: relational questioning, content questioning, content explaining, and relational disclosure. Allowing the student to open up about his/her frustration, goals, hopes, worries, etc., allows the tutor the opportunity to gauge what needs to be done, and how the tutor might best go about helping the student learn. This concept was further illustrated when Burnett (2003) stressed that rather than a tutor "simply transmitting knowledge, s/he should promote dialogue that helps students arrive at new understandings" (p. 249).

Along with the four key behaviors mentioned in Schmidt (2011), the following guidelines demonstrate the importance of both parties in the relationship, although one focuses more on the student and the other set focuses on the tutor. Together with Schmidt's suggestions, the following guidelines can create the basis for the Bill of Rights meant to help and protect both parties.

Dolan, Donohue, Holstrom, Pernell, and Sachev (2009) noted that "effective and personalized support" (p. 94) helps those who enter into an online environment seeking assistance. Although their focus was on technical support for online learners, these suggestions can easily be implemented when seeking success for the online tutoring experience, as technology is an integral part of this process also. They included such hints as offering various means of support, offering "how-to learn online" experiences, and developing an e-Practicum model for student teaching.

E-practicum models are those that are created at the home university or the bricks and mortar office where the teaching, mentoring, or tutoring originates. It is from this location that information is compiled and disseminated to those who need the guidance. Holstrom, Ruiz, and Weller (2007) noted that it was cost-prohibitive to have supervisory faculty at every location. Thus, an e-Practicum model was created to "replicate the mentoring and supervision that occurs in an on-campus student teaching model" (p. 6).

Interactions between students and/or peer tutors, such as those found in a discussion board or similar posting, could be implemented to strengthen the interactions between and among those who use the online portal. Guldberg and Pilkington (2007), based on previous research, noted that discussion is "likely to be more productive when someone monitors discussion, facilitates interaction and summarises [sic] outcomes" (p. 62).

In the same vein, Murphy, Shelley, White, and Baumann (2011) found similar characteristics to Dolan et al., and declared that an online tutor should be instrumental in the formation of a strong tutor-student foundation in an online setting. The main differences between the two studies is that Murphy et al. focused on aspects such as knowledge of Open University systems and distance learning and information technology skills.

Second, in addition to providing guidance in the form of a tutoring "Bill of Rights," comprehensive technological training for the peer tutors is necessary for success. Clark and Whetstone (2014) suggested that those who assist students "need specific advice and training on how to use electronic facilities to provide tutorial support" (p. 4). Guichon, Bétrancourt, and Prié (2012) found that when new tutors were presented with the option to use unfamiliar or more complicated components, such as video, they decided against using it and focused their use on the ways with which they were most familiar and comfortable communicating, such as text and audio modes. Even when multimedia chats were incorporated, they relied more heavily on text because it is a more familiar way to communicate online. Thus, comprehensive training of tutors in the platform, or with the technology to be used, is essential. There might be a time when they must not only teach the student about the subject matter, but they may also need to teach the student how to use the technological platform.

Third, even though a tutor may be well prepared to use the technology through comprehensive training preparation, software and hardware undergo constant change. If a tutor or student were trained under a certain version, and that version changes and adds new options, it can sometimes be frustrating for those trying to use it. As Abbass et al. (2011) wrote, "Both the rapid pace of ongoing software innovation (e.g., version up-dates) and even user interface differences within some of these applications (e.g., OS X vs. Windows versions of Skype) make it difficult to provide a straightforward set of explicit technical instructions that will remain relevant even in the short term" (p. 111). The authors continue with the warning that sometimes bandwidth is reduced or interference of some kind enters into the tutoring session. This creates possibilities for miscommunication. Things like this can be predicted, to some extent, and the expectation of understanding how to use a computer and the programs associated with tutoring should be set ahead of the time that sessions begin so that the student is adequately prepared.

Fourth, a backup plan might need to be introduced into the education plan in the event of technical obstacles, so that the student can be assured of receiving the best support possible regardless of technological difficulties or failures. This could include a phone call or continuing with the audio only portion of the session if the video consumes too much bandwidth. In any situation, the clear communication of a backup plan is a necessary aspect of the tutoring event.

With these four guidelines (creating a "Bill of Rights" as fundamental guiding principles for peer tutoring, providing comprehensive technological training for tutors, realizing that technology is not fail-safe, and having a "Plan B" in case technology becomes a barrier to the peer tutoring process), successful on-line peer tutoring will become a more readily attainable goal. It is, however, essential to remember that none of these guidelines will work effectively if the peer tutor forgets the most basic element to learning: interpersonal communication. This chapter began by stating the overwhelming importance of interpersonal communication in the learning process and the importance of the tutor creating a solid relationship. Once the tutor builds some sort of interpersonal approachability, whether it is for one session or many sessions, the opportunity for productive tutoring can begin.

Conclusion

The primary focus of any tutor-student experience should be focused on the interpersonal relationship and promotion of open communication. Using key strategies such as active listening and empathic listening provide a great start to the session. This enables both parties to learn and come to understand the ways in which each person thrives within the relationship.

The next focus must be on the preparation of the peer tutor. The tutor is the one who will be responsible not only for the subject matter, but also for building a relationship of trust and learning. Additionally, the tutor must be conversant in all the technology available and will often need to assist the student in making sure that technology is functioning correctly for the learning situation.

The peer tutoring center should create a "Bill of Rights" that lays out what is expected by each party, and training should center on this discussion of rights and responsibilities. This protects both the tutor and the student, and allows for each to have a better defined understanding of what is expected within the relationship. Online tutoring is an exciting pedagogical area that merits attention. As technology expands, more and more opportunities will become available for the peer tutoring center to engage students effectively in learning. As these opportunities become available, it will be the responsibility of the peer tutoring center to teach those platforms to the tutors, so they can confidently present themselves as an expert in both the subject matter and technology. Comprehensive tutor training is essential in preparing the tutor to be competent in these multiple aspects of tutoring online.

The focus of this chapter was how to effectively tutor in an online setting. Through the literature, it becomes apparent that effectively tutoring in an online setting begins with extensive off-line preparation. Thus, when creating an online tutoring service, one must first look at the successes and failures of any face-to-face tutoring that occurs, if applicable. Based on what we know from face-to-face traditional tutoring, we can build a solid foundation for creating guidelines for successful online tutoring. Creating a Bill of Rights that clarifies the online forum and its strengths creates an atmosphere of fruitful learning. Ultimately the interpersonal relationship between the student and the tutor will determine the success or failure of the tutoring experience. Understanding the complexities of this relationship will enable the tutor and student to better prepare, and will help immeasurably as both parties navigate the learning environment.

References

Abbass, A., Arthey, S., Elliott, J., Fedak, T., Nowoweiski, D., Markovski, J., & Nowoweiski, S. (2011). Web-conference supervision for advanced psychotherapy training: A practical guide. *Psychotherapy*, 48(2), 109–118.

Berger, C. R., & Calabrese, R. J. (1975). Some explorations in initial interaction and beyond: Toward a developmental theory of interpersonal communication. *Human Communication Research*, 1(2), 99–112.

Boyd, V. (2010). *The retention factor: Retaining the distance education learner* (Doctoral dissertation). Retrieved from ProQuest, UMI Dissertations Publishing. (3409319)

Burnett, C. (2003). Learning to chat: Tutor participation in synchronous online chat. *Teaching in Higher Education*, 8(2), 247–261.

Butler, J. W. (2010). 24/7 on-line learning: Lessons learned. *Techniques*, 85(6), 33–36.

Clark, A. K., & Whetstone, P. (2014). The impact of an online tutoring program on mathematics achievement. *The Journal of Educational Research*, 107(5), 1–5.

Cobb, J. B. (1998). Listening within the social context of tutoring: Essential component of the mentoring relationship. *International Journal of Listening*, 14(1), 94–108.

Cooper, L. O. (2012). Virtual communication centers: A resource for building oral competency. In E. Yook & W. Atkins-Sayre (Eds.), *Communication centers and oral communication in higher education: Advantages, challenges, and new directions* (pp. 199–215). Lanham, MD: Lexington Books.

Cuny, K., Wilde, S. M., & Stephenson, A. V. (2012). Using empathetic listening to build relationships at the center. In E. Yook & W. Atkins-Sayre (Eds.), *Communication centers and oral communication in higher education: Advantages, challenges, and new directions* (pp. 249–256). Lanham, MD: Lexington Books.

December, J. (1997, January). Notes on defining computer-mediated communication. *CMC Magazine*. Retrieved from http://www.december.com/cmc/mag/1997/jan/december.html

De Smet, M., Van Keer, H., & Valcke, M. (2009). Cross-age peer tutors in asynchronous discussion groups: A study of the evolution in tutor support. *Instructional Science*, 37(1), 87–105.

Dolan, S., Donohue, C., Holstrom, L., Pernell, L., & Sachev, A. (2009, November/December). Supporting online learners: Blending high-tech with high-touch. *Exchange*, 190, 90–97. Retrieved from http://www.erikson.edu/wp-content/uploads/Supporting-Online-Learners-FINAL.pdf

Fox, S., & Rainie, L. (2014, February 27). *The Internet at 25*. Retrieved from http://www.pewinternet.org/2014/02/27/part-1-how-the-internet-has-woven-itself-into-american-life/

Guichon, N., Bétrancourt, M., & Prié, Y. (2012). Managing written and oral negative feedback in a synchronous online teaching situation. *Computer Assisted Language Learning*, 25(2), 181–197.

Guldberg, K., & Pilkington, R. (2007). Tutor roles in facilitating reflection on practice through online discussion. *Journal of Educational Technology & Society*, 10(1), 61–72.

Holstrom, L., Ruiz, D., & Weller, G. (2007). A new view: Reflection and student teacher growth through an e-Practicum model. *E-learning*, 4(1), 5–14.

Ishtaiwa, F., & Abulibdeh, E. (2012). The impact of asynchronous e-learning tools on interaction and learning in a blended course. *International Journal of Instructional Media*, 39(2), 141–159.

Kim, Y. (2013). Digital peers to help children's text comprehension and perceptions. *Journal of Educational Technology & Society*, 16(4), 59–70.

Lin, W., & Yang, S. C. (2013). Exploring the roles of google.doc and peer e-tutors in English writing. *English Teaching*, 12(1), 79–90.

Mammadov, S., & Topçu, A. (2014). The role of E-mentoring in mathematically gifted students' academic life: A case study. *Journal for the Education of the Gifted*, 37, 220–244.

McMahan, R. (2011). *Effective communication between Asian ESL tutees and college English tutors* (Masters thesis). Retrieved from ProQuest, UMI Dissertations Publishing. (492107)

Mehrabian, A., & Ferris, S. R. (1967). Inference of attitudes from nonverbal communication in two channels. *Journal of Consulting Psychology, 31*(3), 248–258.

Murphy, L. M., Shelley, M. A., White, C. J., & Baumann, U. (2011). Tutor and student perceptions of what makes an effective distance language teacher. *Distance Education, 32*(3), 397–419.

Peacock, S., Murray, S., Dean, J., Brown, D., & Girdler, S. (2012). Exploring tutor and student experiences in online synchronous learning environments in the performing arts. *Creative Education, 3*(7), 1269–1280.

Radicati, S., & Buckley T. (2012, October). *Email market 2012–2016 executive summary.* Retrieved from http://www.radicati.com/wp/wp-content/uploads/2012/10/Email-Market-2012-2016-Executive-Summary.pdf

Rainie, L. (2013, November 5). The state of digital divides. *The Pew Research Internet Project.* Retrieved from: http://www.pewinternet.org/2013/11/05/the-state-of-digital-divides-video-slides/

Retna, K. S., Chong, E., & Cavana, R. Y. (2009, July). Tutors and tutorials: Students' perceptions in a New Zealand university. *Journal of Higher Education Policy and Management, 31*(3), 251–260.

Rheinheimer, D. C, Grace-Odeleye, B., Francois, G. E., & Kusorgbor, C. (2010). Tutoring: A support strategy for at-risk students. *Learning Assistance Review, 15*(1), 23–34.

Roscoe, R. D., & Chi, M. T. H. (2007). Understanding tutor learning: Knowledge-building and knowledge-telling in peer tutors' explanations and questions. *Review of Educational Research, 77*(4), 534–574.

Schmidt, H. (2011). Communication patterns that define the role of the university-level tutor. *Journal of College Reading and Learning, 42*(1), 45–60.

Schwartzman, R. (2013). Reviving a digital dinosaur: Text-only synchronous online chats and peer tutoring in communication centers. *College Student Journal, 47*(4), 653–667.

Tait, J. (2004). The tutor/facilitator role in student retention. *Open Learning, 19*(1), 98–109.

Vogel, G., Fresko, B., & Wertheim, C. (2007). Peer tutoring for college students with learning disabilities: Perceptions of tutors and tutees. *Journal of Learning Disabilities, 40*(6), 485–493.

Walther, J. B. (1992). Interpersonal effects in computer-mediated interaction: A relational perspective. *Communication Research, 19*(1), 52–90.

Yook, E. L. (2006). Assessment as meta-listening at the communication center. *International Journal of Listening, 20*(1), 66–68.

Young, S. (2006). Student views of effective online teaching in higher education. *American Journal of Distance Education, 20*(2), 65–77.

THEORY INTO PRACTICE

CASE 6

PEER TUTOR TRAINING ACTIVITY

Addressing Various Audiences[1]

Molly McHarg

Due to university policy and curricular changes that emphasize globalization, a demographic shift is taking place in many universities, changing the traditional student population. The author shares an activity that has worked at her writing center for international and English as a Second Language students who are multilingual learners supporting their multilingual peers.

The proliferation of American universities abroad in recent years has also prompted the growth and development of writing centers in international contexts (Bazerman et al., 2012; Eleftheriou, 2011; McHarg, 2011; Thaiss, Brauer, Carlino, Ganobcsik-Williams, & Sinha, 2012). This expansion has transformed the way writing centers are established and shaped, as many of the clients are multilingual learners. While it is not unusual for writing centers worldwide to devote a considerable amount of time to international and English as a Second Language students, it is a relatively new phenomenon to have multilingual learners supporting their multilingual peers (Eleftheriou, 2011; Ronesi, 2009, 2011). This demographic shift has transformed the nature of peer tutor training, and this project seeks to contribute to the development of this shift. In this article, I describe one training activity I developed and implemented at Virginia Commonwealth University in Qatar's Writing Center.

The impetus for this training activity was the concern I had for maintaining the integrity and strength of our new peer tutor program. When I originally suggested starting a tutoring program, faculty repeatedly issued warnings that "The students' English is not strong enough" and "They are busy students and they don't have time." However, with the future budget always an uncertainty, the reports of success with peer tutoring at other institutions, and the increased workload for our understaffed center, I decided it was worth an attempt.

Virginia Commonwealth University in Qatar launched its first semester of peer tutoring during the spring 2012 semester. When training was complete and the tutors began holding their own tutorial sessions, I felt that the VCUQatar Writing Center was on the path to developing a culture of collaboration, peer support, and writing—everything the current writing center literature indicates centers should strive to achieve. Unfortunately, I quickly discovered a weakness when I began reading the submitted tutorial reports. All tutorial sessions are reported to the faculty unless the student requests it remain confidential.

Although they had been selected for the peer tutor positions because of their relatively strong English abilities, report writing is a specialized genre to which peer tutors had previously not been exposed sufficiently. In reviewing the written summaries, I could see that they were weak in their tutorial report writing skills. It concerned me that this was what faculty would be seeing. As this was the first semester launch of the peer tutor employment, I felt the pressure to establish a solid program foundation.

Many of the reports written by tutors were repetitive in that they covered the same topic. This became a ripe opportunity for our next training workshop. As I struggled with how to approach the issue, I reverted to standard English as a second language (ESL) classroom techniques by providing written models.

The result was my development of a template chart. This chart includes three columns: "What you're thinking," "What you might say in a tutorial," and "What you might write in a report." The scenarios in the left column, "What you're thinking …," came directly from the tutors themselves; these comments had been repeated to me many times verbally, so they were good launching points for discussion. Working together, we drafted language in order to appropriately and professionally respond to the potential client verbally, as well as in writing to the instructor. While the peer tutors worked to complete the chart, I offered some suggestions, posed questions, and we worked through revisions collaboratively and interactively. The final production resulted in a reference chart with template language that can be tailored for individual conferencing and reports.

This activity served a wide variety of purposes. Specifically, it provided a low-stakes environment for learning and collaboration during training, solid language structures for sensitive conferences and report writing, and a developmental step for tutors to become professionals. Tutors became more aware of the genre of report writing, with a distinct attention to audience, purpose, and tone. We were also able to discuss the value of writing templates and how they differ from plagiarized work. Tutors are now able to comfortably and confidently speak with peer clients as well as send written reports to faculty. Many tutors have commented on how helpful the chart was in showing how to thoughtfully, appropriately, and effectively handle difficult tutorials with students. Finally, it became a time-saving tool. Tutors are often under pressure to finish working with clients and complete tutorial session reports before their shift ends. Having the report template language can facilitate faster responses and lead to a more effective use of tutor time. Furthermore, the consistency in reporting language can be helpful for faculty receiving the reports. This training tool can easily be adopted and adapted at other institutions around the world.

References

Bazerman, C., Dean, C., Early, J., Lunsford, K., Null, S., Rogers, P., & Stansell, A. (Eds.). (2012). *International advances in writing research: Cultures, places, meaures*. Fort Collins, CO: The WAC Clearinghouse and Parlor Press.

Eleftheriou, M. (2011). *An exploratory study of a Middle Eastern writing center: The perceptions of tutors and tutees* (Unpublished doctoral dissertation). University of Leicester, Leicester.

McHarg, M. (2011). Money doesn't matter. *Praxis: A Writing Center Journal*, 8(2). Retrieved from http://www.praxisuwc.com/vintage-praxis/

Ronesi, L. (2009). Theory in/to practice: Multilingual tutors supporting multilingual peers: A peer-tutor training course in the Arabian Gulf. *The Writing Center Journal*, 29(2), 75–94.

Ronesi, L. (2011). "Striking while the iron is hot." A writing fellows program supporting lower-division courses at an American university in the UAE. *Across the Disciplines*, 8. Retrieved from http://wac.colostate.edu/atd/ell/ronesi.cfm

Thaiss, C., Brauer, G., Carlino, P., Ganobcsik-Williams, L., & Sinha, A. (Eds.). (2012). *Writing programs worldwide: Profiles of academic writing in many places*. Fort Collins, CO: The WAC Clearinghouse and Parlor Press.

Note

1. This article has been adapted from its original publication in the Second Language Newsletter and can be found here: http://newsmanager.commpartners.com/tesolslwis/issues/2013-10-07/3.html

CASE 7

"NOT HOW, BUT WHY"

Training Consultants to Work Thoughtfully Online

Jennifer Whitaker

The author wrote this piece because she recognized the typical problems many administrators face when setting up online communication centers: external pressure, panic about the *how* of online sessions, and finally, revamped training. In this piece she suggests two successful aspects of training consultants to work online: making the connection between platform and philosophy explicit and anticipating student expectations for online tutoring.

Our Online Writing Center (OWC) first grew out of an ethical obligation: if we stayed true to our mission to work with all writers across the university, then we had to include the needs not just of face-to-face, on-campus students (or "terrestrial" students, as we've taken to fondly calling them), but also those of the growing distance-learning population. And so, in 2006, we embarked on what we thought would be the hardest work of running an online peer-consulting center: the upstart. We surveyed how colleagues at other schools offered online sessions, tested multiple models, decided (finally!) on one that fit our needs, and—not without a feeling of brief triumph—presented it to our consultants as we trained them in the procedures and policies we'd designed to support that model.

But—and you knew this was coming—when we started actually *doing* online sessions, the consultants' reflections were, at best, underwhelmed (and underwhelming); indeed, conversations had taken place with writers, and writers seemed to leave the online center thinking differently about their work than when they'd started the session. However, the typical energy for the work—usually palpable among consultants—was missing. When pressed, one consultant admitted, "there wasn't anything *wrong* with my [online] session, but there wasn't really anything *right*, either."

Of course, in hindsight, the problem presented itself obviously: we'd trained consultants in the logistics of connecting with writers (fetishizing the steps of using the chat client or highlighting text in Google Docs, for instance), but neglected to train them to consider the implications of working online. We had carefully designed strategies that supported online peer conversations, but we hadn't yet made the thinking behind those decisions apparent to consultants. We were so worried about the *differences* between online and face-to-face work that we forgot to train consultants to rely and build on the *similarities* in all of our work with writers, regardless of venue.

I offer this piece of history of my own center—the University of North Carolina-Greensboro's University Writing Center—because, after talking with countless colleagues at conferences and in conversation forums, I recognize it to be so typical of the progression many administrators face when setting up online communication centers: from external pressure, to panic about the *how* of online sessions, finally to revamped training. To that end, I offer the two most successful facets I've found for training consultants to work online: the connection between platform and philosophy, and the anticipation of student expectations online.

Essential to training consultants to work effectively online is making visible the connection between administrators' choice of online platform and the center's philosophy. Because our philosophy focuses on conversation as the key to good peer consulting, a synchronous model provided the only way we felt we could do online work. (We would never consider giving feedback on a piece of writing absent a conversation with the writer in our face-to-face center, so we didn't feel that we could, in good conscience, choose an asynchronous model of emailing feedback, for instance.) Once we made evident in training the connection between our center's overall philosophy and our choice of a synchronous online model, consultants could begin to see for themselves how they would make choices in online sessions, relying on their already deep understanding of how to engage students in conversation, how continually to assess and equalize the power dynamics of a session, and how to make sure authority over the piece in question stays with the student.

Of course, making the most of an online session necessitates an awareness of what we expect from online interactions and how we're positioned when we are online (see Benson, 2014). In training, consultants now work their way through the implications of how our usual online activity (such as online shopping, social media, and internet-based research) affects the space of the online peer-to-peer conversation. Consultants tease out the latent expectations that students (and for that matter, all of us!) have in the online environment—expectations that include consumerism (encouraging a stance of passive recipient rather than active participant within the session) and encyclopedic knowledge (reinforcing the idea that knowledge is located external to the student). In doing so, consultants see how the center's policies, procedures, and consulting strategies can counter the expectations so inimical to peer conversation.

As one consultant offered following the revamped training: "I feel more confident now that I know not just *how*, but *why* we do what we do in our online center." Pulling back the curtain on our administrative choices when training consultants to work online returns the focus to a productive conversation between two engaged peers and that, of course—face-to-face or online—is always our goal.

Reference

Benson, A. (2014). "We also offer online services at Interpellation.edu": Althusserian hails and online writing centers. *Southern Discourse in the Center: A Journal of Multiliteracy and Innovation, 19*(1), 11–25.

CASE 8

PEER CONSULTANT EVALUATION

Nicole Magee and Carley Reynolds

Evaluations are crucial for improving overall quality of the staff and for internal and external assessment purposes. This form contains questions on details of the peer tutoring consultant's behaviors and skills. The questions cover aspects of initial interactions, listening, and feedback, among others. The form can become the basis for creating more complex or simple evaluation forms to match the particular needs of a specific peer tutoring center.

Peer Consultant Evaluation				
	Excellent	Good	Fair	Poor
Initial Interaction—A thoughtful first interaction between the consultant and the client will allow rapport to develop.				
Greeting—promptly addresses client with friendly greeting and introduction				
Engagement—questions are asked to get client comfortable with talking				
Inquiry—questions are asked that are specific to assignment				
Agenda setting—goal(s) are set for the appointment				
Effective Listening—A consultant needs to be comfortable listening more and talking less.				
Attention—undivided attention is given to client				
Encouragement—verbal and nonverbal support offered (smiling, nodding, eye contact, saying "Go on," "yes," etc.)				
Silence—strategically uses silence in order to encourage client to elaborate				
Note taking—notes are taken when necessary to help facilitate appointment				

Peer Consultant Evaluation				
	Excellent	Good	Fair	Poor
Feedback—Feedback allows both the client and consultant to discuss problem areas and to develop a plan.				
Self-reflection—begins by asking clients how they think they did, allowing them to make suggestions first				
Evaluation—distinguishes between higher and lower order concerns				
Critique—uses sandwich method to present strengths and weaknesses of work				
Prioritize/Focus—advice is focused on what client can accomplish				
Critical Thinking—Consultants should ask the clients specific questions to encourage critical thinking.				
Understanding—makes sure the client fully understands the objective of the task. Ex: Could you elaborate further? Could you be more specific?				
Relevance—asks questions about the relation of client's argument to the issues. Ex: How does that relate to the problem? How does that help us with the issue?				
Breadth/Depth—leads client to see problem in a different way. Ex: What factors make this a difficult problem? Do we need to look at this in other ways?				
Logic—leads client to question validity of argument. Ex: Does this make sense all together? Does what you say follow from the evidence?				
End Remarks—It is vital to end the appointment with positive and encouraging words.				
Review agenda—discusses what was and still needs to be accomplished				
Positive finish—consultant ends appointment on a positive note				
Motivation—client is motivated to continue working on assignment and/or making additional appointments				
Personal reflection—consultant reflects on what went well and what can be improved for future appointments				
Overall Effectiveness—Consultant must remain professional and on task during an appointment.				
Time management—appointment time is efficiently and appropriately used				
Organization—appointment follows clear direction from beginning to end; does not jump between different topics and problems				
Professionalism—consultant maintains professionalism during appointment				
Goals met—goal(s) set at beginning are accomplished				

Peer Consultant Evaluation				
	Excellent	Good	Fair	Poor
Consultant-Client Connection—Allows client to be at ease and have confidence while working with consultant.				
Personable—consultant is open and friendly throughout appointment				
Trustworthy—consultant provides accurate information and reliable advice				
Credibility—consultant speaks and gives advice with confidence and sincerity				
Collaboration—client and consultant work together toward completing goals				

PART 3
CREATING A SUPPORTIVE AND PRODUCTIVE TUTORING ENVIRONMENT

· 1 1 ·

BUILDING TRUST IN TUTORING THROUGH EFFECTIVE INTERPERSONAL COMMUNICATION

Becky L. Omdahl

Abigail has confidence in her overall ability as a student, but "derails" when she tries to work the assigned college algebra problems. She knows her campus has a Math Tutoring Center. She's willing to try it, but she's anxious: What if the tutor finds out she's three weeks behind on her homework? What if the tutor asks her to work problems that she doesn't even understand?

David's instructor has written in the margin of his paper, "I can't follow your argument. What's your point and where's your supporting evidence? I'd suggest getting some help in the tutoring center before you submit your next paper." David thought he was a good writer who was ready for college-level assignments. His next paper is due in two weeks. If he doesn't improve his skills *fast*, what will happen to his grade in this class?

LaTasha is a new graduate student in political science. One of the more advanced graduate students told her that the tutoring center is excellent at helping students with APA format. Her attitude is to use all the help that is available.

Students come to peer tutoring appointments with a wide range of motivations, prior experiences, and beliefs about their skills and abilities. As illustrated by the opening vignettes, Abigail comes to tutoring with an entrenched belief that she is "bad at" a certain subject. David shows up feeling deflated by a comment from an instructor who exposed a weakness. LaTasha sees tutoring as a great resource to build an important skill set.

Across all students, highly skilled peer tutors work on both content and process levels. On the content level, peer tutors assess how the student is performing on desired skill sets, triage the skill sets that warrant focus, and structure the tutoring session/s to incrementally help the student advance on the target skill/s. On the process level, the tutor gathers information about how the student is thinking and feeling, and carefully works with the information to sustain faith in the process and continued motivation to learn. Peer tutors must monitor both levels and make effective decisions about which level to focus on at any given moment in the tutoring process.

Peer tutoring structures range from one-to-one scheduled appointments to group tutoring sessions, from individual to multiple tutors working together, from tutoring working in traditional centers to highly specialized field or clinical tutoring, from tutors embedded within classes to completely extra-curricular structures (Boud & Cohen, 2001; Falchikov, 2001; Fougner, 2012). Peer tutoring, as opposed to peer learning, encompasses situations in which "advanced students facilitate the learning of less-advanced students" (Fougner, 2012, p. 292).

Across all of these structures for peer tutoring, trust is essential. Trust is defined as "a willingness to place oneself in a relationship that establishes or increases vulnerability with reliance on someone or something to perform as expected" (Jones, 1996, p. 4). Students must trust to make a tutoring appointment, work with the tutor throughout the session, and return for additional appointments. This chapter takes a close look at trust, what leads to trust, and how peer tutors can communicate in ways that promote and maintain trust.

What Is Trust?

Trust has been discussed in every discipline that involves the actions and decisions of people. Most akin to tutoring is the literature of the helping professions. Dinc and Gastmans (2012) review 17 different definitions appearing in the helping professions literature between 1980 and 2010. In trying to understand the reasons for differences in the definitions, they identified some of the underlying debates (e.g., Dinc & Gastmans, 2012; Simpson, 2012). Given that the goal of this chapter is to learn what is needed to build trust in the tutoring process, the debates provide a wealth of information.

One of the key debates focuses on whether trust involves a leap of faith or a rational choice. Anthony Giddens (1991) defines trust as, "the vesting of confidence in persons or abstract systems, made on the basis of a 'leap of faith' which brackets ignorance or lack of information" (p. 244). In contrast, James Coleman (1990) argues that people are rational actors gathering information and deciding whether or not to place a bet on the potential trustee. Those arguing for leap of faith often argue that as social beings, we begin making these leaps at birth and continue them (Simpson, 2012). Others argue that trusting can be a rational decision; people can deduce the likelihood of a desired outcome being met or not, and the costs of counting on the other to assist or not.

From a tutoring perspective, do students simply leap to tutoring or do students carefully assess whether tutoring is a good bet (i.e., the rewards outweigh the costs)? Mayer, Davis, and Schoorman (1995) offer a definition that gives us an escape from answering this question. Their definition allows for both leaping and assessing: "Trust is the willingness of a party to be vulnerable to the actions of another party based on the expectation that the other will perform a particular act important to the trustor, irrespective of the ability to monitor or control that other party" (p. 712). However, the take-away for tutoring is promoting its services both to students ready to make a leap, and those reading the fine print about the potential costs and rewards (e.g., confidentiality, accessibility, nature of tutoring sessions, etc.).

The qualities of the person on whom trust is placed have also been hotly debated. Benevolence is commonly identified as a key quality by the trustee. Baier (1994) writes, "…when I trust another, I depend on her goodwill toward me" (p. 99). Others point to competence as a more important quality, and in cases of professional codes, one that may subsume benevolence. Following this last idea, Simpson (2012) raises the question of whether we need to see benevolence in a well-trained professional operating under a code of conduct that obligates them to apply their knowledge and skill to the situation.

However, in the end, it is clear that both benevolence and competence must exist in the eye of the beholder. For example, Jones (1996) defines trust as "an attitude of optimism that the goodwill and competence of another will extend to cover the domain of our interaction with her, together with the expectation that the one trusted will be directly and favourably moved by the thought that we are counting on her" (p. 4).

The third quality important to those trusting is integrity, meaning that the agent has belief systems or standards leading to the consistent execution of competence and benevolence on his/her behalf. Again, the debates cycle through whether the reliability arises due to social convention, professional requirements, and/or something central to the person (core values, beliefs, and/or and personality); regardless of its impetus, reliability is a quality important to trust (Dinc & Gastmans, 2012).

What Leads to Trust?

The qualities of competence, benevolence, and integrity are not only evident in definitions of trust, but they are also identified as the antecedents to trust. Mayer, Davis, and Schoorman (1995) assert that organizational trust is based on three antecedents: ability, benevolence, and integrity. Jarvenpaa, Knoll, and Leidner (1998) define these antecedents as follows:

> Ability refers to the group of skills that enable a trustee to be perceived competent within some specific domain. Benevolence is the extent to which a trustee is believed to feel interpersonal support and concern, and the willingness to do good to the trustor beyond an egocentric profit motive. Integrity is adherence to a set of principles (such as study/work habits) thought to make the trustee dependable and reliable, according to the trustor. (p. 31)

In the following sections of the chapter, I look at how these three components play out in the tutoring process and how peer tutors can promote them.

Competence

Competence, or the capability of tutors to help students learn, involves many different knowledge and skill sets. Four categories of knowledge and skill required for competent tutoring are: 1) subject or disciplinary; 2) scaffolding and structuring learning progressions; 3) managing time within the tutoring appointment; and 4) tutoring in different modalities (phone, email, Skype, face-to-face). Given the volumes of information that would be required, this chapter will not address subject or disciplinary competence; rather it will focus on overviewing the competencies shared across subject areas.

Scaffolding and Structuring Learning Progressions

Setting the stage for competent learning progressions begins before interactions with students begin. Tutoring centers/coordinators have the responsibility to triage requests and appropriately match students with tutors who possess the appropriate expertise. S. Nielsen (personal communication, June 14, 2014), Tutor Coordinator for the Center for Academic Excellence at Metropolitan State University says, "Centers typically know the capabilities of their tutors and make efforts to find out the subject of focus, the nature of the assignment, and the general level of the student, before assigning a tutor appointment." A graduate student working on a nursing literature review probably needs a different tutor than an introductory composition student working on a short assignment.

Once interactions with the student begin, tutors also engage in triage. What is the assignment? What does the student's current work on the assignment demonstrate in terms of competence on skills and sub-skills? Which skill needs attention first?

While it is an engaging and validating approach to ask students what they would like to work on first, students may offer inaccurate reads based on grades or comments. For example, a student seeing circled grammatical mistakes may state, "I need to work on grammar." The tutor's trained eye might quickly assess that higher order skills need to be a priority. Faculty who were pressed for time might not have spent the thirty minutes required to direct the focus to construction of the main points and subpoints. Circling misspelled words and pointing out grammatical errors is much less time intensive.

The competence of the tutor is reflected and observed in how they identify skills that need focus, and how they guide students throughout the process of their work. "Scaffolding is a process whereby structured guidance is provided that allows the learner to reach a higher level of understanding or competence; it can subsequently be taken away and the learner is able to achieve that level independently" (Winstone & Millward, 2012, p. 59). Scaffolding is best constructed "by providing the environment in which learners can reach new levels of understanding, without being prescriptive and providing all the answers" (Winstone & Millward, 2012, p. 60). A study by Smith (2011) demonstrated that emotional scaffolding may be integrally linked to content scaffolding; students feeling supported by tutors were able to take greater risks with lower levels of negative affect and stress than those working with tutors unable to provide adequate levels of safety and support.

How do tutors scaffold? They analyze the knowledge and skills students have acquired and provide support while students are stretched to work problems, analyze cases, write, or engage in any task that relies on but requires a new application or extension of the knowledge and skills (Winstone & Millward,

2012). Scaffolding involves both content (e.g., Does a student understand the concept of supporting evidence? Can the student identify and incorporate supporting evidence for a subpoint in a paper?) and affect (e.g., encouragement in response to a student identifying statistical evidence for a subpoint). For common skill sets, tutors may use well-developed activities (e.g., series of guided reading questions, sequences of more and more difficult math problems), but in other cases, tutors use highly individualized approaches, even mindful that they are constantly building and supporting the progress. Overall, scaffolding has been found to significantly increase the performance of students in a wide variety of academic tasks (Winstone & Millward, 2012).

Managing a Time-Bound Appointment

The ability of a peer tutor to orchestrate the appointment time impacts evaluations of competence. Students need to complete protocols for the tutoring center (check in, complete short survey about purpose of the visit, etc.) before meeting with the tutor. Tutors need to greet students, provide the opportunity for a minute or two of chatting, and then begin the session. Many tutors find it helpful to manage expectations at the outset (e.g., "We have about 50 minutes to work on your assignment, and we'll need the last five minutes to lay out next steps"). Asking the student for a first focus is a common technique ("What would you like to start with today?"). If the students identifies a starting place that proves to be far from where the tutor's expertise would point (e.g., grammar rather than a thesis), the tutor often steers the student gently to the new focus ("While we're looking out for grammar, what would you think of trying to figure out how we might word the thesis statement?") (S. Nelson, personal communication, June 30, 2014). For the last five minutes, the tutor needs to summarize the work completed ("Great work on the thesis statement and coming up with three main points") and move toward next steps ("During this next week, do you want to work on finding supporting evidence for the main points?").

Often tutoring centers, either due to staffing resources or based on a pedagogical argument that students increase learning through dialogue among students, use group sessions. In group sessions, new members join and old members leave sessions as time progresses. Tutors must be prepared to welcome each new member and orient them to the current focus of the group. As each member leaves, the tutor will need to validate their investment and effort, and clarify next steps.

Tutoring through Different Modalities

Given cost considerations, most academic administrations are aware of the range of tutoring options and the research on their effectiveness. Increasingly, studies are examining the effectiveness of software packages called Intelligent Tutoring Systems (ITS) which can figure out how well a student is performing on skill subsets and assign problems to move them forward in their skill development. ITS are already being used in math and statistics (e.g., ALEKS, WISE, ITS), and they are starting to be used in reading and writing (READ 180, iSTART, and RWISE [Steenbergen-Hu & Cooper, 2014]). Studies are directly comparing the effectiveness of ITS and human tutoring, and how ITS and human tutoring compare to success when no tutoring is offered (e.g., Steenbergen-Hu & Cooper, 2014). To date, studies have found that human tutoring is more effective than ITS tutoring, and both types of tutoring lead to greater student success than no tutoring (Steenbergen-Hu & Cooper, 2014).

As the institutional (e.g., the rise in online and hybrid courses, multi-campus institutions) and individual factors (e.g., time, driving, comfortability with technology) heighten the desire for remote services, the competence of human tutors will be increasingly compared to competence of alternatives like ITS or opportunities to watch a video of a teacher/mentor explaining a concept or working math problems (e.g., Kahn Academy).

Tutors working remotely need to develop skills in effectively using technology. Math tutors need to become fluent in sketching out problems using iPads or white boards projected through Skype. Fax or email plus phone is often an effective modality for writing tutors. While fluency using the technology contributes to the perception of competence, so too does being able to navigate when the technology fails. Knowing how to structure a session that goes from Skype to phone, or other contingencies, is important.

Benevolence

In building trust in peer tutoring relationships, benevolence is critical. In large part this is due to the vulnerability students feel when they are exposing under-developed skills and working to improve them. In addition, given that peer tutors circulate in many of the same social circles, concerns about confidentiality may be heightened. Spence Laschinger, Leiter, Day, Gilin-Oore, and Mackinnon (2012) point out that trust is the critical variable in effective working relationships when vulnerabilities are involved. Rousseau, Sitkin, Burt, and Camerer (1998) state that people "accept vulnerability based on positive expectations of the intentions or behavior of another" (p. 395). In this section of the chapter, the focus will be on four different ways that peer tutors can bolster students' perceptions of benevolence: 1) by offering supportive comments; 2) by understanding the normative process of relationship development and helping students build affective scaffolding; 3) by framing the tutoring process as backstage work; and 4) by understanding shame and how to avoid pushing shame buttons.

Offering Supportive Comments

At the outset of the tutoring process, there are many opportunities for peer tutors to establish their benevolence by offering supportive comments. At its core, benevolence is acting with the other's best interests at heart, desiring to benefit him/her. In tutoring interactions, this can be framed as communicating a desire to help the student attain goals, learn skills, and/or succeed in a class. Based on decades of research on helping and social support, Burleson (2003) concludes that the features of helpful messages are: 1) openly expressing the desire to provide support or help (e.g., "I really want to help you with your writing/math skills"); 2) declaring positive regard for the target (e.g., "I care about helping you"); 3) expressing concern about the current situation faced by the target (e.g., "I am concerned about the distress you feel when you don't know what to do with your math problems"); 4) expressing availability to the target (e.g., "I'm available for appointments Monday and Tuesday afternoons" or "The center is open for appointments every day except Sunday"); and 5) expressing alliance with the target (e.g., "We'll work together to figure this out"). As illustrated by the examples, these can be accomplished easily by comments made during the tutoring session.

Burleson's (2003) research on supportive messages continues, and his focus is now on the factors making these messages the most impactful. According to Bodie, Burleson, and Jones (2012), message content will have the greatest impact when people think about a message a great deal. Increased thinking is typical when people face highly difficult and challenging events. In these situations, the extent to which the message is person-centered (i.e., focused on the well-being and needs of the message receiver) is expected to significantly improve emotions. The applications from the research by Bodie, Burleson, and Jones (2012) to peer tutoring are easy to draw: When students are at low points (e.g., feeling like failures, struggling in their quest for new skills), the ability of a peer tutor to offer highly personal supportive messages will have the greatest impact in changing the student's emotional experience and relative pride in their developing skills.

Understanding Normative Relationship Development

Even when comments are made to heighten the perception of the peer tutor's goodwill or helpfulness, students are likely to have moments of feeling vulnerable. Understanding how the content and nature of tutoring differs from typical relationship development provides a context for understanding this vulnerability. Over four decades ago, Altman and Taylor (1973) posited a theory of relationship development. The Social Penetration Theory posits that relationships develop through self-disclosure, and progress from shallow levels of disclosure characterized by exchanges of less vulnerable information (e.g., "I'm from Wisconsin") to deeper levels of disclosure in which people share information that makes them highly vulnerable (e.g., "I tried so hard in algebra, and I just couldn't understand what the instructor was saying. I flunked my test last week"). Progressing from shallow to deep information allows people to manage risks (potential costs) in comparison to rewards (Altman & Taylor, 1973). The costs of being negatively evaluated or having confidential information shared must be balanced against the positive outcomes of being heard and validated.

The resulting progression is a sequence of stages, with each subsequent stage involving greater risks and rewards (Altman & Taylor, 1973). If emotional safety falters or fails, the relations may be aborted, or the progression reverts to an earlier stage or further testing at the current stage. In the orientation stage, highly reciprocal self-disclosures follow established norms. The parties provide one another with relatively risk-free information that would typically be deemed socially desirable. At the exploratory affective stage, the self-disclosures progress to include experiences and attitudes that, although still largely consistent with social norms, provide the conveyer with a glimpse of the acceptance, supportiveness, and trustworthiness of the other. If the responses at the exploratory affective exchange reflect acceptance and/or support, the relationship progresses to the affective stage. At this stage, the participants become more open in conveying riskier thoughts, feelings, opinions, and experiences. If interactions over time at this stage continue to lead to acceptance, support, and trustworthiness, the relationship may progress to stable exchange. This is the stage at which there is open exchange of even highly risky information, with little monitoring and/or concern about how the other will respond.

Comparing this progression of relationship development with what often happens during the initial stages of tutoring explains some of the vulnerability many students feel. Almost all information about deficits in academic skills or competence would be regarded to involve more risk than the disclosures typical of initial interactions. In initial tutoring sessions, students are frequently jettisoned into conversations about what they don't understand, and skill deficits, which are more characteristics of the stage called affective exchange. They arrive in a stage without having developed the affective scaffolding that supports it.

Using Social Penetration Theory (Altman & Taylor, 1973) as a guide of what to do, tutors would be advised to take some time to build affective scaffolding in the initial session/s. By inviting some phatic communication (e.g., "How's your semester going?" "What's your major?") that transitions into opinion and attitude questions ("What do you like best about your major?"), and responding in highly supportive ways helps build the scaffolding needed for skill and performance-based conversations.

In cases of highly sensitive or anxious students, tutors may also find that suggesting next steps leads to more effective interactions than asking highly open-ended questions. Questions like "What would you like to work on today?" while highly appropriate and effective for many, may go to the heart of some students' challenges and struggles. For struggling students, a simple statement or question such as "go ahead and work the next step" or "what is the central idea of your essay?" can spark anxiety.

Establishing Tutoring as a "Backstage" Process

As tutors begin to move into questions likely to tap perceived weaknesses, peer tutors can also establish their benevolence by framing the context of the interaction. Erving Goffman (1959) talked about all social interaction as being performance based. Called the Dramaturgical Approach, Goffman argued that humans are actors on the stage of life, and across all performances, there is a desire to create impressions by managing performances. In addition to explicating how performances and impressions are managed with costumes, props, and effective performances of rituals, Goffman also argued there can be offstage settings in which actors learn lines and receive coaching on future performances.

Drawing on this metaphor, tutoring is an off-stage performance. Often at the start of tutoring appointments, students may be attempting to perform (i.e., trying to say and do the right things to be perceived as capable). It is a wonderful gift when a peer tutor coaxes a student off the stage and into a side room. By helping the student understand that "we get to work completely off-stage to develop the skills for your test/paper," the student gains essential freedom to take risks. Clear statements like, "In our tutoring sessions, our goal is to learn without evaluations," enable students to try and fail, and try again. Often students need to hear that mistakes are a constructive part of the learning process.

In establishing the tutoring relationship and space as backstage, peer tutors should be prepared to clearly explain the confidentiality assured by their tutoring center. At my university, students are assured that their instructors will never be told that they sought tutoring unless the student wants that information provided to an instructor. At other institutions, instructors are told, and the pledge of confidentiality will need to clarify that the conversations and work done are never shared, and that instructors see it as a sign of dedicated learning to know their students have visited the center. It is an act of benevolence to clearly establish tutoring as a back-stage process in which everyone is free to make mistakes as they work toward goals.

Minimizing Shame

Although supportive communication and establishing tutoring as a back-stage arena do much to establish benevolence, there will still be times when tutors need to exhibit high levels of emotional intelligence in recognizing and responding to emotions. Being effective at working with people around performance issues requires the ability to recognize and work with the emotions in appropriate, constructive, and supportive ways.

One of the most powerful emotions likely to emerge in the tutoring process is shame. Shame arises from the perception that self is flawed, or doesn't measure up. Retzinger (1991, 1995) offers one of the well-developed models of shame. She argues that as social beings, the ability to preserve relationships is key to well-being and success. When a person perceives threat to an important relational bond, shame is triggered.

For many students, an important relational bond is formed with the tutor, as the tutors work with them to achieve their academic goals. Sometimes, students who seek tutoring become very attached to people who are supportive and encouraging. The relationship gains even more importance in the mind of the student if the tutee is truly afraid or concerned about his/her success in a class, as the tutor may represent the last hope, the only known strategy, and/ or the only strategy that the student can afford or enact. When the tutoring is related to a required class that could determine whether the student ends up on probation or is academically dismissed, the importance is ramped up all the more.

Retzinger (1991) identifies two occurrences that are likely to trip shame in interactions with important others: 1) when information is requested or exposed that could lead to an undesirable depiction of self (e.g., telling a tutor about negative instructor feedback, admitting that this is the second time taking the class; and 2) when the other signals a threat to a relational bond (e.g., "For the next couple of weeks, you'll need to work with another tutor." "Next semester when you are working with proofs, there are tutors who would be of greater help").

Examples of what might trip shame during tutoring sessions could fill volumes. Among the most difficult is when a student is making serious mistakes that must be corrected. Burleson (2003) addresses "features of unhelpful messages," and they include: telling people that their feelings are wrong; telling people that they are behaving/performing badly; ordering the person to stop emotional displays; telling the person how to think, behave, or act.

Questions or statements that allow the student to drive the focus are often the least threatening in tutoring (e.g., "Talk to me about the key idea for your paper." "Did your teacher give you any guidelines for this assignment?" "Can you talk me though what you are doing as you work this step of the math problem?"). These types of questions give students the ability to control the information and do not as obviously expose deficits. In addition, in cases in which the student will need to work with different tutors, by asking students about their availability and/or their needs for skill development, attention can be placed on finding the tutor who will best meet the student's needs going forward.

In general, peer tutors will avoid many shame buttons by creating and maintaining a supportive rather than defensive climate (Gibb, 1970) to mitigate shame. In a supportive communication climate, the following characteristics are present: 1) comments are descriptive rather than evaluative (e.g., "When I read this paragraph, I'm picking up three ideas."); 2) provisional rather than certain suggestions are offered ("One idea would be to break this paragraph into three."); 3) the interaction is spontaneous rather than strategic

("Do you want to start here?"); 4) there is a problem orientation rather than a control orientation ("When you were talking, you said that a problem with your paper is the lack of a clear focus. What do you think the focus should be?); 5) empathy rather than neutrality is evident ("I am hearing that you are really frustrated with your teacher's feedback."); and 6) the relationship is between equals rather than one of power difference ("We can brainstorm together, and then you can figure what you want to do.").

Through supportive comments, facilitating as much affective scaffolding as possible, helping students see tutoring as "backstage work," and navigating shame buttons with supportive climates, peer tutors can create tutoring environments in which students perceive their tutors and the tutoring center as benevolent agents. As explored earlier, this benevolence will contribute to increased levels of trust.

Integrity

Integrity is the third antecedent to trust, and another key aspect for tutoring centers. Consistency in professionalism is crucial to integrity at a tutoring center. To increase integrity, training of peer tutors needs to place great emphasis on bringing their best to every tutoring session. They need to commit to a core set of beliefs that every student can learn, that every student deserves quality tutoring, and that they need to continuously hone the complex tutoring skill set. With this emphasis on consistent professionalism across the board, working with the same tutor should not be necessary, although it may affect the comfort level of some students.

There are advantages and disadvantages in allowing students to work with the same tutor across multiple sessions. Among the advantages of working with the same tutor are developing the affective scaffolding that allows a student to be vulnerable while working on skill development, better sequencing of skill development across multiple sessions, and increased accountability, with a tutor who can see whether work has or has not been done. A system of working with different tutors enables students to see triangulated assessments of where they need to focus skill development, and if multiple courses are involved, can lead to potentially better tutor matches for the content matter.

Arguing for established one-to-one tutoring relationships across the entire first year is a recent nursing study, which documented the enhanced retention and performance of students assigned to their personal tutor on day one of courses ("Personal Tutor Support," 2012). The key finding of the study by Jayne Evans was that good relationships with individually assigned tutors reduced the numbers of students leaving the program because they had not integrated academically or socially into higher education ("Personal Tutor Support," 2012). However, most institutions are unable to ensure that the same student will be able to consistently work with the same tutor, mainly due to the financial costs of such a system, so the reliability of competent and benevolent tutoring being provided rests on the center.

Part of this responsibility for consistent quality, and therefore enhanced integrity of the tutoring center, can be fulfilled by managing expectations. Literature provided by the tutoring center should clearly state that over the course of a semester, students are encouraged to work with the center multiple times, and that they are likely to work with different tutors on different visits. Discussions with students should likewise clarify whether the peer tutors assigned in classes will remain consistent for entire semesters. Regardless of the specific tutor assigned, centers need to train their tutors to deliver consistently high quality services so that students have consistently good experiences.

Peer tutors may also benefit from identifying the forces giving rise to their integrity. The tutoring center is likely to be a force through effective training and clear standards. Standards of ethics, embodied in an ethical code, is one way of enhancing integrity. This topic, as well as how to use a code of ethics in tutor training, is discussed in Chapter 12 "Communicating Ethos at the Center" of this book. Personal values centered on their desire to nurture the development of other students are also central to many peer tutors' commitment to their work.

Conclusion

In the tutoring process, trust is essential if students are to make appointments, engage in the work required for skill development, and return for more visits. Trust is engendered when students encounter peer tutors who are competent, benevolent, and operate with consistent integrity. Peer tutors demonstrate competence through their disciplinary expertise, ability to scaffold student learning, structure sessions effectively, and demonstrate effectiveness in the modality selected (e.g., face-to-face, email, Skype). Benevolence is displayed through supportive comments, respect for vulnerabilities introduced, establishing that tutoring is "backstage" work, avoiding the needless tripping of shame buttons, and instead focusing on the creation of a supportive climate. Finally, integrity requires careful work by both the center directors and peer tutors.

It is largely the responsibility of center directors and tutor coordinators to train and set standards so as to ensure the consistent competence and benevolence of all peer tutors. However, most importantly, peer tutors themselves must be committed to ensuring a quality tutoring experience for all students. The demonstration of these qualities promises to build peer tutoring that enables students to seek and receive help that contributes greatly to their academic journeys.

References

Altman, I., & Taylor, D. (1973). *Social penetration: The development of interpersonal relationships*. New York, NY: Holt.

Baier, A. C. (1994). *Moral prejudices: Essays on ethics*. Cambridge, MA: Harvard University Press.

Bodie, G. D., Burleson, B. R., & Jones, S. M. (2012). Explaining the relationships among supportive message quality, evaluations, and outcomes: A dual process approach. *Communication Monographs, 79*, 1–22.

Boud, D., & Cohen, R. (2001). *Peer learning in higher education: Learning from and with each other*. London, UK: Kogan Page.

Burleson, B. R. (2003). Emotional support skill. In J. O. Greene & B. R. Burleson (Eds.), *Handbook of communication and social interaction skills* (pp. 551–594). Mahwah, NJ: Lawrence Erlbaum Associates.

Coleman, J. S. (1990). *Foundations of social theory*. Cambridge, MA: Belknap Press.

Dinc, L., & Gastmans, C. (2011). Trust and trustworthiness in nursing: An argument-based literature review. *Nursing Inquiry, 19*(3), 223–237.

Falchikov, N. (2001). *Learning together*. London, UK: Routledge Falmer.

Fougner, A. (2012). Exploring knowledge through peer tutoring in a transitional learning community: An alternative way of teaching counseling skills to students in social work education. *Social Work Education, 31*, 278–301.

Gibb, J. (1970). Sensitivity training as a medium for personal growth and improved interpersonal relationships. *Interpersonal Development, 1*, 6–31.

Giddens, A. (1991). *Modernity and self identity: Self and society in the late modern age*. Cambridge, MA: Polity Press.

Goffman, E. (1959). *Presentation of self in everyday life*. New York, NY: Anchor Books/ Doubleday.

Jarvenpaa, S. L., Knoll, K., & Leidner, D. (1998). Is anybody out there? Antecedents of trust in global virtual teams. *Journal of Management Information Systems, 14*(4), 29–64.

Jones, K. (1996). Trust as an affective attitude. *Ethics, 107*, 4–25.

Mayer, R. C., Davis, J. H., & Schoorman, F. D. (1995). An integrative model of organizational trust. *Academy of Management Review, 20*(3), 709–734.

Personal Tutor Support from the Start Reduces Student Attrition. (2012). *Nursing Standard*, 27(6), 6.

Retzinger, S. (1991). *Violent emotions: Shame and rage in marital quarrels*. Newbury Park, CA: SAGE.

Retzinger, S. (1995). Identifying shame and anger in discourse. *American Behavioral Scientist*, 38, 1104–1113.

Rousseau, D. M., Sitkin, S. B., Burt, R. S., & Camerer C. (1998). Not so different after all: A cross-discipline view of trust. *Academy of Management Review*, 23, 393–404.

Simpson, T. W. (2012). What is trust? *Pacific Philosophical Quarterly*, 93, 550–569.

Smith, V. (2011). It's the relationship that matters: A qualitative analysis of the role of the student-tutor relationship in counseling training. *Counseling Psychology Quarterly*, 24, 233–246.

Spence Laschinger, H. K., Leiter, M. P., Day, A., Gilin-Oore, D., & Mackinnon, S. P. (2012). Building empowering work environments that foster civility and organizational trust: Testing an intervention. *Nursing Research*, 61(5), 316–325.

Steenbergen-Hu, S., & Cooper, H. (2014). A meta-analysis of the effectiveness of intelligent tutoring systems on college students' academic learning. *Journal of Educational Psychology*, 106, 331–347.

Winstone, N., & Millward, L. (2012). The value of peers and support from scaffolding: Applying constructivist principles to the teaching of psychology. *Psychology Teaching Review*, 18, 59–67.

· 1 2 ·

COMMUNICATING ETHOS
AT THE CENTER

Kristen Hoerl, Mercedes Kolb,
Ethan Gregerson, and William Butler

Tutoring center staff must communicate their credibility to effectively assist students. Ethos is a term used within the discipline of rhetoric to describe the process of demonstrating one's good character and credibility. Based on the works of Aristotle, ethos is one of three devices or modes of argumentative support. *Ethos* refers to the character of the speaker, whereas *logos* concerns effective reasoning and *pathos* relates to the use of emotional appeals. Although they are often considered separately, appeals to ethos, logos, and pathos may function collectively to persuade an audience. While a speaker's prior reputation influences audience perceptions, the concept of ethos fundamentally concerns how speakers demonstrate their character through discourse. Like logos and pathos, ethos is constructed rhetorically through the process of interaction (Baumlin, 1994). Ethos is a matter of practical importance for tutors; in order to believe that a visit to a tutoring center is valuable, students need to believe that tutors are knowledgeable and trustworthy. In this chapter we describe different dimensions of ethos and explain how they might apply to peer tutoring centers, particularly for those that employ undergraduate tutors.

Communicating Wisdom

Smith (2004) identifies wisdom and goodwill as two dimensions of ethos that have particular salience to peer tutoring practice. Wisdom is a multifaceted dimension of ethos that involves both specific knowledge of the subject under consideration and practical wisdom, or the "capacity to apply a rational principle to practical situations that call for a choice about actions" (p. 11). As Smith explains, wisdom is grounded in "knowledge based on the speakers' experience that guides good practice … in a contingent and diverse world" (p. 11). Effective tutors should convey specific knowledge about the subject matter under discussion and they must demonstrate tutoring ability by providing appropriate feedback and advice to students.

Tutor education and training can provide an important foundation to develop skills necessary to communicate wisdom.[1] Practical wisdom in tutoring situations calls for adaptive communication that is sensitive to the variety of relationships that structure student learning, including relationships between tutors and tutees, faculty and students, and student groups outside the classroom. Furthermore, tutors should be able to offer guidance and feedback that enables tutees to develop their own critical thinking capacities and skills. Effective tutors also exercise practical wisdom as they ask questions that help them determine what aspect of their assignments tutees understand, how tutees approach their own learning process, and what their instructors expect of them. When students visit a tutoring center to fulfill an instructor's requirement, it is particularly important that tutors assess the tutee's own goals and investments in their learning process. As Locke and Latham (2002) argue, students with specific goals pay more attention to and learn more from educational activities. Assessing students' goals and investments in the outcome of the session requires careful audience adaptation, which is a point that we will discuss in the following passages.

Communicating Goodwill

Goodwill is another dimension of ethos. Smith (2004) defines goodwill as the demonstration of offering advice without the expectation of reciprocation from the audience. In other words, goodwill communicates that the tutor has the tutee's best interests at heart. Hyde's (2004) definition of ethos in terms of a dwelling place, or radical openness to the other, elaborates on the philosophical dimensions of goodwill. The concept of unconditional positive regard addresses this principle from a psychological perspective. Regarding therapists' relationships with their clients, Rogers (1992) defines unconditional positive regard as "caring for the client, but not in a possessive way or in such a way as to simply satisfy the therapists' own needs" (p. 829). Cuny, Wilde, and Stephenson (2012) argue that peer tutors must convey unconditional positive regard to establish an effective tutoring relationship with tutees. They suggest that nonverbal communication practices including "maintaining comfortable eye contact and pleasing facial expressions" increase unconditional positive regard (p. 253). These authors also recommend that tutors refer to tutees specifically by name and start and end their consultations on time (p. 253).

As the above discussion suggests, the process of constructing the tutor's credibility is grounded in the process of interaction between tutors and tutees. Since determining the audience's beliefs is the key to building credibility, ethos develops not only through what the speaker says but through the relationship between the speaker and the audience, as well. Consequently, ethos is grounded in identification, or the process of establishing common ground between the tutor and tutee. As Burke (1969) observes, "you persuade a man [sic] only insofar as you can talk his language by speech, gesture, tonality, order, image, attitude, [and] idea, *identifying* your ways with his" (p. 55). These communication strategies provide the "'signs' of character needed to earn the audience's good will" (pp. 55–56). Likewise, tutees may be convinced of a tutor's advice only when they believe that the tutors understand and identify with them. Establishing identification occurs in the process of building positive relationships between tutors and tutees during a tutoring session.

Our desire to build identification with students visiting our peer tutoring center informs the language we use to describe staff and visiting students. We have decided to adopt the more traditional model of a "tutor-tutee" relationship rather than the corporate language describing one-to-one education in terms of "consultant-client" communication. In the process of making this decision, staff members commented that the language of "consultants" and "clients" implicitly suggested a hierarchical relationship between the educator and the student. They reasoned that "consultants" refer to specialists who provide their expertise for a fee to "clients." Alternatively, the labels of tutors and tutees foregrounded their mission of helping their peers through the process of interaction and the mutual exchange of ideas. Centers that use the language of consultant-client relationships may certainly be committed to educational development and student engagement. Our own decision should not imply strict rules or guidelines for determining language strategies used to establish ethos in tutoring centers; rather, these strategies require practical judgment that is rooted in tutors' and center directors' adaptation to the contextual factors that shape their interactions with students and others involved with the center. This approach draws upon the assumption of communication accommodation theory that communication is effective when interactants accommodate their communication behavior "to the interlocutor's perceived individual and group preferences" (Gallois, Ogay, & Giles, 2004, p. 136). The language a peer tutoring center uses to describe its mission and staff roles should respond to the needs and perspectives of its particular campus community.

Our effort to identify with students visiting the center also guides tutors' decisions to not enforce a specific staff dress code. Staff members typically wear clothing that they would wear to class in an effort to communicate approachability and to reinforce their peer relationship with tutees. Adapting nonverbal communication style including dress to mirror the tutor's behavior to the tutee's behavior may be useful to create and maintain positive personal and social identities in the tutoring center (Gallois et al., 2004). However, some of our newer tutors sometimes prefer to wear business-casual attire to communicate their credibility. Some sophomores comment that wearing slacks or skirts instead of jeans conveys their authority to juniors and seniors who might otherwise question the wisdom of their advice. These students echo findings that employees often select attire to manage impressions and self-perceptions in the workplace (Peluchette, Karl, & Rust, 2006). However, there are no universal standards for appropriate professional attire because different forms of dress convey different professional characteristics that are important to particular workplace situations (Peluchette et al., 2006). Although dressing professionally to increase ethos for younger tutors may make sense in some cases, in general we believe that efforts to identify with tutees through less formal attire has enabled our tutors to build rapport with students.

Generative Ethos

Just as goodwill is established through the interactions between tutors and tutees, tutors' wisdom is communicated in the context of the tutoring session. Corder (1994) suggests that knowledge itself is not universal and does not exist somewhere a priori outside of human experience. "When we speak, we stand somewhere, and our standing place makes both known and silent claims upon us. We make truth, if at all, out of what is incomplete, or partial" (p. 128). Corder thus argues for a "generative" model of ethos that is constructed when a speaker "gives the hearer free room to live in" (p. 128).

For tutors, attention to generative ethos means recognizing that their own advice is drawn from knowledge that is a product of their particular location within the university. In other words, tutors' understandings of what constitutes appropriate communication and academic excellence depend upon their prior experiences and education. No one single strategy will work equally for each tutor, nor will one particular strategy be equally appropriate for every tutee. Training sessions and staff meetings provide an opportunity for tutoring staff to share different ideas for approaching specific tutoring situations with the understanding that each session will require some degree of adaptation and flexibility.

To some extent, Corder's (1994) interest in the position of the speaker parallels standpoint epistemology's attention to the ways in which knowledge is structured by one's social location. As Jarratt and Reynolds (1994) argue, ethos is informed by our position within asymmetrical social structures such as race, class, and gender from which we speak. They conclude that "the ideas of place, position, and standpoint in feminist theory offer us a way of reconceiving ethos as an ethical political tool—as a way of claiming and taking responsibility for our positions in the world, for the ways we see, for the places from which we speak" (p. 52). Tutors and tutees are positioned "within networks of gender, class, and power" that structure the university (p. 57). Thus, peer tutors should recognize that their own educational experiences may differ from other tutors and tutees depending on their age, race, class, and gender. This information should guide tutors in providing responsive feedback without showing partiality to any particular tutees.

Another aspect of generative ethos is the mutually constitutive nature of knowledge construction that emerges through persuasive communication. Corder (1994) writes that, "generative language seeks to … stretch words out beyond our private universe" (p. 128). When tutors and tutees exchange ideas, both speakers and audiences' worldviews expand. Within the tutoring context, both tutors and tutees should expect to have their perspectives changed through their interactions during a tutoring session. Generative ethos is critical to the tutor's role as a facilitator of student learning. Rather than provide answers to questions, a tutor's job is to provide feedback that helps tutees develop new insights and arrive at their own conclusions.

This perspective on ethos aligns with Cuny et al.'s (2012) emphasis on empathetic listening as a critical tutoring practice. Empathetic listening requires the tutor to understand the tutee's point of view. Drawing from the work of Stewart and Logan (2002), Cuny et al. describe focusing, encouraging, and reflecting as three competencies of empathetic listening. Focusing refers to the full attention that tutors should give to tutees. Encouraging involves motivating tutees to elaborate on their ideas by asking them "clarifying and open questions" (p. 252). Reflecting refers to the tutor's ability to articulate and respond to the tutee's perspective through "paraphrasing the speakers' words or adding an example that the peer tutor believes illustrates the speakers' perspective" (p. 252). Because ethos construction is a process by which both the tutor and tutee's worldviews are transformed, effective tutors should not only convey openness to their tutees' communication and goals, but also reflect on their own experiences and draw lessons from them. Tutors should expect that their own communication and advice will develop over time as they learn from their experiences.

Communicating Ethos during the Tutoring Session

In the following discussion, we elaborate on specific strategies that tutors at our particular center use to build ethos during tutoring sessions. Because ethos construction depends on effective audience adaptation, we provide a brief discussion of our student body to contextualize our strategies. Our institution is a mid-sized private college located in a large city in the Midwest. Although 2.8% of the student body is international, the majority of our students grew up in the Midwestern United States, 59% of our students are female, and 82% are White. Our peer-to-peer tutoring center is staffed exclusively by undergraduate students who are representative of the demographics of the larger student body (although approximately 50% of our staff is female). Our recommendations represent those strategies that we have found useful on a consistent basis. However, we also recognize that these strategies also reflect the social norms and expectations of the demographics of our student body.

Constructing Ethos during Session Introductions

The first minutes of interaction during an initial tutoring session are crucial to establish ethos because this communication sets the tone for the rest of the session. Our tutors recommend a couple of strategies to generate goodwill early during sessions. Their first recommendation is to build rapport. Tutors could begin their sessions by engaging tutees in brief conversations about subjects unrelated to their reason for visiting the center such as weather conditions, events on campus, other projects they are working on, or semester schedules. Tutors could also observe points of commonality between themselves and the tutees. These conversations often create a welcoming environment and ease potential discomfort tutees might have in seeking advice and help from a peer for the first time.

It is often helpful to inquire about how students are feeling when they visit the center because this also helps tutors determine how to approach the rest of the session. For instance, if a student reports feeling apprehensive about the assignment, tutors could provide strategies for approaching the assignment that may help to reduce this anxiety. However, sometimes students who appear apprehensive or disengaged express concern about issues unrelated to the session, or report feeling physically unwell. In these instances, tutors could offer strategies to help them focus or, in some cases, recommend rescheduling the session.

Once tutors believe that they have established rapport, they could seek information about the tutee's reasons for visiting the center and ask questions to discern the tutee's attitude toward the visit. In order to respond empathetically to students' concerns, tutors might find it helpful to start by having a conversation about what tutees want to accomplish. Likewise, tutors could ask students to identify aspects of their assignment they feel confident about and aspects of their assignment that they would like to refine or develop further. Tutors should discuss the assignment with the tutees to determine a primary goal for the tutoring session.

From there, tutors should invite the tutee to work together to build an agenda and allocate time for each item that builds toward that goal. When an agenda is set, "the phases of the tutoring session are made explicit so that there's a better chance for mutual input and understanding" (Macauley, 2005, p. 3). The tutor should refer back to the agenda often to properly allocate time and stay on task. It is often the case that the tutor is not able to address all of the points identified on the agenda. When this happens, tutors could encourage tutees to continue working on the agenda on their own. As Macauley (2005) notes, an agenda is almost more important for a tutor's success after a session has ended because it coaches the student to learn to work successfully without the tutor's help.

By asking tutees to articulate their own goals, tutors help students develop their academic voice. In order to develop their communication skills and intellectual abilities, tutees should take ownership of their learning process. Providing an opportunity for tutees to discuss their own investments in their learning gives their own "room to live" (Corder, 1994, p. 128). By asking tutees what they want to accomplish, tutors indicate that their role is not to provide instruction but to explore how students might expand on or revise their own skills and understanding.

Tutees' explanations could also provide useful information for tutors to respond to in order to effectively communicate practical and generative wisdom. Students' comments about their own goals helps tutors determine how much effort to put into encouraging tutees' participation during the session. A students' goal orientation influences the amount of time and the quality of their engagement in learning (Ames, 1992; Butler, 1987). Students primarily concerned about mastering material tend to be more involved in the learning process than students who are most interested in receiving high grades (Butler, 1987). Thus, students who express interest in learning may be more involved in the session than students who express an interest in getting a better grade on an assignment. In these instances, a tutor might anticipate spending more time providing constructive criticism with them.

Frequently, students' first visits to a tutoring center have been required by a faculty member to complete a class assignment. Although most students who visit our center arrive to sessions with positive attitudes, students who are required to visit the center sometimes seem reluctant or disengaged from the process. Students provide a variety of reasons for being disengaged. For example, some students do not believe that their school work requires any additional development or improvement, some students dislike or are apprehensive about the subject matter, and some students dislike the instructor who gave the assignment. In these circumstances, we recommend several strategies to elicit tutees' involvement. Tutors could encourage them to discuss their feelings of discomfort and then invite them to elaborate on the content of the assignment itself. By allowing tutees a moment to vent their frustrations, tutors establish their role as empathetic listeners.[2]

After a tutee has had a moment to describe his or her concerns, tutors could respond by expressing their interest in assisting the tutee and in providing a positive learning experience. For instance, one tutor worked with a student who believed that her instructor's teaching style was the primary impediment to her receiving a good grade in the class. This tutor responded by suggesting, "Let's figure out how you can demonstrate responsiveness to what your professor had to say." Another tutor once worked with a student who initially suggested that the tutor would not be able to offer any useful feedback. This tutor responded by sharing an anecdote about a previous session in which a reluctant student gained new insight about an assignment. By recounting previous positive interactions with tutees, the tutor communicated wisdom and goodwill toward the tutoring process and prompted the tutee to anticipate a productive experience.

Another useful approach is to ask students to explain what he or she thinks is meaningful or interesting about the assignment topic. If tutees have chosen the topic for a written or speech assignment, asking them about their decision can generate enthusiasm toward the session. Having an informal conversation about the assignment topic helps students realize their passion for a subject and encourages them to improve upon the assignment. If conversations about the merits of students' topics fail to elicit responsiveness from the tutees, tutors could appeal to more instrumental motives for student participation in the session such as getting a good grade or completing the course. One tutor frequently appeals to students' goals outside of the classroom when they express disdain for their instructors by discussing how completing the assignment might help them meet their professional goals after graduation.

Constructing Ethos While Providing Feedback

The process of providing appropriate feedback during a tutoring session also involves the tutor's demonstration of goodwill and wisdom. To maintain goodwill, tutors should strive to provide feedback that is responsive to the tutee's own goals. They should also offer feedback that demonstrates specific knowledge about tutees' assignments. Since many instructors require students to visit the center as part of their coursework, tutors could familiarize themselves with those assignments in advance. During the session, many tutors at our center recall the assignment criteria from memory; if they are uncertain, they refer to copies of instructor's assignments that are kept on file (even though we would prefer that students take ownership of their education by bringing copies of their assignments to the sessions themselves). By communicating specific understanding of the assignment criteria, tutors demonstrate their competence in the subject matter. Referencing assignment criteria also promotes generative ethos because it sometimes encourages tutees to take a more active interest in their sessions.

Before providing feedback to students, tutors should ask tutees to explain any specific feedback they might have received from their instructors. Instructors teaching the same or similar courses sometimes evaluate assignments using different criteria or by weighing criteria differently, so learning about the feedback that tutees have received from their instructors enables tutors to provide responsive and adaptive comments and suggestions. They also help tutors avoid undermining or contradicting the instructor, which is necessary to maintain the center's credibility with both the instructor and the tutee after the session has ended.

In order to provide encouraging feedback, tutors recommend what they refer to as a "critique sandwich." During a session, a tutor could initially respond to the tutee's work by identifying the tutee's strengths. This approach communicates positive regard for the tutee and could build the tutee's morale. Then, the tutor could point to aspects of the tutees' work that could use improvement. The types of suggestions for improvement could vary depending on the assignment and the tutee's expressed goals for the session. Tutors could conclude the feedback session with a reminder of the strengths of the assignment in order to generate the tutee's enthusiasm for the remaining work to be done.

Finally, to maintain rapport and identification, tutors could offer feedback that reflects the tutee's level of enthusiasm and communication style. If students demonstrate an interest in having a longer conversation about their performance or want to bounce some ideas around during the session, tutors could ask more probing questions about their ideas; however, if a student expresses a desire to leave the session early, they could choose not to pursue further conversation. Letting tutees direct the length of the session promotes generative ethos by reinforcing the importance of the tutees' own goals and investments in learning outcomes.

Constructing Ethos during Session Conclusions

Several communication strategies to end a session can reinforce tutors' wisdom and goodwill toward students. We believe that these strategies contribute to students' decisions to make repeat visits to the tutoring center. Although students' first visits to our center are usually required by an instructor, many students voluntarily return for follow up appointments. Some students also return to the center in following semesters. Tutors should announce the end of a session by asking tutees what they learned from the session and what they plan to work on later as a result. We recommend that tutors ask tutees what they learned, rather than remind them of what they worked on for a variety of reasons. Asking tutees to summarize what they learned reinforces the center's identity as a space for collaborative learning. By asking tutees to assess their own progress, tutors emphasize the tutee's ownership over the knowledge generated during the session. Finally, tutees' responses can help tutors assess their own effectiveness in communicating advice. If tutees are unclear about what they learned from the session, tutors could then summarize two or three central recommendations for improvement.

Before students leave the center, tutors could remind tutees of the days that they work in the center and encourage them to schedule follow-up appointments for additional feedback. They could also remind tutees of their strengths and the feasibility of meeting their goals. Tutors could also mirror the rapport-building behaviors that they used to introduce the session. For example, tutors could end the session with a brief reference to the small talk that opened the session in order to demonstrate an interest in the student's general well-being and happiness. Such rapport-building reestablishes identification between the tutor and tutee and reinforces the tutor's unconditional positive regard for the tutee.

Conclusion

We began this chapter by asserting that tutors must communicate their ethos to effectively fulfill their roles. As the rest of the chapter elaborated, a tutor's ethos is constructed *through* a tutor's interaction with a tutee. Communicating ethos is not something that a tutor does in addition to other tutoring activities during a session, but is inextricable from the process of listening to and providing feedback to tutees. Wisdom is communicated via tutors' abilities to demonstrate familiarity with the subject matter at hand and through their adaptation to the particular circumstances of the session. Goodwill is established through tutors' expressed interests in helping students' achieve their own goals. Because no two students share the exact same goals and perspectives, no single approach to establishing ethos will be fitting for every tutoring session. Our emphasis on generative ethos foregrounds a collaborative model of education in which people generate greater awareness of themselves and their social worlds through deliberation with others. Corder (1994) notes that generative ethos brings a listener "into a world that he or she can live in, that has living space and time" (p. 128). For Corder, a speaker's generative ethos issues to audiences "an invitation to a commodious universe" (p. 128). By giving tutees a room to live in, tutors expand their own perspectives. Generative ethos creates environments in which tutors and tutees alike might identify solutions to their academic puzzles and recognize underexplored resources to face their challenges.

References

Ames, G. (1992). Classrooms: Goals, structures, and student motivation. *Journal of Educational Psychology, 84*, 261–271.

Baumlin, J. S. (1994). Positioning *ethos* in historical and contemporary theory. In J. S. Baumlin & T. F. Baumlin (Eds.), *Ethos: New essays in rhetorical and critical theory* (pp. xi–xxxi). Dallas, TX: Southern Methodist University Press.

Burke, K. (1969). *A rhetoric of motives*. New York, NY: Prentice Hall.

Butler, R. (1987). Task-involving and ego-involving properties of evaluation: Effects of different feedback conditions on motivational perceptions, interest, and performance. *Journal of Educational Psychology, 79*, 474–482.

Corder, J. W. (1994). Varieties of ethical argument, with some account of the significance of ethos in the teaching of composition. In R. E. Young & Y. Liu (Eds.), *Landmark essays on rhetorical invention in writing* (pp. 99–134). Davis, CA: Hermagoras Press. (Original work published 1978).

Cuny, K. M., Wilde, S. M., & Stephenson, A. V. (2012). Using empathetic listening to build client relationships at the center. In E. L. Yook & W. Atkins-Sayre (Eds.), *Communication centers and oral communication programs in higher education: Advantages, challenges and new directions* (pp. 249–256). Lanham, MD: Lexington Books.

Gallois, C., Ogay, T., & Giles, H. (2004). Communication accommodation theory. In W. B. Gudykunst (Ed.), *Theorizing about intercultural communication* (pp. 121–148). Thousand Oaks, CA: SAGE.

Hyde, M. J. (2004). Introduction: Rhetorically, we dwell. In M. Hyde (Ed.), *The ethos of rhetoric* (pp. xi–xxvii). Columbia, SC: University of South Carolina Press.

Jarratt, S. C., & Reynolds, N. (1994). The splitting image: Contemporary feminisms and the ethics of ethos. In J. S. Baumlin & T. F. Baumlin (Eds.), *Ethos: New essays in rhetorical and critical theory* (pp. 37–63). Dallas, TX: Southern Methodist University Press.

Locke, E. A., & Latham, G. P. (2002). Building a practically useful theory of goal setting and task motivation: A 35-year odyssey. *American Psychologist, 57*, 705–717.

Macauley, W. J. (2005). Setting the agenda for the next thirty minutes. In B. Rafoth (Ed.), *A tutor's guide: Helping writers one to one* (pp. 1–8). Portsmouth, NH: Boynton/Cook Publishers.

Peluchette, J. V., Karl, K., & Rust, K. (2006). Dressing to impress: Beliefs and attitudes regarding workplace attire. *Journal of Business Psychology, 21*, 45–63.

Rogers, C. R. (1992). The necessary and sufficient conditions of therapeutic personality change. *Journal of Counseling and Clinical Psychology, 60*(6), 827–832.

Smith, C. R. (2004). *Ethos* dwells persuasively: A hermeneutic reading of Aristotle on credibility. In M. J. Hyde (Ed.), *The ethos of rhetoric* (pp. 1–19). Columbia, SC: University of South Carolina Press.

Stewart, J., & Logan, C. (2002). Empathetic and dialogic listening. In J. S. Stewart (Ed.), *Bridges, no walls: A book about interpersonal communication* (8th ed., pp. 208–229). Boston, MA: McGraw-Hill.

Troillett, R., & McIntyre, K. (2012). Best practices in communication center training and training assessment. In E. L. Yook & W. Atkins-Sayre (Eds.), *Communication centers and oral communication programs in higher education: Advantages, challenges and new directions* (pp. 257–272). Lanham, MD: Lexington Books.

Notes

1. See Troillett and McIntyre (2012) for a discussion of best practices recommended for tutor training and training assessment.
2. However, we do not want to suggest that we encourage tutors to mirror students' dissatisfaction with a particular instructor or assignment.

· 1 3 ·

ENGAGING IN EFFECTIVE INSTRUCTIONAL COMMUNICATION BEHAVIORS IN THE TUTORING RELATIONSHIP

Scott A. Myers, Jordan Atkinson, Hannah Ball,
Zachary W. Goldman, Melissa F. Tindage,
and Shannon T. Carton

For decades, instructional communication scholars—whose focus is on the examination of communication variables that affect the teaching process across grade levels, subject matter, and instructional settings (Staton, 1989)— have concentrated their research efforts on examining the link between instructors' use of in-class communicative behaviors and student learning outcomes (Myers, 2010). Collectively, these scholars have found that when instructors simultaneously utilize several rhetorical and relational communication behaviors in the college classroom, students not only view these instructors favorably in terms of perceived instructors' credibility, approachability, and teaching effectiveness (see Mottet, Richmond, & McCroskey, 2006, for a review), but they also report gains in their affective learning (i.e., students' positive attitudes toward instruction, learning, and instructors), cognitive learning (i.e., students' retention of content and information delivered through instruction), and state motivation (i.e., students' attempts to obtain knowledge or skills from instruction) as well as an increase in their levels of communication satisfaction with their instructors (Myers, Goodboy, & Members of COMM 600, 2014; Waldeck, Plax, & Kearney, 2010).

An alternative venue for applying the study of rhetorical and relational instructional communication behaviors is the peer tutoring context. According to Roscoe and Chi (2007), peer tutoring involves the "the recruitment of one student to provide one-on-one instruction for another student," with the idea that peer tutors are "more expert or advanced" (p. 535) than their clients. Given the parallels that exist between in-class instruction and peer tutoring (e.g., both instructors and peer tutors are viewed by students and clients as content experts, the instructional session focuses primarily on content mastery, the instructional content is curriculum based), it stands to reason that if peer tutors are mindful of these rhetorical and relational instructional communication behaviors and integrate them into their tutoring repertoire, the positive views, gains, and increases in learning, motivation, and satisfaction as reported by college students would be reported by their clients as well.

The purpose of this chapter is to review five specific instructional communication behaviors that peer tutors should utilize with their clients during their tutoring sessions. To do so, this chapter is divided into two sections. In the first section, we examine the rhetorical and relational approaches to teaching in general. We then identify, define, and explain the five behaviors essential to the student learning process. In the second section, we offer several recommendations for how peer tutors can specifically use these behaviors with their clients.

The Rhetorical and Relational Approaches to Teaching

Viewed best as complementary rather than competing perspectives, the assumption behind the rhetorical and the relational approaches to teaching is that when both sets of instructional communication behaviors are utilized jointly in any learning environment, both the quality and the effectiveness of instruction are enhanced (Beebe & Mottet, 2009). In their conceptualization of these approaches, Mottet and Beebe (2006) posited that instructors enter a learning situation with two goals in mind. The first goal is rhetorical (i.e., the rhetorical approach) and centers on the messages that instructors create as a way to influence or persuade their students to learn; the second goal is relational (i.e., the relational approach) and focuses on how instructors and students mutually create and share meaning as a way to enhance student learning (Beebe & Mottet, 2009). The emphasis of the rhetorical approach is on message design that facilitates effective instruction whereas the emphasis of the relational approach is on collaborative communication that facilitates affective instruction (i.e., the expression of shared emotions and feelings) between instructors and students (Mottet & Beebe; Myers, 2008).

Although there are multiple effective instructional communication behaviors from which instructors and peer tutors can draw upon when teaching, we highlight two rhetorical behaviors (clarity and humor) and three relational behaviors (power, nonverbal immediacy, and affinity seeking) that we believe are particularly appropriate for the peer tutoring context. For peer tutors to be effective, they must possess several abilities. Not only must they be able to "transform their prior knowledge into instructive messages that are relevant, coherent, complete, and accurate" (Roscoe & Chi, 2007, p. 545), but also they should be able to explain things clearly, use appropriate and relevant examples, and develop rapport with their clients (Bell & Mladenovic, 2008). The five behaviors we have selected best encapsulate these abilities. Because peer tutors typically are undergraduate students who have no prior formal training in education or pedagogy, although they may possess the requisite oral communication skills and interpersonal ability needed for effective tutoring (Wilson, 2012), becoming acquainted with these five instructional behaviors is one way in which peer tutors can develop further their effectiveness. The information below can serve as useful guidelines for them to follow in their training sessions.

Teaching from the Rhetorical Approach

The rhetorical approach is instructor-centered, meaning that student learning occurs when instructors intentionally design messages that stimulate student learning (Beebe & Mottet, 2009). Clarity and humor are perhaps the most essential instructional behaviors when teaching from the rhetorical approach.

Clarity

Clarity refers to the instructional messages that instructors use to present information in a way that facilitates students' understanding (Simonds, 1997). For the effects of clarity to be maximized, instructors must be able to differentiate between their use of low-inference behaviors and high-inference behaviors. Low-inference behaviors are those behaviors that can be easily observed by students and include using transition statements between points, providing advanced organizers, and outlining a lecture (Bush, Kennedy, & Cruickshank, 1977). Conversely, high-inference behaviors are those behaviors that are not easily observable, can diminish student understanding (Powell & Harville, 1990), and include lecturing in a vague manner (e.g., using unclear sets of words, lacking precision in word choice), using utterances (i.e., vocalized pauses such as "um," "uh," and "like"), and providing insufficient examples (Land & Smith, 1979). Both these behaviors can emerge in the form of either oral (e.g., lectures, discussion, and feedback) or written (e.g., syllabus, course objectives, exam questions, and course assignments) messages (Sidelinger & McCroskey, 1997).

Perhaps the greatest benefit of instructor clarity is that it affords students the opportunity to better grasp the course material. Because students spend a great amount of time in their classes listening to instructor lectures, taking notes, and making sense of the course material, oral organizational cues provided by the instructor are particularly important. When instructors use organizational cues (e.g., signposts indicating main points, transition statements) during class discussions, students record more organizational points and details in their notes (Titsworth, 2004). In fact, when students listen to lectures containing clearly stated organizational cues, they record twice as many details and four times as many organizational points in their notes than students who listen to lectures that do not contain these cues (Titsworth & Kiewra, 2004).

Humor

Humor is defined broadly as verbal or nonverbal messages that make people laugh (Martin, 2007). Central to comprehending this notion is that for humor use to be effective, both instructors and students must demonstrate an appreciation for humor and they must be able to enact it. Occurring often in tandem, *humor appreciation* refers to an individual's ability to enjoy humorous messages (Miczo, 2012), whereas *humor enactment* refers to a person's intentional creation of verbal or nonverbal humorous messages (Booth-Butterfield & Booth-Butterfield, 1991). In the college classroom, instructors enact humor in many forms. Early research revealed that instructors generally limited their humor attempts to jokes, riddles, puns, funny stories, and funny comments (Bryant, Comisky, & Zillman, 1979). Later research identified additional forms, including instructor use of brief tendentious or disparaging comments directed at a variety of targets, anecdotes (either personal or general) related or unrelated to course content, jokes, and verbal or vocal comedy (Gorham & Christophel, 1990). Other humor forms include cartoons, sarcasm, professional humor, sexual humor, ethnic humor, and aggressive/hostile humor (Torok, McMorris, & Lin, 2004).

How instructors use humor has implications for students' perceptions of classroom instruction and the classroom environment. Instructors who demonstrate the ability to engage in humor are perceived as possessing credibility (i.e., being competent, having character, and being caring; Dunleavy, 2006) and communicating with their students in a competent manner (Wanzer & Frymier, 1999). Students also are more likely to initiate out-of-classroom communication (OCC) with their instructors and to find this OCC more communicatively satisfying when their instructors are humorous (Aylor & Oppliger, 2003). Humor use does have its consequences, though. When instructors use humor aggressively, students perceive them as competitive, controlling, defensive, unsupportive, disorganized, and unclear (Darling & Civikly, 1987; Stuart & Rosenfeld, 1994); when instructors use humor infrequently, students perceive them as neutral and detached (Darling & Civikly).

Teaching from a Relational Perspective

The relational approach is student-centered, meaning that student learning occurs when instructors and students work together to create and nurture a professional working relationship as a way to increase student learning (Beebe & Mottet, 2009; Myers, 2008). Although the research literature is replete with relational instructional behaviors, power, nonverbal immediacy, and affinity seeking are among the more salient behaviors to use when teaching from the relational perspective.

Power

Power refers to those instructor behaviors that either influence or have the potential to influence students to behave in such a way that they otherwise normally would not (McCroskey & Richmond, 1983). Key to understanding the concept of instructor power is that it is both relationally-based and receiver-based; that is, power exists within the instructor-student classroom relationship, but only to the extent that students perceive their instructors to hold it (Richmond & McCroskey, 1984).

Using French and Raven's (1959) typology of relational power as a foundation, McCroskey and Richmond (1983) identified five ways that instructors communicate power in the classroom: reward, coercive, legitimate, expert, and referent. *Reward power* is based on students' perceptions that their instructors can introduce a benefit or take away something negative; *coercive power* is based on students' perceptions that their instructors can introduce a punish-ment or take away something positive; *legitimate power* is based on students' perceptions that their instructors' title or position justifies the requests or demands instructors make of their students; *expert power* is based on students' perceptions of their instructors' competence and knowledge of the subject matter; and *referent power* is based on students' perceptions that they like their instructors or identify with them in some way.

Research findings suggest that in the U.S. college classroom, students con-sider instructors' use of reward, expert, and referent power to be more effective and appropriate than instructors' use of coercive and legitimate power (Roach, Richmond, & Mottet, 2006). This confirms previous recommendations that instructors should utilize reward, expert, and referent power—also referred to as prosocial forms of power—rather than coercive and legitimate power, which are referred to as antisocial forms of power (Richmond & McCroskey, 1984). Indeed, when instructors use prosocial forms of power, they tend to be perceived more favorably by their students. These instructors are consid-ered to be credible (Teven & Herring, 2005), behave in a confirming manner toward their students (Turman & Schrodt, 2006), express understanding in response to student contributions (Finn, 2012), and treat students fairly when communicating with them (Paulsel, Chory-Assad, & Dunleavy, 2005). When instructors use antisocial forms of power, they are regarded as less confirming and less interpersonally fair, and tend to express more misunderstanding in response to their students.

Nonverbal immediacy

Nonverbal immediacy refers to an individual's simultaneous use of several nonverbal behaviors that help to create the perception of interpersonal close-ness with another person (Andersen, Andersen, & Jensen, 1979). Instructors should remember that these nonverbal behaviors act as a vehicle through which they communicate closeness and warmth toward students, signal whether they are available to interact with students, and indicate whether they are approachable (Andersen & Andersen, 1982). As such, nonverbal immediacy plays a primary role in whether students either are drawn to, or feel the need to distance themselves from, their instructors.

In the college classroom, instructors engage in nonverbal immediacy pri-marily as a way to reduce both the psychological distance and the physical proximity that exists between them and their students (Andersen, 1979).

They do so by utilizing several nonverbal immediacy behaviors with their students, which include gesturing, engaging in direct eye contact with students, smiling, moving around the classroom while talking, having a relaxed body position, using a variety of vocal expressions, being facially expressive, nodding encouragement when students answer questions, and turning their body toward students while lecturing (McCroskey, Sallinen, Fayer, Richmond, & Barraclough, 1996; Richmond, Gorham, & McCroskey, 1987; Smythe & Hess, 2005).

Perceived instructor immediacy is tied to the impressions that students make about their instructors, namely instructor credibility, homophily (i.e., the perceived amount of similarity that exists between two individuals), and attractiveness. When instructors engage in nonverbal immediacy behaviors, students perceive them as having competence and character as well as being caring (Thweatt & McCroskey, 1998). They also are perceived to be similar in attitude and background as students and are regarded by students as being physically, socially, and task attractive (Rocca & McCroskey, 1999). More importantly, nonverbally immediate instructors generally are rated as more effective than nonimmediate instructors. For example, Henning (2012) found that instructors who were rated as effective have a calm voice, show enthusiasm for the course material, walk around the classroom, maintain eye contact with students, and use sweeping gestures to illustrate points.

Affinity seeking

Affinity seeking refers to "the active social communicative process by which individuals attempt to get others to like and feel positive toward them" (R. A. Bell & Daly, 1984, p. 91) and is one way in which instructors can easily build relationships with students. Understanding how affinity seeking works in the classroom requires instructors to acknowledge that not only is it considered to be an active (rather than passive) process rooted in their use of verbal and nonverbal communication behaviors, but also that they have a choice in regard to the strategies they can use when seeking affinity from their students (Daly & Kreiser, 1992).

Based on Bell and Daly's original typology of 25 affinity-seeking strategies used in the interpersonal communication context, instructional communication researchers have modified these 25 strategies for use in the classroom. Of these 25 affinity-seeking strategies, Frymier and Wanzer (2006) recommended that college instructors consistently use 10 strategies to elicit students' affinity:

altruism (i.e., striving to assist students), *assume equality* (i.e., making attempts to establish social equality), *comfortable self* (i.e., appearing relaxed and authentic during interactions), *conversational rule-keeping* (i.e., following appropriate conversational norms), *dynamism* (i.e., appearing active and enthusiastic while teaching), *elicit other's disclosure* (i.e., encouraging students to talk), *facilitate enjoyment* (i.e., keeping interactions fun and enjoyable), *listening* (i.e., paying attention to students), *optimism* (i.e., maintaining a positive outlook and attitude), and *sensitivity* (i.e., showing empathy toward students).

Generally, when instructors use affinity-seeking strategies effectively, students rate them more positively. Students perceive instructors who engage in affinity seeking as being competent and trustworthy (Frymier & Thompson, 1992), they evaluate the course positively (Roach, Cornett-DeVito, & DeVito, 2005), they perceive the classroom climate as supportive more so than defensive (Myers, 1995), and they are likely to engage in out-of-class communication with their instructors (Myers, Martin, & Knapp, 2005). Relatedly, when instructors engage in affinity seeking, they are less likely to be perceived as utilizing instructor misbehaviors (Dolin, 1995), which refers to distracting or ineffective behaviors that deter students from learning and participating in the course. Similarly, Cuny, Wilde, and Stephenson (2012) suggest that tutors be taught such affinity-seeking behaviors to increase student satisfaction with the tutoring session in that they were affirmed and listened to attentively by the tutor.

Using Rhetorical and Relational Behaviors during Tutoring Sessions

Embracing teaching from both a rhetorical and a relational approach is advantageous for both instructors (and more specifically for peer tutors) and students. As Beebe and Mottet (2009) concluded, when instructors use clarity, humor, power, nonverbal immediacy, and affinity seeking in their classrooms, the results are mutually beneficial: "[T]eachers become better teachers and students become better students" (p. 356). Similar results should occur in the tutoring context as well. When peer tutors utilize low-inference clarity behaviors, use appropriate forms of humor, operate from prosocial power bases, and employ nonverbal immediacy behaviors and affinity-seeking strategies in their tutoring sessions, clients should respond favorably.

To enhance the peer tutoring experience, we offer five recommendations peer tutors should heed when tutoring clients. Because clients need their tutors to provide feedback that is instructive, helpful, and encouraging, these recommendations should assist peer tutors in doing so. Two caveats accompany these recommendations, however. First, peer tutors must recognize that these five behaviors—clarity, humor, power, nonverbal immediacy, and affinity seeking—do not *and* should not occur in isolation. That is, while it is fairly common for effective instructors to utilize some or all of these behaviors simultaneously, these behaviors do indeed work best when they are used in conjunction with each other.

Second, peer tutors must understand that the effectiveness of each behavior is undermined should they lack the sincerity, competence, or confidence to engage in each behavior. If peer tutors find any of these five behaviors difficult to adopt, or if they feel uncomfortable engaging in any of the behaviors, then they should refrain until they feel comfortable with its use, as the effects of "faking" the behavior could be more detrimental than if it had not been used at all. Continued training, simulation, and practice will help to build competence and confidence in these behaviors and skills. Additionally, these behaviors will more likely become second nature sooner if a genuine interest in helping the client exists. This is where tutor selection becomes important.

Clarity

When it comes to clarity, peer tutors should take pains to engage in both the structurally clear and the verbally clear message behaviors identified by Chesebro (2003).

Structurally clear message behaviors are those behaviors that focus on the organizational aspects of lectures by previewing main ideas before beginning a lecture, stopping to summarize ideas, and explaining the learning objectives of each unit. These structurally clear message behaviors assist clients in organizing information so they are able to successfully integrate the course material into their existing schemata. Peer tutors should make efforts to summarize key information covered throughout the tutoring session and provide information in an organized way. Tutors also could provide clients with advance organizers, graphical representations, or additional handouts.

Verbally clear message behaviors refers to the words used by peer tutors to enhance clarity by being straightforward when explaining the material, pacing the lesson so clients have time to comprehend, and refraining from introducing tangential information that is unrelated to the content. Peer tutors also can use stories and anecdotes to clarify material, take the time to answer questions thoroughly, and pose follow-up comments to clients' contributions to enhance their verbally clear message behaviors. Perhaps the best way, however, for peer tutors to engage in verbally clear message behaviors is by ensuring that their comments, examples, and questions are relevant to their clients' personal interests, educational needs, and career goals. Frymier and Shulman (1995) identified several relevance behaviors, such as having clients apply their own experiences as a way to demonstrate a concept, using current events to supplement how peer tutors teach a concept, or having tutors explicitly make the connection between the material and some aspect of the client's life. Peer tutors who take the time to reflect on how they can make the content relevant likely will clarify the content for their clients.

Humor

While students demonstrate higher levels of long-term retention when instructors are humorous (Kaplan & Pascoe, 1977), peer tutors need to be mindful that their humorous attempts are appropriate, given their relationship with their clients. Whether humor is deemed as appropriate or inappropriate often depends on both the content and the target of the humor. According to college students, appropriate instructional humor takes one of four forms: humor that either is relevant (e.g., showing a humorous video clip to reinforce the course material) or irrelevant to the course (e.g., sharing a whimsical anecdote about one's family), humor in which instructors self-disparage by either making fun of themselves (e.g., referring to himself or herself as "an idiot" when making a mistake in class) or sharing embarrassing stories about something that happened to them, or humor that emerges unintentionally and spontaneously based on what instructors or students may have said or done during a class session (Wanzer, Frymier, Wojtaszczyk, & Smith, 2006).

Conversely, college students perceive humor to be inappropriate when instructors use it to disparage students (e.g., teasing students for making mistakes), ridicule others (e.g., offering racial or gender stereotypes in class), or appear offensive (e.g., making vulgar or sexual comments) (Wanzer et al., 2006). To be most effective, peer tutors should rely solely on utilizing appropriate forms of humor. A word of caution, however: Although students view self-disparaging humor as both appropriate and inappropriate, peer tutors may want to avoid using this form of humor altogether as frequent or extensive use could affect negatively their credibility with their clients.

Power

To use power effectively, peer tutors should focus on integrating strategies that highlight their expert and referent power during conversations with their clients. These strategies, which are known as behavioral alteration techniques (BATs), are used by instructors to gain compliance from their students (Kearney, Plax, Richmond, & McCroskey, 1985). McCroskey, Richmond, and McCroskey (2006) identified several examples of BATs that can apply to peer tutoring sessions. To integrate *expert* power, peer tutors should use BATs that emphasize how their prior experience engaging in a recommended behavior will benefit the client (e.g., "From my experience, memorizing this acronym is the best way to remember this information") or allow the tutor to confirm what the client has learned (e.g., "Why don't you repeat that back to me so I can compare your understanding of the definition to mine?"). To integrate *referent* power, peer tutors should use BATs that emphasize either how their own behaviors can help their clients become academically successful (e.g., "I always organize my class notes this way and find it very helpful") or how engaging in a behavior will increase rapport with the tutor (e.g., "I'd really appreciate it if you would think about my suggestions when you revise your paper"). Peer tutors also should consider using positive *relational* BATs, which emphasize that they are pleased with their clients' behavior (e.g., "If you can solve this next problem without my help, I will be impressed"). Using these prosocial BATs is one way in which peer tutors can directly influence their clients' study behaviors.

Nonverbal Immediacy

In a similar vein, students are more likely to comply with their instructors' requests when these requests are made by instructors who are considered to be either moderate or high in their use of nonverbal immediacy behaviors (Burroughs, 2007). Although some of the suggestions for promoting immediacy in the classroom (e.g. turning the body toward students while lecturing) might not be as relevant for the tutoring context, many of the immediacy behaviors such as smiling and eye contact are also suggested by Cuny et al. (2012) as important for creating rapport between tutor and tutee in the context of the tutoring session.

Although nonverbal immediacy behaviors help build rapport between tutor and tutee, these behaviors should be used with caution. There are three drawbacks associated with using nonverbal immediacy behaviors, particularly when the behaviors are perceived to be highly immediate, that are especially relevant for the tutoring context (Richmond, 2002; Richmond & McCroskey, 2004). First, clients may interpret their peer tutors' use of nonverbal immediacy behaviors as *intimate* rather than as *immediate*. Peer tutors need to be aware that when they are highly nonverbally immediate (e.g., sitting too close; keeping a light and humorous tone; looking, smiling, or nodding excessively) with a client, they run the risk of being perceived as flirtatious. Second, nonverbally immediate peer tutors are considered approachable, and clients may connote a tutor's approachable demeanor with someone who is a push-over. When peer tutors use these immediacy behaviors, they must continue to be firm and hold onto the standards they have set forth for their clients to discourage this connotation. Third, students tend to communicate more frequently with nonverbally immediate instructors than with nonimmediate instructors. Because the amount of time peer tutors are able to spend with their clients is limited, peer tutors need to focus on the content of the lesson and the time on task by refraining from engaging in nonverbal behaviors that invite peripheral, albeit possibly interesting, conversation. Peer tutors must learn to strike a balance between being nonverbally immediate and being *too* nonverbally immediate to prevent these drawbacks from occurring.

Affinity Seeking

Although peer tutors may be inclined to utilize particular affinity-seeking strategies as a way in which to gain liking from their clients, they also need to realize that affinity seeking can be used as a way to encourage their clients' liking for the subject matter. As Gorham, Kelley, and McCroskey (1989) found with K–12 teachers, two affinity-seeking strategies in particular—*concede control* (i.e., allowing students to have a voice in decision making) and *facilitate enjoyment*—help to increase students' liking of the subject matter because they promote an autonomous learning environment in which students are able to recognize course material as something that can be fun, enjoyable, and even entertaining. As such, students are more likely to participate in class and find the material more interesting, thereby enhancing their ability to learn the course content. Similar results should occur in the tutoring context.

However, regardless of the strategies peer tutors decide to use with their clients, we recommend that they avoid using the *self-inclusion* (i.e., joining clients in social activities), *reward association* (i.e., providing clients with incentives or favors), *perceptions of closeness* (i.e., leading clients to misinterpret their relationship as a friendship), and *inclusion of others* (i.e., inviting clients to participate in social activities outside the tutoring session) strategies as these communication techniques simply are not appropriate for the peer tutor-client relationship (Frymier & Wanzer, 2006). By selecting and using appropriate affinity-seeking strategies, as well as avoiding inappropriate strategies, peer tutors can effectively promote a more effective working relationship with their clients.

Conclusion

It should be noted that the much of the research discussed and cited in this chapter has been studied in the instructional communication context by researchers interested in examining the communication that occurs between instructors and students in the college classroom, which we subsequently applied to the peer tutoring context, given the aforementioned parallels between in-class instruction and peer tutoring. Because effective instruction requires instructors to simultaneously use several rhetorical and relational communication behaviors, it would behoove researchers who are interested in studying the role communication plays in effective peer tutoring to focus their research more specifically on some of these rhetorical and relational communication behaviors. The behaviors identified and reviewed in this chapter represent a starting point for peer tutors, and can be used to provide peer tutors with the opportunity to reflect upon their current communicative practices with their clients and devise ways in which they can incorporate the rhetorical (i.e., clarity, humor) and the relational (i.e., power, nonverbal immediacy, and affinity seeking) instructional communication behaviors into their existing inventory of communication behaviors. Doing so will not only result in student clients who develop an appreciation for the content, but who also report gains in their learning, motivation, and satisfaction from the peer tutoring session.

References

Andersen, J. F. (1979). Teacher immediacy as a predictor of teaching effectiveness. In D. Nimmo (Ed.), *Communication yearbook* (Vol. 3, pp. 98–120). Englewood Cliffs, NJ: Prentice-Hall.

Andersen, J. F., Andersen, P. A., & Jensen, A. D. (1979). The measurement of nonverbal immediacy. *Journal of Applied Communication Research, 7,* 153–180.

Andersen, P., & Andersen, J. (1982). Nonverbal immediacy in instruction. In L. Barker (Ed.), *Communication in the classroom* (pp. 98–120). Englewood Cliffs, NJ: Prentice-Hall.

Aylor, B., & Oppliger, P. (2003). Out-of-class communication and student perceptions of instructor humor orientation and socio-communicative style. *Communication Education, 52*, 122–134.

Beebe, S. A., & Mottet, T. P. (2009). Students and teachers. In W. F. Eadie (Ed.), *21st century communication: A reference handbook* (Vol. 1, pp. 349–357). Thousand Oaks, CA: SAGE.

Bell, A., & Mladenovic, R. (2008). The benefits of peer observation of teaching for tutor development. *Higher Education, 55*, 735–752.

Bell, R. A., & Daly, J. A. (1984). The affinity-seeking function of communication. *Communication Monographs, 51*, 91–115.

Booth-Butterfield, S., & Booth-Butterfield, M. (1991). Individual differences in the communication of humorous messages. *Southern Journal of Communication, 56*, 205–218.

Bryant, J., Comisky, P., & Zillmann, D. (1979). Teachers' humor in the college classroom. *Communication Education, 28*, 110–118.

Burroughs, N. F. (2007). A reinvestigation of the relationship of teacher nonverbal immediacy and student compliance-resistance with learning. *Communication Education, 56*, 453–475.

Bush, A. J., Kennedy, J. J., & Cruickshank, D. R. (1977). An empirical investigation of teacher clarity. *Journal of Teacher Education, 28*(2), 53–58.

Chesebro, J. L. (2003). Effects of teacher clarity and nonverbal immediacy on student learning, receiver apprehension, and affect. *Communication Education, 52*, 135–147.

Cuny, K. M., Wilde, S. M., & Stephenson, A. V. (2012). Using empathic listening to build relationships at the center. In E. L. Yook & W. Atkins-Sayre (Eds.), *Communication centers and oral communication programs in higher education: Advantages, challenges, and new directions* (pp. 249–256). Lanham, MD: Lexington Books.

Daly, J. A., & Kreiser, P. O. (1992). Affinity in the classroom. In V. P. Richmond & J. C. McCroskey (Eds.), *Power in the classroom: Communication, control, and concern* (pp. 121–143). Hillsdale, NJ: Erlbaum.

Darling, A. L., & Civikly, J. M. (1987). The effect of teacher humor on student perceptions of classroom communicative climate. *Journal of Classroom Interaction, 22*, 24–30.

Dolin, D. J. (1995). An alternative form of teacher affinity-seeking measurement. *Communication Research Reports, 12*, 220–226.

Dunleavy, K. N. (2006). The effect of instructor humor on perceived instructor credibility, student state motivation, and student motives to communicate in the classroom. *Kentucky Journal of Communication, 25*, 39–56.

Finn, A. N. (2012). Teacher use of prosocial and antisocial power bases and students' perceived instructor understanding and misunderstanding in the college classroom. *Communication Education, 61*, 67–79.

French, J. R. P., Jr., & Raven, B. H. (1959). The bases of social power. In D. Cartwright (Ed.), *Studies in social power* (pp. 150–167). Ann Arbor, MI: University of Michigan.

Frymier, A. B., & Shulman, G. M. (1995). "What's in it for me?": Increasing content relevance to enhance students' motivation. *Communication Education, 44*, 40–50.

Frymier, A. B., & Thompson, C. A. (1992). Perceived teacher affinity-seeking in relation to perceived teacher credibility. *Communication Education, 41*, 388–399.

Frymier, A. B., & Wanzer, M. B. (2006). Teacher and student affinity-seeking in the classroom. In T. P. Mottet, V. P. Richmond, & J. C. McCroskey (Eds.), *Handbook of instructional communication: Rhetorical & relational perspectives* (pp. 195–211). Boston, MA: Pearson.

Gorham, J., & Christophel, D. M. (1990). The relationship of teachers' use of humor in the classroom to immediacy and student learning. *Communication Education, 39,* 46–61.

Gorham, J., Kelley, D. H., & McCroskey, J. C. (1989). The affinity-seeking of classroom teachers: A second perspective. *Communication Quarterly, 37*, 16–26.

Henning, Z. T. (2012). From barnyards to learning communities: Student perceptions of teachers' immediacy behaviors. *Qualitative Research Reports in Communication, 13*, 37–43.

Kaplan, R. M., & Pascoe, G. C. (1977). Humorous lectures and humorous examples: Some effects upon comprehension and lecture. *Journal of Educational Psychology, 69,* 61–65.

Kearney, P., Plax, T. G., Richmond, V. P., & McCroskey, J. C. (1985). Power in the classroom III: Teacher communication techniques and messages. *Communication Education, 34,* 19–28.

Land, M. L., & Smith, L. R. (1979). The effect of low inference teacher clarity inhibitors on student achievement. *Journal of Teacher Education, 31*, 55–57.

Martin, R. A. (2007). *The psychology of humor: An integrative approach.* Burlington, MA: Elsevier Academic Press.

McCroskey, J. C., & Richmond, V. P. (1983). Power in the classroom I: Teacher and student perceptions. *Communication Education, 32*, 175–184.

McCroskey, J. C., Richmond, V. P., & McCroskey, L. L. (2006). *An introduction to communication in the classroom: The role of communicating in teaching and training.* Boston, MA: Pearson.

McCroskey, J. C., Sallinen, A., Fayer, J. M., Richmond, V. P., & Barraclough, R. A. (1996). Nonverbal immediacy and cognitive learning: A cross-cultural investigation. *Communication Education, 45*, 200–211.

Miczo, N. (2012). Humor and message production. In R. L. DiCioccio (Ed.), *Humor communication: Theory, impact, and outcomes* (pp. 35–49). Dubuque, IA: Kendall Hunt.

Mottet, T. P., & Beebe, S. A. (2006). Foundations of instructional communication. In T. P. Mottet, V. P. Richmond, & J. C. McCroskey (Eds.), *Handbook of instructional communication: Rhetorical and relational perspectives* (pp. 255–282). Boston, MA: Pearson.

Mottet, T. P., Richmond, V. P., & McCroskey, J. C. (Eds.). (2006). *Handbook of instructional communication: Rhetorical and relational perspectives.* Boston, MA: Pearson.

Myers, S. A. (1995). Students' perceptions of teacher affinity-seeking and classroom climate. *Communication Research Reports, 12*, 192–199.

Myers, S. A. (2008). Classroom student-teacher interaction. In W. Donsbach (Ed.), *The international encyclopedia of communication* (Vol. II, pp. 514–520). Malden, MA: Blackwell.

Myers, S. A. (2010). Instructional communication: The emergence of a field. In D. L. Fassett & J. T. Warren (Eds.), *The SAGE handbook of communication and instruction* (pp. 149–159). Thousand Oaks, CA: SAGE.

Myers, S. A., Goodboy, A. K., & Members of COMM 600. (2014). College student learning, motivation, and satisfaction as a function of effective instructor communication behaviors. *Southern Communication Journal, 79,* 14–26.

Myers, S. A., Martin, M. M., & Knapp, J. L. (2005). Perceived instructor in-class communicative behaviors as a predictor of student participation in out of class communication. *Communication Quarterly, 53,* 437–450.

Paulsel, M. L., Chory-Assad, R. M., & Dunleavy, K. N. (2005). The relationship between student perceptions of instructor power and classroom justice. *Communication Research Reports, 22,* 207–215.

Powell, R. G., & Harville, B. (1990). The effects of teacher immediacy and clarity on instructional outcomes: An intercultural assessment. *Communication Education, 39,* 369–379.

Richmond, V. P. (2002). Teacher nonverbal immediacy: Uses and outcomes. In J. L. Chesebro & J. C. McCroskey (Eds.), *Communication for teachers* (pp. 65–82). Boston, MA: Pearson.

Richmond, V. P., Gorham, J. S., & McCroskey, J. C. (1987). The relationship between selected immediacy behaviors and cognitive learning. In M. L. McLaughlin (Ed.), *Communication yearbook* (Vol. 10, pp. 574–590). Newbury Park, CA: SAGE.

Richmond, V. P., & McCroskey, J. C. (1984). Power in the classroom II: Power and learning. *Communication Education, 33,* 125–136.

Richmond, V. P., & McCroskey, J. C. (2004). *Nonverbal behavior in interpersonal relations* (5th ed.). Boston, MA: Pearson.

Roach, K. D., Cornett-DeVito, M. M., & DeVito, R. (2005). A cross-cultural comparison of instructor communication in American and French classrooms. *Communication Quarterly, 53,* 87–107.

Roach, K. D., Richmond, V. P., & Mottet, T. P. (2006). Teachers' influence messages. In T. P. Mottet, V. P. Richmond, & J. C. McCroskey (Eds.), *Handbook of instructional communication: Rhetorical and relational perspectives* (pp. 117–139). Boston, MA: Pearson.

Rocca, K. A., & McCroskey, J. C. (1999). The interrelationship of student ratings of instructors' immediacy, verbal aggressiveness, homophily, and interpersonal attraction. *Communication Education, 48,* 308–316.

Roscoe, R. D., & Chi, M. T. H. (2007). Understanding tutor learning: Knowledge-building and knowledge-telling in peer tutors' explanations and questions. *Review of Educational Research, 77,* 534–574.

Sidelinger, R. J., & McCroskey, J. C. (1997). Communication correlates of teacher clarity in the college classroom. *Communication Research Reports, 14,* 1–10.

Simonds, C. J. (1997). Classroom understanding: An expanded notion of teacher clarity. *Communication Research Reports, 14,* 279–290.

Smythe, M.-J., & Hess, J. A. (2005). Are student self-reports a valid measure for measuring teacher nonverbal immediacy? *Communication Education, 54,* 170–179.

Staton, A. Q. (1989). The interface of communication and instruction: Conceptual considerations and programmatic manifestations. *Communication Education, 38,* 364–371.

Stuart, W. D., & Rosenfeld, L. B. (1994). Student perceptions of teacher humor and classroom climate. *Communication Research Reports*, *11*, 87–97.

Teven, J. J., & Herring, J. E. (2005). Teacher influence in the classroom: A preliminary investigation of perceived instructor power, credibility, and student satisfaction. *Communication Research Reports*, *22*, 235–246.

Thweatt, K. S., & McCroskey, J. C. (1998). The impact of teacher immediacy and misbehaviors on teacher credibility. *Communication Education*, *47*, 348–358.

Titsworth, B. S. (2004). Students' notetaking: The effects of teacher immediacy and clarity. *Communication Education*, *53*, 305–320.

Titsworth, B. S., & Kiewra, K. A. (2004). Spoken organizational lecture cues and student notetaking as facilitators of student learning. *Contemporary Educational Psychology*, *29*, 447–461.

Torok, S. E., McMorris, R. F., & Lin, W-C. (2004). Is humor an appreciated teaching tool?: Perceptions of professors' teaching styles and use of humor. *College Teaching*, *52*, 14–20.

Turman, P. D., & Schrodt, P. (2006). Student perceptions of teacher power as a function of perceived teacher confirmation. *Communication Education*, *55*, 265–279.

Waldeck, J. H., Plax, T. G., & Kearney, P. (2010). Philosophical and methodological foundations of instructional communication. In D. L. Fassett & J. T. Warren (Eds.), *The SAGE handbook of communication and instruction* (pp. 161–180). Thousand Oaks, CA: SAGE.

Wanzer, M. B., & Frymier, A. B. (1999). The relationship between student perceptions of instructor humor and student's reports of learning. *Communication Education*, *48*, 48–62.

Wanzer, M. B., Frymier, A. B., Wojtaszczyk, A., & Smith, T. (2006). Appropriate and inappropriate uses of humor by teachers. *Communication Education*, *55*, 178–196.

Wilson, S. (2012). The role becomes them: Examining communication center alumni experiences. In E. L. Yook & W. Atkins-Sayre (Eds.), *Communication centers and oral communication programs in higher education: Advantages, challenges, and new directions* (pp. 55–67). Lanham, MD: Lexington Books.

PEER TUTORING AND CUSTOMER SERVICE

Students as "Partial Employees"

C. Erik Timmerman

When peer tutors and students work together, this interaction may be described by some as a type of customer service. Peer tutors perform the role of the service provider by sharing their knowledge of content, giving advice about strategies for learning, managing the relationship with their student peer, and so on. Conversely, students perform the role of customer by contacting the tutor, consuming relevant expertise and advice, being an active participant in the process, and compensating the service provider (via the organization/institution) for services rendered.

Using the language of customer service to describe education-based relationships, such as those that exist between students and their peer tutors, is somewhat controversial. Although discussions of this issue typically focus upon instructor-student exchanges, the positions held by proponents and critics of the "student as customer" perspective can also be applied to a peer tutoring context. On the one hand, advocates praise the "student as customer" metaphor by arguing that a customer-focused approach can effectively improve the quality of content, instructional approaches, and learning achievements (e.g, Gremler & McCollough, 2002). On the other hand, detractors express concern about the appropriateness of customer-based approaches in educational settings, arguing that notions such as "the customer is always right" are neither applicable nor appropriate to the processes of teaching and learning (Svensson & Wood, 2007).

Rather than create an either/or argument about the roles of peer tutors and students in this form of service exchange, this chapter will adopt a perspective that draws from key features of the customer metaphor, but adapted to be appropriate to the tutoring context. Whereas a peer tutor is a representative of an organization and, as such, is a service provider, I will suggest that a student is not the same as a customer. Rather, a student's requisite involvement in the tutoring process is best characterized as that of a "partial employee" or, more accurately, a "partial tutor." By conceptualizing the student role in this way, it is possible to apply knowledge drawn from customer service literature to improve the process and outcomes of peer tutoring.

The chapter begins by explaining concepts from customer service literature and how the concepts can be applied to understand the tutoring process. Next, I introduce the notion of the customer as partial employee and how this shift in perspective can apply to peer tutoring. The paper concludes with a series of recommendations that explain (1) how peer tutors can benefit from treating students as partial employees/tutors and (2) how tutors and tutoring centers can best prepare students to work as a partial employee in a way that will maximize the likelihood of success for all parties.

Customer Service

First, it is necessary to clarify what is meant by customer service. Definitions of the term vary, but many (e.g., Gibson-Odgers, 2008; Jothi, 2011; Wong & Perry, 1991) classify what "counts" by describing features of: (1) provider-client relationships, (2) the service delivery process, and/or (3) outcomes of service exchange. Definitions that are oriented toward provider-client relationships generally explain that customer service is a process of managing the relationship between an organization (or relevant service provider) and a customer/client. For example, one definition of customer service explains it as "the long-term person-to-person relationship between [an organization], its distributors and its customer" (Wong & Perry, 1991, p. 11). Second, definitions that center upon delivery of service emphasize the techniques used to share information and effort in an effective and efficient manner. A fairly representative definition from the service delivery perspective describes customer service as "the process by which your organization delivers its services or products in a way that allows the customer to access them in the most efficient, fair, cost effective, and humanly satisfying and pleasurable manner possible" (Jothi, 2011, p. 111). A third category of definitions puts greatest emphasis upon the qualities of service by emphasizing the outcome or result of the transaction. This perspective primarily addresses how effective the organization is at providing the service or, perhaps more precisely, how positively or negatively a customer experiences it. For example, Gibson-Odgers (2008) puts strong emphasis upon the customer experience stating, "customer service is the process of satisfying the customer, relative to a product or service, in whatever way the customer defines as meeting his or her need, and having that service delivered with efficiency, understanding, and compassion" (p. 6).

One element that is often neglected in definitions of service is the idea that, at the core, service *is* communication (e.g., Ford, 1998; Gutek, 2000). Whether dealing with a simple transaction in which a customer places an order for a standardized prepared meal at a fast-food restaurant, or engaging in complex negotiations with a real estate broker, participants are involved in the process of information exchange. However, most characterizations of service neglect the clearly communication-based feature of service. To remedy this, I would add a fourth definition, and one that will be utilized in this chapter, to describe service as a "communication process in which an organizational representative presents products or professional assistance in exchange for another individual's money or cooperation" (Ford, 1999, p. 341).

Customer Service Encounters and Relationships

The most basic form of service is that which occurs in a service encounter, which is an interaction between a customer and an organization (Gutek, 2000; Gutek, Groth, & Cherry, 2002). There are seven distinguishing characteristics of service encounters (Czepiel, Solomon, Suprenant, & Gutman, 1985). First, service encounters are purposeful—they occur for a reason and are goal-oriented. Second, they are not altruistic. The purpose of service is to provide a service to a client, and the client in turn pays for the services provided via tangible (e.g., money) and/or intangible (e.g., cooperation) means. Third, prior acquaintance between parties is not required to engage in this form of encounter. Customers generally understand that, upon encountering a need, they may approach a service provider, typically, without prior invitation. Fourth, the range of tasks covered by a service encounter is limited in scope. The nature of the service constrains what is usually asked of a service provider. For example, a math-focused tutor will generally not be asked for advice on Spanish homework. Fifth, task-related information exchange is prominent. Although non-task information can be found in many transactions (e.g., when engaged in tutoring, peer tutors may discuss a range of topics that go beyond information related to the task at hand), service encounters center around communication about a task. Sixth, in service interactions, roles of client and provider tend to be well defined for participants. The rules that direct interaction between client and provider are determined by the roles that each party fills. Finally, in service interactions, a temporary status differential occurs as the provider controls service delivery in a manner that must be requested from a customer.

Characteristics of service encounters are applicable to the exchanges between peer tutors and students. First, peer tutoring has the purpose of allowing students to consult a party with expertise to improve understanding and skills. Second, although most peer tutoring configurations do not involve compensation that is delivered directly from a student to a tutor, students do pay for academic tutoring services, often via student fees that are directed toward student support services. Third, one of the primary benefits of having an active tutoring center on campus is the fact that it provides a singular location where students can approach trained personnel and seek assistance, usually in a context of support and confidentiality. Fourth, although peer tutors may have expertise in a range of topics, the majority of students utilize the tutoring services to seek assistance with academic matters that typically include a single course at a time (or a single part of a course). Fifth, as with all service encounters, there is potential for some degree of non-task information exchanged in peer tutoring transactions; however, efficient tutoring is often centered around a core task, which is the discussion of content, strategies for improving understanding, and so forth. Sixth, in general, peer tutors and students assume their respective roles and develop expectations for behavior that are based upon those roles. Certainly, there are many cases in which roles reverse as a tutor learns from the student, but this exchange is usually temporary rather than the primary feature of the interaction. And, seventh, although the peer tutoring configuration is specifically designed to decrease status differentials between tutor and student, there is still a distinction in status as the tutor holds an organizationally-sanctioned role that is performed in accordance with a center's relevant policies and procedures.

Customer Participation

In general, peer tutoring matches up well when considering whether it meets the criteria for being classified as a service encounter. But, as mentioned earlier, there tends to be some disagreement about whether it is appropriate to classify education-based relationships in this fashion. Part of the reason for this is a belief that education-based interactions do not fit the mold of service that a customer requests and receives, in exchange for something of value (for a more extensive review of the arguments on either side of the "student as customer" metaphor, see Hoffman & Kretovics, 2004). Instead, education typically works best when students are actively involved in the learning process, rather than passive recipients of content.

An important construct in customer service literature that helps to address these types of concerns is *customer participation*. When focused upon customers' contributions, participation is "a behavioral concept that refers to the actions and resources supplied by customers for service production and/ or delivery" (Rodie & Kleine, 2000, p. 111). All service transactions require some degree of customer participation, but the quantity tends to vary across different types of service.

There are three general levels of participation that distinguish service types from one another (Bitner, Faranda, Hubbert, & Zeithaml, 1997). At the lowest level of participation, the primary participation requirement from customers is mere presence. In these types of transactions, products are typically standardized and are usually going to be available regardless of an individual consumer's decision to purchase or not. For example, upon purchasing a ticket to see a movie, a customer needs to do little more than arrive and find a seat for the service to be delivered. In general, the need for more extensive participation suggests that it is not likely that most one-to-one peer tutoring would occur at the low level of student involvement.

At a moderate level, a somewhat increased level of customer input is required in order to complete the transaction (Bitner et al., 1997). Service that requires moderate customer participation involves customer input that allows for the customization of what would otherwise be a standard service. Unlike low participation service for which services will be delivered regardless of purchase, moderate participation transactions are only initiated when a customer makes a request and, usually, provides payment. For the service to be delivered, a customer must give some degree of information input, but the service organization maintains the full responsibility for completing the service itself. Examples of moderate participation service would include going to a dentist for an annual check up. In this case, a customer's presence is required and s/he must provide information to place the request for examination, and so on. However, a dentist or staff member performs all of the necessary activity (e.g., cleaning, X-rays) while the client maintains a generally low level of activity. It is possible that some peer tutoring could occur at the moderate level of involvement, possibly in circumstances where a peer tutor is trained to deliver content to students without extensive customization to a student's specific learning needs.

At high levels of customer participation, a customer is an active participant in service delivery who co-creates the service along with the service provider (Bitner et al., 1997). These forms of service are highly customized to a client's specific needs and requirements. Like service types at the moderate level, highly participative service only takes place when a client makes a request and engages in all necessary behaviors. Any outcome that results from the service process is achieved because of the customer's participation. Examples of high customer participation would include family counseling, physical therapy, and, in all likelihood, different forms of tutoring. For example, a peer tutor would likely meet with a student to learn his/her particular tutoring requirements, develop a plan for study and future tutoring, and review content as needed. Upon departure, the student assumes responsibility for adherence to the study plan, and completion of any activities that are included in the plan.

At all three levels, customer/student participation represents a type of input into the service process. Customer participation generally has varying degrees of mental, physical, and emotional input (Jiménez, Voss, & Frankwick, 2013; Keh & Teo, 2001; Rodie & Kleine, 2000). Mental inputs consist of cognitive effort and information that is used to complete the service. For example, when participating in peer tutoring, a student must provide information about what it is that s/he is hoping to master as well as engage in active cognition to analyze and understand material and learning strategies as presented by the peer tutor. Physical inputs include not only actual bodily presence but also any physical efforts. If a peer tutor is working with a student on a series of math-based problems, it may be necessary for a student to provide physical effort when working through problems to reach a solution. Last, emotional input is any form of effort that a customer must provide to maintain pleasant interaction with the service provider. Although a student may be experiencing stress and frustration while engaging in the learning process, emotional effort to manage these emotions allows a tutor to focus the exchange upon the learning process.

Partial Employees and Peer Tutoring

Service interactions between peer tutors and students require a high level of participation from both parties. In circumstances where a client has an influential and instrumental role in the service process, some scholars suggest that service providers should view customers as partial employees (e.g., Bowen, 1986; Hsieh, Yen, & Chin, 2004; Kelley, Donnelly, & Skinner, 1990; Mills & Morris, 1986) or even as the sole producer of the service transaction (Namasivayam, 2003). This transition from viewing the customer as strictly an external component, to that of an active contributor to the service outcome creates a degree of overlap between the roles of "customer" and "service provider" (Mills & Morris, 1986; Namasivayam, 2003). As such, concepts and practices that are traditionally applied as management or employee development may have practical application for enhancing the peer tutoring process. Essentially, viewing students as an active and critical component of the tutoring process, rather than as a passive consumer, identifies a new form of resource that can be drawn upon by peer tutors. No longer is a tutor dependent upon only his/her own knowledge and training, s/he can also depend upon the idea that part of the work is going to be done by the student who seeks tutorial advice.

In the general service context, a partial employee makes contributions to the service process by (a) completing work that would otherwise be completed by a service provider or (b) acting as a partner with a service provider to share labor (Halbesleben & Buckley, 2004). Often, when technology is incorporated into the service process, a customer takes on the role of the service provider to complete a transaction. For instance, the recent implementation of self-checkout lines in grocery stores has made it possible for the customer to fulfill all of the functions of the service provider by scanning items, bagging, and paying. In a tutoring context, technologies may provide some opportunity for replacement, but teaching students a set of techniques for teaching themselves would also suffice. If, for example, a student is working with a peer tutor to improve writing skills, the tutor may spend time reviewing writing and providing the student with feedback so that s/he may improve in the future. But, the same ends are also achieved by teaching the student about various tools that may be available to assist with the writing process (e.g., explaining how grammar check tools function). Should a student become competent at the use of these tools as a result of the tutoring intervention, the tutor has essentially been replaced by a set of skills that are performed by the student.

More often, a peer tutor and student are likely to form a partnership that allows them to share resources toward the completion of a task. When a customer and service provider work together to share information and effort, they are essentially collaborators. An example from a typical service context would be the case in which, upon discovering a leak coming through their ceiling, a customer may contact a roofing contractor to address the problem. Upon arrival, the customer and contractor must share effort to analyze the causes of the leak, often through a period of information exchange until a decision is made about possible solutions. At this stage, the parties may again need to collaborate as they collect information about various roofing products (shingles, etc.) that are appropriate. Both parties perform necessary functions in the service process. Without shared effort, the overall level of service quality would decrease.

By conceptualizing students as partial employees, or partial tutors, they too can be viewed as collaborators (rather than recipients) in the tutoring process. During an initial encounter, a well-trained tutor often asks a series of questions aimed at getting a solid grasp upon a student's needs and objectives. As a participant, a student must actively consider his/her own previous levels of effort, feedback on assignments, and so forth in order to provide accurate information about how to proceed. Without active engagement in this task from the student, a peer tutor may not be able to efficiently focus upon any areas where subsequent attention should be focused. Thus, both student and peer tutor benefit from the shared effort.

Techniques for Working with Students as Partial Tutors

Thus far, this chapter has focused upon a set of concepts from the customer service literature to suggest that peer tutoring is a service process that should acknowledge the idea that there is a requirement for extensive participation from students. When examined from this perspective, students can be viewed as fulfilling a portion of the tutoring role, which allows them to be classified as partial tutors in the process. Although peer tutors are often provided with substantive training so that they may be effective tutors, there is not usually a very extensive discussion of the essential participatory role for students in the overall tutoring exchange. Thus, this next section provides four recommendations that should be considered by peer tutors in order to maximize the benefits of student tutoring collaborators.

Recommendation 1: Recognize Students as Collaborators in the Tutoring Experience

When framing the role of potential peer tutors, much of the focus is upon the responsibilities of the peer tutor for facilitating effective tutoring. Although this focus is necessary, there should be a clear acknowledgment that students are as responsible as peer tutors for assuring the effectiveness of the tutoring process. By depicting the student as a service participant who shares in the delivery of the service, peer tutors may be able to more accurately position themselves in the tutoring relationship. Specifically, they can acknowledge their own role as a facilitator of learning, rather than as a party who is individually responsible for assisting a student with his/her learning needs.

Recommendation 2: Acknowledge That a Primary Function of a Peer Tutor Is to Create a Learning Structure

A key factor that can be linked to service outcomes is role clarity, or the degree to which an individual understands the behaviors that s/he is expected to perform in a given circumstance (Donnelly & Ivancevich, 1975). For students who are beginning the tutoring process, it is likely that there will be some degree of ambiguity about how the process will develop. Because role clarity is a key factor that can positively influence the service experience (Fonner & Timmerman, 2009), peer tutors should spend some time during initial encounters to make sure that both student and peer tutor understand their role functions.

This type of discussion can take place either before or after determination of student tutoring needs, but should take place early in the process. A strong focus should be placed upon discussion of the structure of the tutoring session(s), with clarification that one of the peer tutor's tasks (both within each meeting as well as across multiple sessions, when appropriate) will be to help create and adhere to a plan that may address the topics to be examined, approximate time allocation, and intended outcomes. By putting emphasis upon the structural components of tutoring sessions, as well as any individual work that a student must complete between sessions, both student and peer tutor create a heightened sense of clarity about which behaviors are appropriate and expected during given stages of the tutoring process.

Recommendation 3: Openly Discuss the Need for Student Effort and Division of Labor

Related to the previous recommendation, some portion of the discussions of role and structure should clarify the importance of student effort and the tasks that each party will perform. Essentially, time should be taken to teach the role that the student is to perform. This conversation should clearly address the notion of the partial employee role, customer participation, and coproduction of effort (Hoffman & Kretovics, 2004) and highlight the direct relationship between participation and customer perceptions of quality and satisfaction (Cermak, File, & Prince, 2011). Because students may initially approach tutoring as a situation in which a service provider is solely responsible for service, tutors may help students understand the importance of their participation by clarifying the reasons for as well as benefits of staying actively engaged in tutoring sessions.

Recommendation 4: Value and Reward Student Input

Complex service that is tailored to individual customer requirements requires a high level of participation from customers (Bitner et al., 1997). Without positive feedback to encourage continued involvement, students' interest in the process may decrease. Indeed, due to the importance of student input, forms of service that are similar to peer tutoring put an even heavier workload on customers than upon the organizational representative (Namasivayam, 2003). Positive feedback may be useful in order to maintain the high level of participation in co-production efforts (Kuppelwieser & Finsterwalder, 2011). Feedback from peer tutor to student may focus upon both contributions to learning (e.g., successfully completing a problem set) as well as actions that advance the tutoring process (e.g., completing any extra work between sessions). When appropriate, positive feedback could be as simple as acknowledgment of the effort or identifying any positive benefits that resulted from the student contributions.

Techniques for Preparing Students to Be Partial Employees

Although this chapter is mostly focused upon the perspective of the peer tutor when relating to students, ideas drawn from the notion of the partial employee also can be used to focus upon better preparing students for participation in the tutoring process. These recommendations can be implemented by peer tutoring centers as well as peer tutors to better equip students for the partial employee/tutor role.

Recommendation 5: Engage Students in Socialization, Before the Tutoring Process Begins

In the workplace, employee socialization involves an organization's attempts to provide new members with information that allows them to better understand and assimilate into the workplace (Chao, O'Leary-Kelly, Wolf, Klein, & Gardner, 1994). As customers learn their role as partial employee, processes of socialization and assimilation occur in a manner that is similar to those experienced by organizational members (Fonner & Timmerman, 2009). Socialization of partial employees may improve both behavioral as well as affective experiences (Kelley et al., 1990). To assist with their own socialization, customers (as partial employees) seek information from a variety of sources, including direct questions, observation, and conversations with others (Fonner & Timmerman, 2009).

In order to increase students' understanding of peer tutoring services, tutors and tutoring centers may wish to engage in a variety of socialization strategies. The strategies may vary from formal training sessions that are focused exclusively upon the nature of the tutoring process and participation requirements, to informal efforts to encourage students to share word-of-mouth experiences with peer tutors and tutoring centers. For instance, tutoring centers may help form student expectations by providing website-based explanations about what students may expect during a tutoring appointment and how they can best prepare. Or, even allowing students to observe either live or recorded video of the tutoring process may demonstrate appropriate behaviors and increase the likelihood that students will perform in a similar fashion.

Recommendation 6: Inform Students about Important Outcomes and How You Will Work Together to Achieve Them

One of the primary arguments against the "student as customer" metaphor points to the idea that the emphasis upon customer satisfaction is not appropriate for educational settings (Hoffman & Kretovics, 2004). Although satisfaction may be a beneficial outcome, among some educators the more favored objectives are typically related to student learning. But, it is important to acknowledge that the positive attitudes about learning outcomes may also be held by students, especially those who are willing to approach a tutoring center to improve their grasp of course content and to improve study skills.

Tutors and tutoring centers have great potential to highlight the types of outcomes that they seek to achieve through the tutoring process, but students should be informed of the targeted outcomes. By managing attention to the intended outcomes, students have the ability to monitor their progress according to standards that go beyond their own level of satisfaction with the experience. For example, if a key emphasis is upon teaching students effective time management skills so that they may focus their studies in a more efficient manner, this objective should be clarified. If the objective is expressed to students and a student finds that s/he is not achieving the desired gains, this information can be beneficial for revising the tutoring process.

Recommendation 7: Encourage Students to Share Stories about How Active Participation Led to Success

When customers and students share their perceptions of a service experience with others, it is referred to as word-of-mouth (Clewes, 2003). Sharing of experiences serves to help others understand how the service process works and essentially serves as a form of vicarious, or observational, learning (Bandura, 1977). In addition to providing students with an understanding of how the service process works, it also provides a form of positive reinforcement for anticipated behavior. In other words, if a student shares a story indicating that they were able to deliver significant, focused effort because a peer tutor provided a structured environment for success, it is likely that individuals who hear the story will have a clear expectation about what they will need to do to also achieve success. Encouraging students to "spread the word" about their experience develops accurate expectations, as well as positive affect about the tutoring process.

Conclusion

Peer tutors and students are part of a service relationship that is focused upon completing a complex task. Although peer tutors receive training to be able to effectively participate in the tutoring process, less attention is typically directed to the role of the student. By examining peer tutoring as a form of service, additional attention can be placed upon the level of participation that is required of students. The concept of the "partial employee" or "partial tutor" clarifies the division of labor in tutoring exchanges and points to the importance of student involvement for achieving tutoring outcomes.

Putting attention on student participation makes it possible to better understand how peer tutors can structure work and provide a context for student participation, as well as how tutors and tutoring centers can prepare students to be effective contributors to the tutoring process. Peer tutoring centers can implement this service-based approach by recognizing students as active collaborators (rather than passive observers), acknowledging the tutor's role in creating and maintaining structure, openly discussing the need for student effort and the division of labor, and providing students with positive feedback. Students, too, can be further prepared for their partial tutor role as tutoring centers work to clarify the tutoring process through socialization, identify desired outcomes for students, and encourage students to share stories about their experience.

References

Bandura, A. (1977). *Social learning theory*. Englewood Cliffs, NJ: Prentice-Hall.

Bitner, M. J., Faranda, W. T., Hubbert, A. R., & Zeithaml, V. A. (1997). Customer contributions and roles in service delivery. *International Journal of Service Industry Management, 8*, 193–205.

Bowen, D. (1986). Managing customers as human resources in service organizations. *Human Resource Management, 25*, 371–383.

Cermak, D. S., File, K. M., & Prince, R. A. (2011). Customer participation in service specification and delivery. *Journal of Applied Business Research, 10*, 90–97.

Chao, G. T., O'Leary-Kelly, A. M., Wolf, S., Klein, H. J., & Gardner, P. D. (1994). Organizational socialization: Its content and consequences. *Journal of Applied Psychology, 79*, 730–743.

Clewes, D. (2003). A student-centered conceptual model of service quality in higher education. *Quality in Higher Education, 9*, 69–85.

Czepiel, J. A., Solomon, M. R., Suprenant, C. F., & Gutman, E. G. (1985). Service encounters: An overview. In J. Czepiel, M. Solomon, & C. Suprenant (Eds.), *The service encounter: Managing employee/customer interaction in service businesses* (pp. 3–15). Lexington, MA: Lexington Books.

Donnelly Jr., J. H., & Ivancevich, J. M. (1975). Role clarity and the salesman. *The Journal of Marketing, 39*, 71–74.

Fonner, K. L., & Timmerman, C. E. (2009). Organizational newc(ust)omers: Applying organizational newcomer assimilation concepts to customer information seeking and service outcomes. *Management Communication Quarterly, 23*, 244–271.

Ford, W. S. Z. (1998). *Communicating with customers: Service approaches, ethics, and impact.* Cresskill, NJ: Hampton.

Ford, W. S. Z. (1999). Communication and customer service. In M. E. Roloff (Ed.), *Communication yearbook 22* (pp. 341–375). Thousand Oaks, CA: SAGE.

Gibson-Odgers, P. (2008). *The world of customer service* (2nd ed.). Mason, OH: Thomson.

Gremler, D. D., & McCollough, M. A. (2002). Student satisfaction guarantees: An empirical examination of attitudes, antecedents, and consequences. *Journal of Marketing Education, 24*, 150–160.

Gutek, B. A. (2000). Service relationships, pseudo-relationships, and encounters. In T. Swartz & D. Iacobucci (Eds.), *Handbook of services marketing and management* (pp. 371–381). Thousand Oaks, CA: SAGE.

Gutek, B. A., Groth, M., & Cherry, B. (2002). Achieving service success through relationships and enhanced encounters. *The Academy of Management Executive, 16*, 132–144.

Halbesleben, J. R., & Buckley, M. R. (2004). Managing customers as employees of the firm: New challenges for human resources management. *Personnel Review, 33*, 351–372.

Hoffman, K. D., & Kretovics, M. A. (2004). Students as partial employees: A metaphor for the student-institution interaction. *Innovative Higher Education, 29*, 103–120.

Hsieh, A. T., Yen, C. H., & Chin, K. C. (2004). Participative customers as partial employees and service provider workload. *International Journal of Service Industry Management, 15*, 187–199.

Jiménez, F. R., Voss, K., & Frankwick, G. L. (2013). A classification schema of co-production of goods: An open-systems perspective. *European Journal of Marketing, 47*, 1841–1858.

Jothi, A. L. (2011). A comprehensive study on life insurers' services in India. *EXCEL International Journal of Multidisciplinary Management Studies, 1*, 111–121.

Keh, H. T., & Teo, C. W. (2001). Retail customers as partial employees in service provision: A conceptual framework. *International Journal of Retail & Distribution Management, 29*(8), 370–378.

Kelley, S. W., Donnelly, J. H., & Skinner, S. J. (1990). Customer participation in service production and delivery. *Journal of Retailing, 66*, 315–335.

Kuppelwieser, V. G., & Finsterwalder, J. (2011). Psychological safety, contributions and service satisfaction of customers in group service experiences. *Managing Service Quality, 21,* 617–635.

Mills, P. K., & Morris, J. H. (1986). Clients as 'partial' employees of service organizations: Role development in client participation. *Academy of Management Review, 11,* 726–735.

Namasivayam, K. (2003). The consumer as "transient employee": Customer satisfaction through the lens of job-performance models. *International Journal of Service Industry Management, 14,* 420–435.

Rodie, A. R., & Kleine, S. S. (2000). Customer participation in services production and delivery. In T. A. Swartz & D. Iacobucci (Eds.), *Handbook of services marketing and management* (pp. 111–125). Thousand Oaks, CA: SAGE.

Svensson, G., & Wood, G. (2007). Are university students really customers? When illusion may lead to delusion for all! *International Journal of Educational Management, 21,* 17–28.

Wong, S. M., & Perry, C. (1991). Customer service strategies in financial retailing. *International Journal of Bank Marketing, 9,* 11–16.

· 1 5 ·

DESIGNING AND DELIVERING EFFECTIVE FEEDBACK

Making the Most of Your Consultation Time

Jennifer Butler Ellis and Angela Grimaldi

Designing and delivering effective feedback requires utilizing leadership and communication skills. Communication skills are critical for the success of peer tutoring centers (Atkins-Sayre & Yook, Chapter 1 in this volume), and peer tutors must also draw upon various leadership skills (e.g., goal-setting, organizing, problem-solving) as they guide and coach tutees through consultations. Although leadership and communication skills are central to the peer tutoring situation, the ability to influence others by identifying specific areas of strength and areas for improvement for a peer is a skillset that many struggle to master. Stone and Heen's (2014) book entitled *Thanks for the Feedback* argues that providing feedback is a lost art, and that it is often "unfair or off base. It's poorly timed and even more poorly delivered" (p. 3). Furthermore, research has shown that feedback interventions, if conducted poorly, can even negatively impact cooperation and relationships (Coens & Jenkins, 2000) and lead to a decline in performance (Kluger & DeNisi, 1996).

Although much of this research examines the organizational situation (i.e., employer-employee relationship), the findings (e.g., feedback messages focused on the task and messages that activate the learning process improve performance) can be applied to the peer tutoring situation and can help tutors better understand the power and perils of designing and delivering effective feedback. This chapter briefly reviews relevant feedback literature and discusses four important principles for designing and delivering feedback in the peer tutoring situation. The chapter concludes with sample scenarios that illustrate the feedback principles and may be used as training material for peer tutors.

Literature on Feedback

Kluger & DeNisi's (1996) meta-analysis revealed that feedback interventions do not always produce the desired results and oftentimes can even hurt performance. Smither, London, and Reilly (2005) examined performance appraisal reviews and found negligible effects on motivation and performance improvement. As mentioned earlier, Coens and Jenkins (2000) argued that performance appraisals can negatively impact cooperation and relationships in organizations. In contrast, feedback-seeking behavior has been found to be related to relationship quality or relationship building, but not to performance (Anseel, Beatty, Shen, Lievens, & Sackett, 2015).

Although the literature paints a rather bleak picture for feedback interventions and performance appraisals, Kluger and DeNisi (1996) provide insight into the complexity of feedback interventions and identify different outcomes associated with different feedback interventions. Specifically, the data were used to develop feedback intervention theory (FIT) which highlights how feedback interventions (i.e., task learning, task motivation, and meta-task) change the receiver's focus. Feedback interventions that direct the focus on the individual or the self were less effective than interventions that focused on the task details and learning. FIT also suggests that feedback "cues that direct attention to the motivational level should improve performance" (p. 268). For example, cues that identify past performance (e.g., "You produced more widgets this month" or "Your report was better organized this week") may help focus the recipient's attention on task goals and motivate them to strive for improvement. Furthermore, feedback "that directs attention to learning processes can also improve performance" (p. 268). Specifically, messages explaining why particular answers are correct are more likely to improve performance. Although FIT is typically applied to the organizational setting, the tutoring situation may also benefit by considering how to design and deliver effective feedback messages.

Designing and Delivering Feedback in the Tutoring Situation

Delivering feedback is a significant component of the tutoring situation. Because students often visit communication centers to improve and expand their communication skills, effectively delivering quality, usable feedback to tutees is a significant component of the tutoring situation. As the feedback literature suggests, feedback interventions do not always yield the desired results (Kluger & DeNisi, 1996). To improve the quality of peer tutoring exchanges, tutors should be trained to design and deliver messages that incorporate principles of supportiveness and sincerity, specificity, significance, and a strategy for improvement.

Supportiveness and Sincerity

Creating a supportive environment for peer-to-peer tutoring is a critical backdrop for delivering effective feedback messages. Although there are many ways to create a supportive and sincere environment, two practical ways for tutors to create a comfortable tutoring situation involve engaging in empathic listening and reducing the use of powerless language.

Cuny, Wilde, and Stephenson (2012) argue for the importance of using the empathic listening skills of focusing, encouraging, and reflecting in peer-to-peer tutoring. Focusing skills or attending to the person you are helping is characterized by the use of effective eye contact, professional communication, and "I" language rather than "you" language when providing constructive feedback during a consultation. Cuny et al. (2012) also suggested that tutors should motivate tutees to talk more by asking clarifying and open questions. Encouraging skills may help tutees feel more comfortable and set "into motion a supportive chain of interactions in which the speaker feels more accepted and validated" (p. 252). In addition, paraphrasing and summarizing a tutee's words or perspective demonstrate reflecting skills that are important for developing effective peer-to-peer tutoring relationships as well as meeting the needs of the tutee (Cuny et al., 2012).

Although creating a supportive environment can often be accomplished by utilizing empathic listening skills, tutors must be careful to avoid using generic supportive terminology in a one-size-fits-all approach that tutees could interpret as insincere. Bronson (2007) highlighted the importance of sending sincere praise, and notes that children over the age of seven can tell if there is a hidden agenda embedded in praise messages. If even children can identify insincere praise or encouragement, surely adults in peer tutoring relationships would be able to recognize praise that feels generic. Thus, tutors should seek to use focusing skills to be attentive and they should strive to tailor supportive, individualized messages to the tutee. For example, messages such as "Good job!" might seem canned, and call to question whether the tutor really paid attention to the presentation or paper. Thus, delivering positive messages tailored for the tutee (e.g., "Good job, I really liked your organizational strategy") will help to create a trusting environment where the tutee feels valued and comfortable as he or she seeks to set and reach personal goals.

Another component that contributes to the creation of a supportive and sincere tutoring environment is the avoidance of powerless language. Holtgraves and Lasky (1999) define powerless language as "a cluster of linguistic features that includes (but is not limited to) hesitations (e.g., umm ...), hedges (e.g., I kinda think...), and tag questions (e.g., right? ... OK?); the absence of these features is referred to as powerful language" (p. 196). While many instances of powerless language can be challenging to avoid, tutors should strive to use more powerful professional communication, rather than powerless speech. Research has shown that listeners consistently rate powerless speakers, and the arguments they present, lower than that of powerful speakers when both deliver the same message (Holtgraves & Lasky, 1999). Furthermore, powerless speakers are seen both as less competent and social (Gibbons, Busch, & Bradac, 1991), and as less credible and dynamic (Haleta, 1996). Clearly, powerless language creates an impression that most speakers would consider undesirable.

If tutors deliver messages that are cluttered with powerless language, tutees may be distracted and feel less comfortable because they question the tutor's credibility and level of comfort in the situation. If the tutor seems nervous, the tutee's own nervousness may be heightened. In addition, Areni and Sparks (2005) found that powerless language can shift the focus to the speaker and lead the receiver to generate more thoughts about the speaker. In the tutoring situation the focus should be on the tutee not the tutor. If the tutee is generating more thoughts about the speaker due to powerless language, the tutee may not internalize the feedback as thoroughly because they are distracted by the speaker's powerless language. Essentially this distraction may negatively impact a supportive environment by shifting the focus away from the tutee.

In the tutoring situation, tutees will likely feel more at ease with tutors whom they perceive as competent and credible. Atkins-Sayre and Yook

(Chapter 1 this volume) argue that effective communication is important for creating a supportive environment, and highlight that "to effectively tutor a client, it is necessary to build credibility and trust between the tutor and the client." In light of the effect that powerless language can have on listeners, this section highlights two examples of powerless language that tutors should avoid.

Hesitations

One common form of powerless language is the hesitation. O'Barr (1982) classified hesitations as the frequent use of nonverbal filler sounds such as *uh, um, ehh,* and *ah,* or verbal word fillers such as *I mean, well,* and *you know.* Verbal or nonverbal hesitations can be quite distracting, especially when used excessively, and they can direct the tutee's attention away from the tutor's message. Hesitations can also convey nervousness, a lack of confidence, and unpreparedness, all of which can detract from a tutor's credibility. Tutors can avoid hesitations by taking the time to breathe and/or pause for a few seconds to catch their train of thought. Oftentimes, speakers hesitate to allow their thoughts to catch up with their speech because they want to avoid awkward pauses, and the same applies to the tutoring situation. However, tutors should remember that while those few seconds may seem like an eternity to the tutor, the tutee will most likely not have that perception. When needed, tutors should take some time to think before responding to the tutee. In sum, tutors should strive for a conversational, yet professional speaking style, and seek to minimize the number of hesitations used when speaking with tutees.

Hedges

Another form of powerless language is the hedge. According to Durik, Britt, Reynolds, and Storey (2008), hedges are noncommittal phrases that "modify the meaning of a statement by commenting on the uncertainty of the information or on the uncertainty of the writers" (p. 218). By conveying uncertainty, hedges can water down a communicator's message. While hedges like *kind of, I think, sort of, I guess, somewhat,* and *possibly* provide protection from confrontation, the more tutors water down their statements with hedges, the more they give the impression that they do not have sufficient confidence in their abilities or in the validity of their message. Portraying a lack of confidence does not create a supportive environment for tutees and may make them feel nervous. Furthermore, Durik, Britt, Reynolds, and Storey (2008) found that hedges placed on data statements led to negative perceptions of the policy, source, and argument, ultimately undermining persuasive attempts.

Because hedges invite listeners to question the credibility and competence of the speaker, tutors should seek to avoid them when possible. It is very easy to say "I think" when feeling intimidated, but tutors should remember that they are not expected to be an expert on everything. Additionally, tutors should ask questions or make comments unapologetically when they need more information. This confidence will help put tutees more at ease and create a more comfortable environment for tutors and tutees to communicate.

As with hesitations, tutors can use hedges in certain situations, such as ones where politeness is needed or when counterexamples are available. Interestingly, Durik et al. (2008) found that professional hedges such as *may*, *seem to*, and *likely* as well as hedges on interpretive statements (as opposed to data statements) do not lead to negative perceptions like colloquial hedges (e.g., *sort of*, *kind of*, and *I guess*). Thus, tutors should carefully examine their word choices to maintain credibility and create a positive tutoring environment.

In sum, the first step to creating a comfortable backdrop for the tutoring context is to set a tone that helps tutees feel supported. To accomplish this, tutors should seek to use empathic listening skills, design messages that are sincere, and reduce the use of powerless language when communicating with tutees. In addition to setting a supportive tone, tutors should strive to develop specific feedback messages that allow tutees to internalize the information more effectively.

Specificity

Feedback should be specific for it to be effective. Providing feedback in more general terms often leads to confusion. Research on feedback suggests that messages related to the details of the focal task are associated with performance improvement, while messages focused on the individual or self are associated with performance decline (Kluger & DeNisi, 1996). Thus, tutors should design messages that include specific positive and constructive examples from the student's work to more fully illustrate the tutor's feedback. For example, if a student brings a paper for peer review, the tutor should avoid general messages such as "nice paper," "good flow," or "awkward wording." These generic statements are more difficult to process and often leave a tutee confused. In contrast, highlighting specific sentences or transitional phrases that improved the overall flow of the paper helps a tutee process more clearly what the tutor is referencing. This specificity also allows tutees to internalize the information more effectively. Sometimes we succeed by default, yet if we do not realize that we did something well, we may never repeat the behavior. When tutors point out specific examples of success, not only can this boost a tutee's confidence, but the tutee is also more likely to use a similar approach in the future. Furthermore, identifying specific deficiencies allows a tutee to more clearly understand where to focus his or her efforts.

Significance

Although academic research on feedback does not directly explore the importance of identifying the significance of positive or negative behaviors, practitioners from the Center for Creative Leadership (Situation-Behavior-Feedback Tool, n.d.) developed a feedback tool for feedback delivery. This tool identifies one component that is underdeveloped in the academic literature: impact or significance of the behavior. Discussing the impact or significance involves discussing the effects of the behavior. Although the feedback tool is designed for organizational feedback (i.e., employee-employer), there are some useful suggestions we can apply to the tutoring situation. Namely, tutors should seek to discuss the impact or significance of specific behaviors with their tutees to help them understand the importance and the effects the behavior may have on a particular audience.

Helping students identify areas of strength and areas for improvement is an important starting point; however, the concepts often come to life when a tutor highlights the significance or importance of the component. For example, a tutor may suggest the importance of reducing powerless language such as *ums* and *uhs*. Generally, students know this language clutters a presentation, but when a tutor identifies that *ums* and *uhs* often distract an audience and reduce a speaker's credibility, this helps students understand the importance or significance of making changes. Identifying the significance may also serve to motivate students to change. At times, students may think a tutor is being too picky. Designing feedback messages that include information about significance provides justification for the tutor's suggestion, and may motivate students to make important changes.

Strategies for Improvement

Feedback Intervention Theory highlights the importance of "task learning" (Kluger & DeNisi, 1996). The authors assert that feedback interventions that engage the learning process related to tasks (i.e., task learning feedback interventions) were more effective than feedback interventions that focus on the individual or the self. Thus, tutors should seek to design messages that are focused on the task by offering strategies and instruction that assist the tutee in learning more about the task and exploring strategies for improving his or her performance on current and future tasks. For example, if a tutee struggles with speech organization, the tutor may instruct the tutee about various organizational strategies (e.g., topical, chronological, pro-con, problem-solution). By explaining different organizational patterns, the tutee may better internalize and learn about organizational patterns and utilize these organizational strategies in future presentations as opposed to using the same organizational strategy for every presentation. For example, a topical organization may not be effective when trying to propose a solution to a budget issue. By being aware of the problem-solution organizational pattern the presentation may be more persuasive than if it were organized topically.

In addition to explaining useful strategies related to the task, a tutor should consider the use of examples. Examples can serve to illustrate the concept and engage the learning process by bringing the tutor's words to life. For example, tutors may explain the importance of using visually appealing layouts and graphic highlighting (e.g., headings, bullets), but showing tutees examples of presentation slides with effective layouts, graphic highlighting, and visuals supplements the verbal explanation and illustrates the tutor's ideas. If the tutor does not provide messages that engage the learning process, tutees may continue to make the same mistakes over and over again. Thus, tutors should seek to provide instruction and offer strategies related to the task as often as possible when providing feedback to a tutee.

To help tutors incorporate important communication principles and feedback findings into messages delivered to peers during a tutoring session, the SSSS formula provides a simple way to organize and deliver messages (see Figure 15.1). Supportiveness, Specificity, Significance, and Strategies are four pillars that support designing and delivering effective feedback. Feedback that is supportive and sincere contributes to the creation of a tutoring environment that facilitates the tutee's learning, and feedback messages that are specifically tailored to tutees provide them with useful instruction that is easier to internalize. Additionally, incorporating an explanation of significance into feedback

Figure 15.1. Designing and Delivering Effective Feedback.

messages helps tutees understand *why* they should either change or continue a given communication behavior, and providing strategies for improvement shows tutees *how* to do so. To illustrate the application of the SSSS formula, two scenarios were developed as a training tool for tutors.

Sample Scenario: Written Communication Consultation

Student A comes for a consultation about a research paper she recently completed. Her paper suffers from excessive use of passive voice, but it is well organized. Feedback from her professor states that the paper is "too wordy."

Supportiveness and Sincerity

Following the SSSS model, the tutor should begin the consultation by establishing a supportive environment that exhibits the qualities of empathic listening. To do so, the tutor can begin the discussion by smiling, introducing herself, and asking Student A what she hopes to accomplish during the consultation. Letting Student A set the agenda for the consultation focuses the consultation on the student's needs, contributing to the creation of a supportive environment. The tutor should also be mindful throughout the consultation to avoid powerless language and provide comments about Student A's paper that display sincere attentiveness to the student's needs, such as "Your thorough explanation of this point effectively supported your argument," rather than a generic statement such as "good development of your ideas."

Specificity

The tutor should provide Student A with specific examples from her writing that demonstrate areas of strength and weakness rather than providing generic praise and criticism. For example, when discussing Student A's use of passive voice, the tutor could say, "This sentence here is an example of passive voice. You can tell that this sentence is in passive voice because it uses a form of the verb *to be* and the past participle. Another clue that this sentence is in passive voice is that the subject is not performing the action. In fact, this sentence does not refer at all to the performer of the action." Similarly, the tutor could say, "I like your use of strong, focused topic sentences throughout the paper," rather than simply telling Student A that her paper is well organized.

Significance

As the tutor discusses the strengths and weaknesses in Student A's paper, she should explain why those strengths and weaknesses matter or what their overall impact is. For example, the tutor could state that using passive voice too frequently impacts the overall clarity of Student A's writing. Passive constructions frequently use more words than active constructions, making Student A's writing less concise. As a result, the audience may feel like they have to dig through a lot of words to get to the main ideas, hence her professor's comment about the wordiness of Student A's paper. Additionally, the tutor could mention that passive constructions also obscure the performer of the verb's action, resulting in potential confusion, especially if the subject is not located in the object position of the sentence. Explaining the significance is also critical when providing praise, so when discussing the strengths of Student A's organization, the tutor could explain that having strong, focused topic sentences provides the audience with cues about the main point of each paragraph, making it easier for them to follow Student A's argument.

Strategies for Improvement

After identifying these examples in Student A's writing, the tutor can then help her develop strategies to avoid overusing passive voice in the future. The tutor could begin with some grammatical instruction to ensure that Student A clearly understands what passive voice is, such as explaining what its structural components are (e.g., All passive constructions include a form of the verb *to be* followed by a past participle verb) and how she can identify sentences written in passive voice (e.g., Is there a form of the verb *to be* followed by a past participle? Is the subject of the sentence doing the action or being acted on by someone or something else?). The tutor could also give Student A an example of a passive and an active construction that clearly illustrates the differences between the two sentence structures (e.g., "The bone was eaten by the dog" vs. "The dog ate the bone.")

Once Student A has a better understanding of passive voice, the tutor could ask her to go through her paper and identify additional examples of passive voice. Upon doing so, the tutor could then help her to rewrite those sentences in active voice. Additionally, the tutor can circle back to her earlier discussion of the significance of overusing passive voice and discuss the impact of the revised sentence in comparison with the original sentence.

Sample Scenario: Oral Communication Consultation

Student B comes for a practice presentation consultation. During his practice presentation, Student B speaks clearly and at an optimum volume; however, he rarely makes eye contact due to his public speaking anxiety. Overall, the speech is well organized, and the introduction starts with a humorous, yet appropriate attention-getter.

Supportiveness and Sincerity

As in the written communication scenario, the tutor should begin the consultation by creating a welcoming space in which Student B feels at ease and supported. The tutor can begin the consultation by warmly introducing himself and asking Student B what his goals are for the consultation. Additionally, the tutor can employ encouraging skills, such as self-disclosing that he also feels nervous when giving a presentation, to make Student B feel comfortable despite his anxiety. The tutor should also avoid using powerless language when offering genuine comments about Student B's presentation, such as "I liked how you used humor to start the presentation," instead of saying "Um, nice start."

Specificity

In order to provide Student B with specific examples of his presentation's strengths and weaknesses, the tutor could videotape the practice presentation and cue the video to show Student B the introduction and attention-getter. The video could also be used to show specific instances where he avoids looking at the audience. In addition, the tutor could highlight where the student uses more eye contact and ask him why he thinks eye contact increased during certain parts of the presentation compared to places in the speech where eye contact decreased.

Significance

After showing Student B those examples, the tutor should explain the significance of these strengths and weaknesses. For example, the tutor could state that, "When we don't use eye contact during a presentation, it's very difficult to connect with the audience. Without eye contact the audience may feel that you are simply reciting a script rather than speaking from the heart." The tutor should also highlight how the humorous attention-getter helped the audience and the tutee relax and get the presentation off to a good start. The tutor could also note that attention-getters utilizing appropriate humor help to capture the audience's attention, set the tone, and infuse positive energy into the room. In addition, the tutor should discuss the impact of speaking clearly and loudly enough for the audience to easily hear him. If it is too difficult to hear the speaker, audience members typically tune out and stop listening. Furthermore, speaking clearly and loudly helps to project confidence to the audience. By mentioning the impact of some of the presenter's strengths, the tutor can highlight why these behaviors matter and motivate the tutee to continue these behaviors.

Strategies for Improvement

After discussing the significance of some of the examples, the tutor can discuss strategies for controlling nerves and managing speech anxiety. First, the tutor should highlight the importance of practicing and encourage the tutee to come back for another practice session. The tutor should also highlight that practicing helps presenters feel more comfortable and less nervous. Second, the tutor could suggest that the tutee go through some deep breathing exercises to help his body and mind relax. The tutor could also discuss strategies for maintaining more eye contact with the audience during the presentation. For example, the tutor might suggest picking out a few friendly faces in the audience and work to maintain eye contact with various individuals throughout the room. After discussing these strategies, the tutor could videotape Student B's second practice presentation, identify his areas of improvement, and discuss the impact of his amount of eye contact during the first practice presentation in comparison to the second practice presentation.

Conclusion

Successfully communicating authentic and useful feedback to students can be challenging. Research has shown that feedback interventions are oftentimes unsuccessful (Coens & Jenkins, 2000; Kluger & DeNisi, 1996; Stone & Heen, 2014). By incorporating supportiveness and sincerity, specificity, significance, and strategy into feedback messages, consultants can avoid common pitfalls that negatively affect feedback design and delivery. The sample scenarios above highlight the value that these components add to feedback messages within the tutoring situation. Feedback that is supportive and sincere contributes to the creation of a tutoring environment that facilitates the tutee's learning, and feedback messages that are specifically tailored to tutees provide them with useful instruction that is easier to internalize. Additionally, incorporating an explanation of significance into feedback messages helps tutees understand *why* they should either change or continue a given communication behavior, and providing strategies for improvement shows tutees *how* to do so. Thus, by designing feedback messages that incorporate these four components, tutors can improve the quality of their consultation time with tutees and deliver more effective and beneficial feedback.

References

Anseel, F., Beatty, A., Shen, W., Lievens, F., & Sackett, P. R. (2015). How are we doing after 30 years? A meta-analytic review of the antecedents and outcomes of feedback-seeking behavior. *Journal of Management.* 41(1), 318–348.

Areni, C. S., & Sparks, J. R. (2005). Language power and persuasion. *Psychology & Marketing*, 22(6), 507–525.

Bronson, P. (2007, August). How not to talk to your kids: The inverse power of praise. *New York Magazine*. http://nymag.com/news/features/27840/

Center for Creative Leadership. (n.d.) *Situation-Behavior-Impact Feedback Tool*. Retrieved from: http://www.mindtools.com/pages/article/situation-behavior-impact-feedback.htm

Coens, T., & Jenkins, M. (2000). *Abolishing performance appraisals: Why they backfire and what to do instead*. San Francisco, CA: Berrett-Koehler Publishers.

Cuny, K. M., Wilde, S. M., & Stephenson, A. V. (2012). Using empathic listening to build relationships at the center. In E. L. Yook & W. Atkins-Sayre (Eds.), *Communication centers and oral communication programs in higher education: Advantages, challenges, and new directions* (pp. 249–256). Lanham, MD: Lexington Books.

Durik, A. M., Britt, M. A., Reynolds, R., & Storey, J. K. (2008). The effects of hedges in persuasive arguments: A nuanced analysis of language. *Journal of Language and Social Psychology*, 27(3), 217–234.

Gibbons, P., Busch, J., & Bradac, J. J. (1991). Powerful versus powerless language: Consequences for persuasion, impression formation, and cognitive response. *Journal of Language and Social Psychology*, 10(2), 115–133.

Haleta, L. L. (1996). Student perceptions of teachers' use of language: The effects of powerful and powerless language on impression formation and uncertainty. *Communication Education*, 45(1), 16–28.

Holtgraves, T., & Lasky, B. (1999). Linguistic power and persuasion. *Journal of Language and Social Psychology*, 18(2), 196–205.

Kluger, A. N., & DeNisi, A. (1996). The effects of feedback interventions on performance: A historical review, a meta-analysis, and a preliminary feedback intervention theory. *Psychological Bulletin*, 119(2), 254–284.

O'Barr, W. M. (1982). *Linguistic evidence*. New York: Academic Press.

Smither, J., London, M., & Reilly, R. R. (2005). Does performance improve following multisource feedback? A theoretical model, meta-analysis, and review of empirical findings. *Personnel Psychology*, 59(1), 33–66.

Stone, D., & Heen, S. (2014). *Thanks for the feedback: The science and art of receiving feedback well*. New York: Viking Penguin.

THEORY INTO PRACTICE

CASE 9

TAILORING CONSTRUCTIVE CRITICISM IN THE PEER TUTORING CENTER

Susan Wilson

Based on rhetorical theory and the importance of audience analysis, this piece puts rhetorical theory into action by suggesting two ways to provide feedback: the "positive-negative-positive" method or the more direct feedback style. This piece emphasizes that not only is the feedback content important, but the way that feedback is relayed can be equally, if not more, important in achieving effective results and client satisfaction in peer tutoring.

Providing constructive criticism, like every other rhetorical act, must be carefully constructed. There are several reasons for this. First, there is the inherent power difference. The person who plans to give criticism believes that they are in a position from which their knowledge and expertise can help another. However, to be most effective in sharing their knowledge and expertise they must do some savvy audience analysis to determine the best way to tailor the message for optimum reception. Over time rhetorically sensitive critics figure out the best, or at least better, ways of crafting their messages. However, because peer tutor center consultations are often short, it may be hard to effectively make that determination. Frequently in peer training sessions, critics are instructed to use a PNP pattern (positive, negative, positive), or what some refer to as a praise sandwich. As Scott Berkun (2004) notes this kind of format works well "for dealing with people sensitive or new to receiving criticism." He also identifies a potential problem in that some receivers feel it has a "touchy-feely vibe and it can lead to pretension and insincerity." Other students see the PNP format as being too indirect, and sometimes too lengthy; they would prefer the critic to cut to the chase. Preferences for criticism format are also sometimes related to the culture of origin. While some international students prefer the gentler approach of PNP, others indicate that the consultant is in a position of power and should speak directly about the problems evident in a presentation. Other academic studies (e.g. Carli, 2001; Turner, Dindia, & Pearson, 1995) have suggested that there is a difference in both the way that criticism is given and received depending on the gender of the sender and receiver.

Because of the variance in what type of criticism is optimum for the receiver, our peer tutoring center has instituted a new initiative. When clients come in and begin filling out the session's paperwork, they receive a separate sheet that briefly describes two scenarios in which a consultant provides criticism to a client. After reading the two scenarios, they elect to receive criticism in the style modeled in A or B scenario (see below). When the clients complete their appointment, they are given an opportunity to indicate whether they received criticism in the style they elected and how effective that criticism was for them. Prior to the semester, consultants received training in both methods as well as role-playing practice.

There are several potential benefits to this initiative. Hopefully, criticism will be constructed and delivered in the way most conducive to being heard and acted on by the client. Additionally, clients may begin to assess their own styles. Further, they may feel empowered to ask for the criticism style that works best for them. This could assist not only in our center, but may help them in other areas as well. For example, they may be able to ask a professor, employer, or even people in their social network to use the specific styles of criticism that would enable them to most effectively improve. This initiative is also beneficial to peer center tutors. In actively adapting to the styles that various clients prefer, peer center tutors can expand and refine their own repertoire for delivering criticism. Finally, peer tutors may realize that the way they personally give (and receive) criticism varies depending on the critic, the subject, and the context, thus further enhancing their rhetorical sensitivity.

References

Berkun, S. (2004, September) #35- How to give and receive criticism. [Web log essay] Retrieved from http://scottberkun.com/essays/35-how-to-give-and-receive-criticism

Carli, L. L. (2001). Gender and social influence. *Journal of Social Issues, 57*(4), 725–741.

Turner, L. H., Dindia, K., & Pearson, J. C. (1995). An investigation of female/male verbal behaviors in same-sex and mixed-sex conversations. *Communication Reports, 8*(2), 86–96.

Appendix

Sample Surveys

In order to provide the most effective feedback about your presentation, it would be helpful to know the type of feedback style that would be most effective for you. Please read the following two scenarios. (The scenarios provide samples of the style of feedback. They do not represent the total amount of feedback.) After reading them, select which style you would like the S Consultant to use.

Scenario A: Pat comes into the S Center and gives a presentation. At the conclusion of the presentation, the S Consultant says:

"Nice job, Pat. Your introduction really caught my attention and also provided a good preview of the direction of your speech. I think you may want to work on the organization of your supporting points in the body of the speech. You jumped around between ideas frequently. Your enthusiasm and careful word choice in your conclusion helped to reinforce your thesis."

Scenario B: Pat comes into the S Center and gives a presentation. At the conclusion of the presentation, the S Consultant says:

"Good start, Pat. Here are the things that you can do to make your speech more effective. The organization of the body needs attention. What are your three main points? You wandered around between ideas. This caused you to seem scattered and you lost credibility. It's a good idea to signpost ideas. This helps both you and your audience.

I prefer the S Consultant to give feedback like the S Consultant in

_____ Scenario A
_____ Scenario B

Please tell the S Consultant which Scenario style you have chosen.

After the session an email is sent to the client, asking them to please complete the following:

1. I consider myself to be an experienced and comfortable speaker.
2. I felt comfortable speaking in front of my consultant.
3. The S Consultant gave feedback in the way I indicated would be effective.
4. The S Consultant addressed my specific need.
5. The session was beneficial to my proficiency as a speaker.
6. How would you rate your session on a scale from 1–10 (with ten being the best).
7. Provide any other comments you'd like to share in the space below:

CASE 10

STRENGTHENING TUTORING COMMUNITIES WITH "*THEY SAY / I SAY*"

Lori Walters-Kramer and Bridget Draxler

The authors share a successful idea that helped to build community between written and spoken communication peer tutors when they were placed structurally within one center on campus. They recommend building reciprocity between speaking and writing tutors by co-training the staff using shared materials, in their case "*They Say / I Say*," which is equally relevant for spoken as well as written rhetoric.

    In a peer tutoring center with tutors from various disciplines, with separate training programs, administrative leadership, and/or expectations, it can be challenging to build a sense of community amongst the tutors. However, a shared sense of identity can help tutors feel a sense of responsibility for and affiliation with seemingly dissimilar tutors. At our institution, we are working to house speaking and writing tutors (which have historically been completely separate programs) in a single Communication Center, with tutoring in both disciplines. In order to build a sense of cohesion between tutors in these programs, we have taken steps to use shared readings, host joint speakers, exchange practice tutoring sessions, and use a shared vocabulary within our tutor training programs. One shared reading we have used successfully is Graff, Birkenstein, & Durst's (2012) "*They Say / I Say*" *with Readings: The Moves That Matter in Academic Writing.*" We offer this example as a specific case study that illustrates the broader value of integrating tutor training into a multi-disciplinary tutoring center.

Building connections between speaking and writing tutors makes sense partly because, in terms of the curriculum at our college, our first-year writing and speaking courses emphasize rhetoric. As speakers and writers, students and tutors need to understand strategies of building both written and spoken arguments whether they are building their own argument, guiding someone else in that process, or attending to the arguments of others.

One way to build reciprocity between speaking and writing tutors is to co-train the staff using shared materials, in our case *"They Say/I Say"*—a text that is popular in first-year composition courses. The name of the text itself, with the use of the verb "say" rather than "write," conveys the transferability of its content from writing to speaking contexts. It offers guidelines and insights that are just as useful for speakers as they are for writers. Accordingly, this text is beneficial for communication centers—whether those centers employ speaking and/or writing tutors.

One cross-disciplinary insight the book offers is that when writers write an essay, that text becomes one part of a much larger conversation about that topic. The same can be said for speakers whose speeches are just one contribution to a larger discursive text: "writing well means engaging the voices of others and letting them in turn engage us" (Graff et al., 2012, p. xix). When the authors encourage writers to turn to what others have said (i.e. "They say") before asserting their own position (i.e. "I say"), speakers can be invited to do the same.

Along with these insights, the authors provide short templates for writers to help them structure their arguments. The authors write,

> Templates have a rich history. Public orators from Ancient Greece and Rome through the European Renaissance studied rhetorical topoi or "commonplaces," model passages and formulas that represented the different strategies available to public speakers. In many respects, our templates echo this classical rhetorical tradition of imitating established models. (Graff et al., 2012, p. xxv)

While public speaking textbooks usually dedicate a section to templates such as transitions and signposts, the templates provided in *"They Say / I Say"* are more varied and allow speakers to understand the nuances of, for example, acknowledging dissenting views or asserting one's position. For instance, one of the templates in a section titled "Agreeing and Disagreeing Simultaneously" is "Though I concede that _____, I still insist that _____"

(Graff et al., 2012, p. 65). This is a rhetorical move that can help developing speakers make more complex arguments.

Because all tutors are also speakers, *"They Say / I Say"* also offers all tutors tools to employ when conversing with tutees. For example, a content tutor for a nursing program working with a tutee who is convinced all alcoholics are irresponsible drinkers could turn to one of the templates for "Introducing an Ongoing Debate" (pp. 25–27) to help the nursing student appreciate diverse stances. The tutor could fill in the template's blanks and claim, "In discussions of *alcoholism*, one controversial issue has been *whether or not it is a disease*. On the one hand, *those who claim it is not a disease* argue *that the alcoholic has a behavioral problem*. On the other hand, *those who believe it is a disease* contend *that alcoholism is a medical disorder of the brain.*" Templates such as this one provided in *"They Say / I Say"* could help tutors gently address students' inaccurate understandings of material, flawed reasoning, or gaps in knowledge. For this reason, the book could be a useful resource in any tutor training program.

While this shared text offers one iteration, we hope this model can transfer to other contexts. For example, you might hold a session on visual literacy for speech and math tutors, or use a shared text on anxiety for speech and pre-professional exam tutors. In each of these instances, our biggest piece of advice is this: give the tutors time to parse out how the shared text, speaker, or idea relates to their discipline. If the tutors are able to sort out how the nuances of signposting transitions, phrasing claims, and making arguments differ between speeches and papers, or the way the visual display of information differs between visual aids in presentations and data visualization on posters, or the way anxiety manifests differently in speeches versus tests, the tutors will gain a deeper understanding of the topic, their role as tutors, and the work of their peers in different fields.

Reference

Graff, G., Birkenstein, C., & Durst, R. (2012). *"They say/I say" with readings: The moves that matter in academic writing* (2nd ed.). New York, NY: W. W. Norton & Company.

CASE 11

TUTOR OBSERVATIONS AS A TOOL FOR CREATING A SUPPORTIVE AND PRODUCTIVE TUTORING ENVIRONMENT

Cassandra A. Book and Maureen McCoy

At one center, the center director and tutor coordinator conduct observations of staff members each semester. Their observations have proven to be useful in enhancing the quality of their peer tutoring services, as the observations become a communication tool for the education and assessment of tutors. This case explains the process.

Session observations are an important part of our tutor development strategy in the Bellarmine University Tutoring and Writing Centers. These observations allow the Tutor Coordinator and the Writing Center Director to understand how undergraduate tutors implement strategies learned in training. In particular, we look for signs that they are applying theory to practice. Observations serve as a communication tool for the education and assessment of tutors.

Procedure

Center supervisors conduct observations each semester. Often trained and experienced tutors assist to accommodate large staffs. Supervisors make an announcement that observations will begin, and the staff may review the Tutor Observation form at any time. Observers choose a random appointment, greet the tutor and tutee(s), and ask permission from both parties to sit in on the session. He or she observes the entire interaction from greeting to salutation and records comments on the form. It is important to note that the observers are not entirely invisible during observations because tutors ask for input at times. Following the observation, the observer and tutor meet to discuss strengths, weaknesses, and ways to improve.

Observations as Education and Assessment

Session observations and follow up discussions with the tutors reinforce the connection between theory (as discussed in training) and practice. The Tutor Observation form serves as a guide for connecting theory to practical application in the session. Key practices include: building rapport, listening to students' needs, providing appropriate positive reinforcement, encouraging tutee participation and involvement, and overall helping tutees develop as critical thinkers and writers.

Tutors may not always be aware of their own tendencies; the follow-up discussion allows the observer to point these out. One common suggestion for new content tutors is to talk less and ask more strategic questions in order to get students engaged. When tutors ask strategic questions, tutees become more proactive in finding their own answers. Tutors should provide guidance in using resources and thinking about concepts in a different way. Follow up discussions with writing tutors often illuminate the tutor's disregard for a tutee's stated agenda. In addition, inexperienced writing tutors need to develop their ability to employ non-directive "minimalist" techniques (Brooks, 1991) because they tend to employ overly prescriptive techniques. The dialogue allows tutors to self-reflect on their approach and think about alternatives or additions to improve, which fosters a comfortable atmosphere in a center (Munger, Rubenstein, & Burow, 1996). Overall, follow up discussions allow observers to remind tutors of the center's mission to help tutees become independent—they should foster skills in their tutees that will be transferrable.

Observations and follow up discussions can also be connected with job performance evaluations. The observation provides an example of how the tutor applies theory, best practices, and training techniques to uphold the center's mission. Although the tutor's strengths and weaknesses observed during the session are an important component of the job performance evaluation, supervisors may wish to consider additional factors such as other required tasks, professionalism, communication, and confidentiality.

At Bellarmine University, we have found the observation practices out-lined to be satisfactory in maintaining an atmosphere of professional development and tutor competency across centers. Just as our tutoring sessions focus on the growth of tutees, we design our procedures to foster continual improvement and critical reflection in all tutors. We also allow tutors to give us feedback on our process, and our current practice reflects the incorporation of their suggestions. We look forward to seeing more research into tutor observation practices that works toward the goal of creating a supportive and productive tutoring environment.

References

Brooks, J. (1991). Minimalist tutoring: Making the student do all the work. *The Writing Lab Newsletter, 15*(6), 1–3.

Munger, R. H., Rubenstein, I., & Burrow, E. (1996). Observation, inter-action, and reflection: The foundation for tutor training. *The Writing Lab Newsletter, 21*(4), 1–5.

Appendix
Tutor Observation

Observer: _____ Tutor: _____

Date: _____ Time: _____

Student's name and basic information:

Course, professor, and assignment:

For each criterion, in addition to commenting, the observer rates the tutor as Needs Improvement, Satisfactory, Outstanding or Not Applicable.

Criteria	Comments	Rating
Introduction and Rapport		
Greets the tutee and introduces him/herself.		
Negotiates a realistic agenda.		
Employs language (including body) that is welcoming and respectful.		
Ensures understanding of basic center procedures and corrects misconceptions, if necessary.	*Misconceptions include students expecting paper editing or re-teaching of course material.*	
Possible Strategies		
Discusses assignment and/or course parameters and expectations.		
Identifies and focuses on higher order concerns.	*Writing center theory emphasizes that tutors should focus on improving higher order (or global) writing concerns, such as following assignment guidelines and organization, before lower order (or sentence-level) issues.*	
Provides appropriate and specific positive reinforcement.		
Balances directive and non-directive techniques.	*Non-directive techniques are typically open-ended or Socratic questioning, e.g. "So what is your main point in this introduction?" Directive techniques are typically more instructive, e.g. "You need a thesis in your introduction."*	

Adapts session to problems that arise.		
Refrains from evaluating tutee or tutee's performance.		
Encourages tutee participation and involvement.		
Ensures tutee's understanding of strengths and weaknesses.		
Employs and refers to appropriate resources such as professor or library.		
Connects the session to general writing (or other content area) advice.		
Reaffirms tutees ownership of his/her work.		
Conclusion		
Summarizes session.		
Addresses tutee's final questions.		
Asks if the tutee would like to schedule another appointment.		

Additional observations:

Summary

The tutor's main strengths are:

The tutor may benefit from keeping in mind or working on the following:

LIST OF CONTRIBUTORS

Wendy Atkins-Sayre is associate professor of communication studies and Speaking Center director at the University of Southern Mississippi.

Jordan Atkinson is a Ph.D. student in the Department of Communication Studies at West Virginia University.

Hannah Ball is a Ph.D. student in the Department of Communication Studies at West Virginia University.

Steven A. Beebe is Regents' and University Distinguished Professor of Communication Studies at Texas State University.

Christopher Bell is an assistant professor of media studies in the Department of Communication at the University of Colorado-Colorado Springs.

Jennifer L. Bevan is associate professor of communication studies and director of the Master of Science Program in Health and Strategic Communication at Chapman University.

Alison Fisher Bodkin is assistant professor of communication studies at James Madison University.

Cassandra A. Book is the director of the Writing Center at Bellarmine University.

Carl J. Brown is an affiliate professor in the School of Communications and associate director of the Speech Lab at Grand Valley State University.

William Butler was the former senior tutor educator of the Speakers Lab at Butler University and is currently a Masters of Professional Accounting student at Butler University.

Shannon T. Carton is a Ph.D. candidate in communication studies at West Virginia University.

Kimberly M. Cuny is director of The University Speaking Center, co-director of The Multiliteracy Centers, and Senior Academic Professional in communication studies at the University of North Carolina-Greensboro.

Bridget Draxler is an assistant professor of English, coordinator of Communication Across the Curriculum, and director of the Writing Center at Monmouth College.

Karen Kangas Dwyer is a professor of communication studies, Basic Course director, and Human Resources & Training Graduate Certificate Program chair in the School of Communication at the University of Nebraska-Omaha.

Erin Ellis is a faculty member in the Department of Communication Studies and the Speaking Center assistant director at the University of North Carolina-at-Greensboro.

Jennifer Butler Ellis is the director of professional development in the EY Leadership and Professional Development Center at Northern Illinois University.

Zachary W. Goldman is an assistant professor in communication studies at Illinois College.

Ethan Gregerson was the former technology manager of the Speakers Lab at Butler University and is currently an assurance associate at McGladrey, an accounting firm in Indianapolis.

Angela Grimaldi is the undergraduate academic counselor in the Department of Accountancy at Northern Illinois University.

Jon A. Hess is professor and chair of the Department of Communication at the University of Dayton, and editor of *Communication Education*.

Kristen Hoerl is associate professor of critical communication and media studies and Speakers Lab director at Butler University.

Michael L. King is the associate director of union and programs at the University of Southern Mississippi.

Mercedes Kolb was the former senior manager of the Speakers Lab at Butler University and is currently the business operations coordinator at the National Panhellenic Conference in Indianapolis, IN.

Nicole Magee is an MA student in communication studies and Speaking Center coordinator at the University of Southern Mississippi.

Maureen McCoy is the coordinator of the Tutoring Center at Bellarmine University.

Molly McHarg is an assistant professor of writing at Virginia Commonwealth University in Qatar.

Sherwyn Morreale is associate professor of communication and director of graduate studies at University of Colorado-Colorado-Springs.

Scott A. Myers is a professor of communication studies and Ph.D. graduate studies coordinator at West Virginia University.

Becky L. Omdahl is professor of communication at Metropolitan State University.

Patricia R. Palmerton is professor and chair of communication studies at Hamline University.

Carley Reynolds is a Ph.D. student in communication studies and Speaking Center assistant coordinator at the University of Southern Mississippi.

William J. Seiler is professor of communication studies and director of the introductory communication course at the University of Nebraska-Lincoln.

Theodore F. Sheckels is professor of English and communication and director of the Speaking Center at Randolph-Macon College.

C. Erik Timmerman is an associate professor of communication and the course director for business and professional communication at the University of Wisconsin-Milwaukee.

Melissa F. Tindage is a Ph.D. student in the Department of Communication Studies at West Virginia University.

Kathleen J. Turner is professor and chair of communication studies and director of oral communication at Davidson College.

Steven J. Venette is an associate professor of communication studies at the University of Southern Mississippi.

Jennifer H. Waldeck is associate professor of communication studies and director of graduate teaching assistants at Chapman University.

Lori Walters-Kramer is an assistant professor of communication studies and the basic communication course director at Monmouth College.

Jennifer Whitaker is a poet and director of the University Writing Center at the University of North Carolina-at-Greensboro.

Susan Wilson is professor of communication and theatre and director of the Speaking/Listening Center at DePauw University.

Catherine K. Wright is an associate professor at George Mason University and the faculty director for the Media, Culture, and Society summer study abroad trip to Milan, Italy.

Eunkyong Lee Yook is associate professor of communication studies at George Mason University.

CONTENT INDEX

AUTHOR INDEX